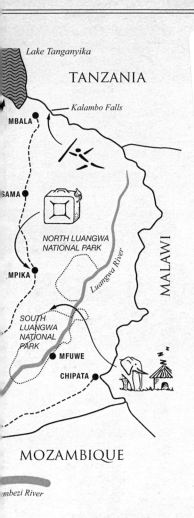

Lake Tanganyika

TANZANIA

Kalambo Falls

MBALA

SAMA

MPIKA

NORTH LUANGWA
NATIONAL PARK

Luangwa River

MALAWI

SOUTH
LUANGWA
NATIONAL
PARK

MFUWE

CHIPATA

MOZAMBIQUE

mbezi River

N

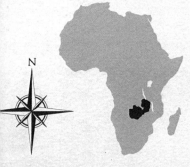

THE Z-FACTOR

A Zambian Episode

THE Z-FACTOR

A Zambian Episode

J B LEE-POTTER

Published by Guy, Barry and Beccy Lee-Potter

Printed by Book Printing UK www.bookprintinguk.com

Remus House, Coltsfoot Drive, Peterborough, PE2 9BF

Printed in Great Britain

ISBN: 978-1-3999-3431-2

For my darling wife Anne
and our children Guy, Barry and Beccy.

To our wonderful parents.

Thank you for giving us such amazing childhood memories. How lucky we were to have had each other, and to have seen and loved Zambia and the wider extraordinary planet with you both.

In 1979 after 20 years in Zambia we all left Africa for good and travelled 'home' to Cornwall in the UK. Dad, you then committed these memoirs to paper, and there they lay dormant on one of your impeccably organised shelves, waiting for something to happen.

In 2022 the three of us decided to bring *The Z-Factor* back to life: Guy was project manager, proofread the copy and created the line drawings. Barry rekeyed it all into digital format during the COVID-19 lockdown, fact checking along the way, and Beccy was our chief designer.

We hope you like it.

29 October 2022

CONTENTS

Chapter 1
AFRICAN ARRIVAL

She lay on her side on the mud floor, flecked with froth, her limbs occasionally twitching with pain, her eyes staring and expressionless. The elegant Dalmatian bitch had been bitten by a snake earlier that day, whilst foraging in the parched bush surrounding the remote exploration basecamp in the north-western province of what was then Northern Rhodesia. No efforts had been spared to save her life, but no-one had seen the snake, and the animal's distress had not been noticed until she had dragged herself through the line of tents to the main thatched hut, which served as our mess and office. She fought long and hard for survival, perhaps helped by the injections of anti-venom serum which were quickly administered, but really she stood no chance and by the morning had died. Later that same morning a large puff-adder, beautiful but sinister, was seen coiled beneath one of the trucks and was quickly despatched, without mercy, in a mood of revenge.

The puff-adder is reputed to account for more deaths, of both animal stock and humans, than any other snake in southern Africa, and is killed without compunction, but I have always found it distressing to have to destroy any life which does not pose an immediate threat. Nevertheless snake-catching is for the experts, and there was no question but that this lethal serpent had to be killed. The slow-moving adders are undoubtedly fascinating to watch, and it is easy to believe stories of mesmerising encounters with these dangerously attractive creatures; but substantiated tales are rare of attacks by snakes without provocation, and in over 18 years in Africa I did not hear a verifiable account of such an occasion.

The death of the Dalmatian was my introduction to life in the African bush and followed a truck journey of some 250 dusty and uncomfortable miles, through mainly flat and featureless bush country. Our sense of relief and pleasure at arriving, in early evening, at the large and well-stocked camp, was dispelled by the gloom of those already there who had been watching the slow but inexorable ebb of life from the plucky bitch, which looked so out of place in such unsophisticated surroundings.

It was unfortunate that I should have been confronted with such a tragedy on my very first day as a field exploration geologist, newly graduated, newly married, and only two short weeks on the African continent, but it was in many respects a lesson well learned as there is nothing like experience to hone one's awareness. But the essence of life in a strange environment is to maintain a sense of proportion, and I was soon to learn more of the ways of the wild places and their indigenous populations of both animal and vegetable kingdoms. Africa is a continent of extremes, and it has long held a fascination for Europeans which grows with familiarity, such that its pleasures are frequently distilled from its harshness.

In fact Africa had long been foremost in my mind as a place that I would one day have to visit. The schoolboy images of a land of deserts and jungles, volcanoes and swamps, inhabited by lions, crocodiles, elephants and flamingos, and other far more bizarre and exotic creatures, had only been slightly mellowed and matured during my three years at Oxford, studying first forestry and then geology. But that these phenomena all still existed in abundance on the African continent could not be denied. More importantly, these superlative sights were becoming more readily accessible than ever before and to work amongst them suddenly became possible with the offer of a job as an exploration geologist, in 1959, to work in the Federation of Rhodesia and Nyasaland. At that time politics could scarcely have been further from my mind, but over the ensuing years it became quite clear to me that despite the awesome magnificence of the natural environment, fully up to my wildest expectations, all that time and natural selection had so splendidly created was becoming increasingly at risk in a continent boiling with nationalism and political expediency. The conservationists and environmentalists of the future will have a massive task in protecting these wonderful wilds for later generations.

Partly to prolong our honeymoon, and partly to see more of Africa, Anne and I chose the long route to Northern Rhodesia, first by sea to Cape Town and then by rail up to the centre of the southern half of the continent, through South Africa, Bechuanaland (now Botswana), and Southern Rhodesia (now Zimbabwe). Having had to borrow sufficient funds from my new employer to pay for my wife's fare we travelled in what felt and sounded like the bowels of the Union Castle mail-ship *Pretoria Castle;* 14 days at sea, with a brief stop at Las Palmas as the only sight of land. Our impression was of a floating holiday camp and at times we found it hard to escape the jolly pressures of being rallied to join the inevitable ping-pong, fancy dress or deck quoits, by well-meaning folk intent on enjoying themselves if it was the last thing they did. Perhaps this was to compensate for anticipated periods of prolonged solitude in remote bush areas, but whatever their reasons we were pleased to escape our enforced confinement on the morning we docked at Cape Town. We felt a thrill of excitement and unease at the sight of dawn and the veil of clouds gradually lifting off Table Mountain in the chill damp morning air.

The port formalities were soon over and entailed little welcome, or even civility, but these places seldom generate in their officials any feelings other than functional suspicion of travellers, and we were too engrossed in all around us to take serious notice of the offhand indifference we mostly encountered. A taxi ride to the railway station with our motley collection of cases and small crates brought us to the next stage of our journey. A quite comfortable, and spotlessly clean sleeper compartment was to be our home for the next four days, first on South African Railways and then Rhodesia Railways, for the 3,000-mile train journey to our destination, Kitwe, on the Northern Rhodesian Copperbelt. Service was adequate if not effusive, and we found ourselves trying hard not to notice the cynical looks cast at us by fellow passengers when we responded with gifts of fruit, biscuits or coins, to the pleas of begging African children who swarmed around the train at the various halts and stations. We were told, condescendingly, that these children had no need to beg and should not be encouraged to do so, but whilst clearly not in desperate need nor in any danger of actual starvation these youngsters were certainly not over-nourished and were delighted with our small offerings, which were given as a sign of friendship as much as charity. Later on, as we learned more of the racial barriers, real and imagined, we were to come to understand better, though never to accept, that friendship between the races in South Africa is even now most often only acceptable in a degrading or patronising sense, and very rarely on a genuine personal basis: since friendship implies equality, anathema to protagonists of apartheid.

Perhaps the highlight of that train journey was the stop at Victoria Falls and the crossing of the bridge over the great Zambezi River. The Falls themselves, 'the smoke that thunders' or *Mosi-oa-tunya,* were not impressive, as the river was low at the end of the dry season and only a few thin veils of water could be seen from the bridge, but the forces responsible for carving out these great canyons from the tough layers of volcanic lava were vividly apparent. Subsequent journeys to the Falls, exploring both banks on foot and flying over the mile-wide precipice, both at low and high river levels, have since reinforced that first impression of enormous natural energy and timelessness as the full flood of the Zambezi, which has been gathering force along its course for over 600 miles by that point, crashes into a single narrow gorge snaking through the dry bush on either side. The river has changed its course many times, and the present mile-wide lip of the Falls is the latest of some seven earlier precipices which are now preserved in the basalt walls of the zigzag canyon downstream. It was fascinating to reflect on the spirit of pioneering and adventure which had prevailed at the time this rail bridge was completed in 1905, and the time 50 years earlier when Livingstone first sighted the Falls themselves. The statue of Dr Livingstone on the southern, Zimbabwe bank, is a permanent reminder of this great explorer and missionary and one feels he would applaud the political realisation of independence for the lands to the north and south of the river, although he would no doubt be saddened by the strife along the border for the past 15 years.

Our arrival in Kalulushi, a small mining town some ten miles from Kitwe, provided a pleasant surprise. We had anticipated accommodation in a flat, and found instead that we had been allocated a delightful bungalow set in a well-tended garden containing brilliant hibiscus, bougainvillea and poinsettia bushes as well as clumps of bamboo, a fair lawn, and a gigantic tree-covered termitary. This house was to be our home for the next three years, and though we didn't know this at the time, we were later to move to four other houses in Kalulushi, the Place of Rabbits, each house larger and more lavish than the last. But our first house still holds a special place in our memory as do the many pets which joined us there from time to time.

October, the month in which we arrived, is the hottest month and the only really uncomfortable time of the whole year when daytime temperatures may reach the low 90sF and are consistently in the 80s: a small penalty to pay for what must be one of the finest climates in the world, since despite being only some 900 miles south of the equator, the Copperbelt is situated on the great Central African plateau at an elevation of 4,000 feet above sea level. However, be that as it may, October was known as 'suicide month' and it was certainly to us unpleasantly hot, so that our first purchase had to be a refrigerator. At the first opportunity we got a lift into Kitwe and swiftly signed a hire-purchase agreement with a salesman in Alf's, a large superstore, and returned home to await eagerly the delivery of our new acquisition. Basic furniture had been provided but this really was basic such that our fridge was to take precedence even over a stove or easy chairs, all of which we had to save for over the next year or so, and all of which were bought on the dreaded never-never. A far cry from today when all expatriate recruits to the mining industry are not only provided with a full house of furniture, but whose company fridge is even filled with food as well. But our precious fridge duly arrived and was switched on after the icetrays had been ceremoniously filled and our meagre stocks of beer and butter had been inserted. Every hour we impatiently checked how cold our fridge was getting and were disturbed that the items inside were indeed no colder than outside. But we persevered, continued to check, and resigned ourselves to having warm beer for our sundowners and later went to bed. First thing next morning we rushed out of bed only to find a pool of molten butter in the fridge, the whole of which had become almost red hot, with alarming accompanying noises. We eventually got a replacement, which served us well, but not before discovering that in Africa as elsewhere, purchase is one thing and service yet another. That protracted encounter with the commercial world made us so infuriated that I permitted myself one of my rare dishonesties either before or since: we purchased four small garden chairs from the same supplier as the fridge, only as we could not get what we wanted elsewhere, and we received an invoice for "four chairs at £4 each – Total 16s." I paid the 16 shillings, fully expecting a corrected invoice, but none came, and I guiltily allowed myself a verdict of justifiable dishonesty.

But there is nothing to compare with the sounds and scents of the African bush for easing one's conscience concerning worldly matters, and sitting on our stoep, or open verandah, on our under-priced chairs with a cold beer in the evening, it was not difficult to forget such things. Even in the busy and noisy mining towns one learned not to hear the ever-present grind and clank of major industry but the truly primeval sounds of birds and insects; and to smell not the fumes of diesel and smelter but the smoke of bush fire and charcoal burning, and the incomparable fragrance of the earth after the first rains following a dry season of six months. It is these intangible pleasures that make the most unforgettable memories, comparable only indirectly with the rural sights and sounds of other continents and unique, in their intensity, to Africa.

One of our greatest pleasures was in discovering for ourselves the source of some new and mysterious sound or smell, and these were in abundance all around us wherever we went; but nowhere as overwhelmingly as deep in the bush and away from man-made interference of any kind. Walking through the forest at different seasons held different rewards for the observant and never failed to provide us with some new experience. Wildlife, except for birds and insects, squirrels and other small mammals, is rarely seen outside the really remote parts of the country or within the vast and magnificent National Parks, but we were to have ample opportunities for visiting such places, and between these times we were happy to observe and enjoy what our gardens and surrounding patches of bush could offer. On a hot day the dominant sound might be the deafeningly shrill hiss of hidden cicadas high in the trees, strangely congregated in belts such that one walks from zones of relative quiet to others of stupendous background noise which drowns out all else. Whether these cicadas remain in larval form underground for many years, only to emerge for a single day of noisy adulthood as in one North American species I am unsure, but whatever their lifecycle they seem determined that theirs shall be a cry heard by all, and few predators seem to dine on these horny beasts to reduce their numbers. Should any of these clumsy but oddly friendly insects become distressed, as sometimes happened when discovered singing away on the verandah's mosquito netting at night by one of our cats, the hideous shriek emitted and the look of almost human terror in the insect's large and limpid eyes always resulted in an instant rescue, and the dispossessed cat leaving in disgust. Other less attractive nocturnal visitors were the cumbersome and bloated sausage flies, actually winged termites, fully half an inch long or more, which penetrated every fortification designed to exclude them, usually in early evening at the start of the rainy season. Swarms would appear, instal themselves on the verandah where they had been attracted by the light, divest themselves of their now useless wings, and squirm in a most unappealing and nauseating display of incompetence. They in fact constituted, so we were told, a palatable source of protein, and the local peoples, as well as our cats and dogs, quite enjoyed them as a wriggling hors d'oeuvre. Being more fastidious and not attracted by the more exotic sources of nourishment we were only once tempted to try this free manna, lightly fried in oil, and found the experiment unpleasant with a lingering flavour of rancid peanut butter as our reward. Nor did we ever venture into culinary excesses with other plentiful and free food sources, so that we merely informed our servants should we locate a supply of the edible caterpillars and grasshoppers which were popular with certain tribes. Why the English palate should be so squeamish is hard to say, and I'm sure we're the poorer for it, but the pale brown writhing sausage fly harvest was to my mind the epitome of poor cuisine.

In direct contrast to the repulsive sausage flies, butterflies are noted for beauty and enhance any landscape. The most lavish and flamboyant central African species are frequently high fliers, in the literal sense, or else prefer the dense and lush jungly vegetation alongside rivers and streams where they may be hard to see. But even the smaller and less garish species provide splendid spectacles, often by virtue of quantity rather than quality. Butterflies are normally seen but not heard, like Victorian children, but the pulsing turmoil of colour produced when these thirsty creatures arise hastily from a patch of moisture on some stream side, or rain puddle, is accompanied by a magical silken rustling of wings quite unlike any other insect noise as they jostle for airspace in an attempt to escape. Dense clumps of Grass Yellows, Citrus Swallowtails or Orange and Lemons, and other numerous species scattering in alarm into the surrounding leafy refuge should be both seen and heard, and are an integral part of the charm of the African insect world.

But it is the birds, more than the insects, which produce the most beautiful sounds of the African bush as well as providing ample visual rewards to the observer. And again, it is not essential to leave the confines of one's own garden to derive such pleasures since a garden is normally an oasis of life, especially during the long dry season. Our own gardens have played temporary or permanent host to diminutive sunbirds and mannikins little larger than my thumb, and to the enormous turkey-sized ground hornbills, with all manner of shapes and sizes in between. It is difficult to select a favourite of course and we learned to enjoy the drab and ubiquitous black drongo as much as the occasional visit of the splendid paradise flycatcher. The fork-tailed drongos are accomplished aerobats and their antics and flying displays were often spectacular, particularly when the winged termites appeared in the evenings after the first early rains. These birds, uniformly black and about the size of a slim British starling, preferred to dine on the wing, swooping to and fro with amazing agility, mopping up several termites at a time, and returning to their elevated perches to digest their mouthfuls before sweeping into the feast again. On one occasion we watched enthralled as a steady stream of whimsically fluttering termites rose from a small hole in our lawn, promptly to become a target for a host of different birds all eager for the pickings which were sufficiently plentiful to sate even the most voracious appetite. The techniques for mopping up this seemingly unending and succulent supply varied enormously between the customers. The drongos, aerial artists supreme, appeared to delight in catching the most elusive and accomplished escapees with unerring accuracy and ease, whilst the elegant woodland kingfisher, providing magnificent flashes of vivid blue, could produce at best a slight swerve from its arrow-like pass through the feast, drawing a bead on its prey from a distance and relying on a rather improbable straight-line flight of the termite to ensure capture. When successful there was a loud click of impact as the luckless insect was caught in the dagger-like beak, but more often than not the almost embarrassed bird swooped up to its vantage point and looked jealously at its more successful rivals. The pied wagtails, always amongst the cheekiest of garden birds, as well as friendliest, would tackle the supply at source and together with the gorgeous plum-coloured starlings and groundscraper thrushes would stake out a pitch on the ground right next to the termites' exit and lower the insects' chances of becoming airborne. The tiny black sunbirds, great artists like the drongos, would twist and turn in mercurial flight as they shared the aerial marketplace. Even at dusk the termites were still streaming into the warm scented air and it became the turn of the silent and extravagantly plumed pennant-winged nightjars to tackle the feast, supplemented by the first of many moths.

In addition to their spectacular aerial displays the drongos also provided great amusement by their accomplished vocal mimicry, their star performance being a perfect feline miaow. These skilful birds would persist in shadowing our cats wherever they went in the garden, disclosing their hiding places to their greatest disgust and frustration: eventually the wretched cats would run indoors for cover, their teeth chattering in thwarted fury. We never witnessed a reverse of fortunes and the wary drongos would always manage like the wagtails to tease the cats with sufficient skill to avoid capture. It would take too long to mention all the many pleasures we gained from our garden birds, from the familiar cry of 'Hello, Georgie' from the elusive emerald cuckoo, and the rippling call like water dripping from a tap, from the rain-bird or coucal; to the crafty pied crows which would drop in unexpectedly to rob the dog's bowls of left-overs; and the golden weaver family which valiantly kept a hawk from robbing their dangling nest for day after day until their young flew to safety. Sufficient to say that with all this wealth of interest all around us a stroll in the garden was never dull. Anne and I soon fell into the habit of what looked to our friends and neighbours' amusement rather like beating the bounds, as we wandered every evening around the property, followed by either our children or pets or both, seeing what the past day had brought or changed. In that superb climate gardening is most rewarding and a patch of rough bush can be transformed in only a few short years into a lovely garden, with high hedges, lush flowering shrubs and lawns, such that overnight changes are certainly often noticeable and not only to be seen in the eye of the believer. It is said that a watched pot never boils, but despite our constant observation our garden pot boiled many times over.

From my apparent preoccupation with the world of natural history it might be surmised that this chronicle will exclude all else, but I have really attempted only to set the scene. To live for long in a foreign land it is necessary, temporarily at least, to divorce oneself from the day-to-day trivia which characterised one's previous existence. Since I had recently left behind an urban academia, in exchange for a rural industria, the transformation was extreme in my surroundings and it was with the natural environment that it became easiest to identify quickly, as it was with this that my job was involved. In many ways the job of an exploration geologist with a concern for the environment provides a conflict, since to be successful one must bring mining development, and all its ancillary industrial and administrative morass, to virgin land. Such is progress, however, and to deny it would be foolish. And so our life in Africa, Anne's and mine, began in a small mining town within a prosperous colonial infrastructure, later to be torn by many and varied turmoils and trials: it is sad that after 18 years only the essence of climate and location remain unchanged. Though many of the gardens of the past are now a poor reflection of their previous throbbing vitality, the drongos and termites, cicadas and sunbirds remain: and though the mining industry, like Zambia's faltering economy, is in disarray, the forests and bush continue their cycle of decay and rejuvenation. And since mineral exploration cannot attract the investment it needs during times of recession, large areas of virgin land have earned a reprieve, however short-lived, from the prying surveys and drills of the geologists.

Chapter 2
DOUGHNUT & DIAMONDS

Doughnut was the unlikely name of my first boss-boy, a worker nowadays more tactfully referred to as a crew-boss, or in the more pompous modern idiom of job description and classification the even more specific and elaborate title of field assistant. However, Doughnut he was, and he remained with me for several years before a vindictive colleague fired him for some trivial incompetence during my absence on leave one year. It took me a month to discover the derivation of his name, and despite many inventive and imaginative hours of enjoyable speculation, the answer was simple. His legal name, or at least that on his *situpa*, or colonial work permit, was Donat, derived not after the famous film star but from Donald, since the Bemba language does not accommodate a sound for a terminal -ld. Disappointing; but many others of the workforce had more descriptive or evocative names, such as Bigshirt, Petrol, Lemon and Bicycle and an exotic collection of obscure biblical names from Philemon to Jeremiah no doubt conferred by past missionaries, but perhaps my favourite name was the unlikely Patrick O'Fumpa, owned by a competent and likeable field assistant with a fortuitous touch of the Irish humour to seal a most successful philological blend of cultures.

The unsophisticated villagers in the rural areas provided a never-ending source of interest and amusement, and it was always a pleasure to be able to laugh with them, rather than at them. They had their own well-developed sense of fun and were never slow to see a joke at whoever's expense. Slapstick custard-pie humour was always a success, but occasionally a sense of cruelty showed through, thinly veiled at times, as when a joke turned sour and someone was perhaps injured as a result. But essentially these are generous and light-hearted people whose values one can respect and appreciate, at least until they become demeaned by the more unattractive aspects of urban existence which is so alien to their traditional way of life. The urban generations of Zambians appear to have divorced much of their light-hearted ebullience and friendliness, and the confection of mixed tribal and cultural values present in the big mining town suburbs, and squatter townships, as well as those circling the administrative and political hierarchy, such as Lusaka or Ndola, is far less attractive. This unfortunately is the side seen most often by visitors and tourists to the country. The Western worship of money has been adopted quite readily as a means of emulating the lifestyle enjoyed by many expatriates, without a corresponding appreciation of the responsibilities inherent in their new-found earning power. This picture can be seen throughout independent Africa and has led to a self-degradation of whole cultures bringing nepotism and corruption and a new range of evil ugliness to previously contented and light-hearted people. The advent of freely available education at primary level has increased aspirations from an early age, leading to frustration with reduced opportunity at secondary level, and an even worse problem as school leavers find no suitable jobs to fit their new and hard-earned qualifications. This seems to be a world-wide problem, not restricted either to the developing countries, but the alternatives are unpalatable and controversial as well as immensely complex. A reversion to labour-intensive methods and a reluctance to adopt the ever-increasing flood of new technology is seen as retrograde and uncompetitive, even though world inflation and the rapid consumption of non-renewable resources points ever more forcefully to the necessity of looking at such alternatives. It is ironic that in Zambia, for instance, satellite communication through Mwembeshi satellite station has made it easier to receive live world championship boxing and football events to television than to produce live broadcasts on Zambian events. Easier too, on occasions, to make an international call than to dial a number in a neighbouring town; and vast areas of this country of course have no telecommunications of any sort. Perhaps, in the long term, they would be better off to remain this way and enjoy their state of incommunicado from the remorseless and bureaucratic and political process of government.

But back to the bush and the faithful Doughnut. To he and his workers there was absolutely no need for concern with technology and politics, as their immediate needs were all provided for by their employers in the best colonial fashion. They were paid to build their own village, provided they maintained a moderate degree of conformity with the needs of health and hygiene, and could live happily in their traditional way. Staple foods were also provided, as were medical supplies for cuts and bruises, coughs and sneezes and other trivial complaints. The daily sick parade soon sorted out both the malingerers and those with an addiction for western medicines. Any really ill villager, man, woman or child, could be quickly evacuated by road or air to missionary or government hospitals, and there was usually an accessible local witch doctor whose traditional medicines could be bought or exchanged, for a pilfered handful of nails or some such item of stores which had a habit of thinning themselves out and vanishing at discrete intervals. This form of minor theft was not seen by the men as a crime, as they felt that camp supplies were provided for their benefit, as indeed they essentially were, and so a blind eye was normally turned in those cases where no flagrant deterioration of supplies was noticed. At the end of each month the men received their wages and were provided with transport to the nearest store where they would often spend the entire sum on clothes or beer, or attempt to attract some female company. Different tribes had different attitudes to the latter form of recreation, and I well remember on one occasion being surprised to see one of my less brawny workers leap out of the bushes at the side of the road, and frantically wave down my vehicle some two miles outside the village a couple of days after payday. It took some time to gather, from his hysterical and virtually incoherent babblings, that the husband of his temporary girlfriend was hunting him with an axe with a very firm promise to chop him into hundreds of pieces. After much pleading I was eventually persuaded to drive him to a town some 25 miles away and pay him off. None of us saw him again, but we all assumed that his head start had been sufficient to guarantee escape form the enraged and cuckolded village axeman.

It was rare for me to find nothing new or of note on each of my regular visits to my workers' village, and Doughnut was always there to explain every happening in excruciating detail. The technique I found most useful in handling local disputes was usually to allow ample time for each party to explain, at length, his version of the story, and it was uncommon during this process for the guilty person to avoid thoroughly committing himself so that a wise judgement, thus enhancing one's own standing, was very simple. But apart from performing as a weekly Solomon, there were many other diversions, as when I arrived to find the village virtually empty due to a speedy evacuation caused by an abnormally large incursion of driver ants, or *seruwe* as they are known. These ferocious red ants can be terrifying, and although seldom as impressive as their relatives in the tropical parts of Central Africa, they do attack the unwary in a most insidious way, waiting until good number are on the poor creature and then biting in unison after some mystic signal and thus perhaps paralysing their prey by shock, sufficient to overcome it before consuming it. But small columns are more usual and pose little real threat unless invading by night, when they might remain unnoticed until the first bite. Many are the battles in house and garden to destroy these organised and vicious insects and my family and I have many memories to do with either stopping them or de-infesting ourselves, or pets, after inadvertently treading on a column on the march. Our daughter Beccy, aged only four, once became covered from head to toe with these red ants in our garden, and was so terrified after the first agonising bites that she just stood and screamed, rooted to the spot, so allowing more and more ants to climb up her limbs: each had to be picked off as rapidly as possible by hand, as their grip is tenacious and no amount of rubbing or hosing down will dislodge them. Hence the empty village, and no-one would return until the ant columns had worked their way through the camp and disappeared once more into the bush. As the *seruwe* will eat any kind of animal matter, from chickens to lice, their purpose as hygiene orderly is perhaps overlooked, and I'm sure the huts and surroundings of that camp were a lot cleaner after their journey, and the village's pest population was no doubt dramatically reduced.

Of course, the principal objectives of my visits to Doughnut's village were to inspect the work of his gang of labourers, or perhaps collect a team for a day's mapping or sampling. Most of the work at the main camp was digging prospect pits, both to obtain deep samples and for the geologist to map the depth, type and attitude of the underlying rocks. Much of this area is covered by thick soil, weathered in place from the rotting rocks, and so digging from the surface was usually quite easy work. But I never ceased to be amazed at the way a pair of labourers would dig a round shaft, some 30 inches in diameter and 60 or more feet deep, using simply a crowbar and a short-handled shovel. One of the team would dig, whilst his partner on the surface would haul up the bucketloads of soil by rope, returning the empty buckets to the bottom. In soft soil progress could be as much as 20 feet a day, but if hard layers were encountered perhaps only six inches would be achieved, and incentive bonuses were then paid. This work was essentially dangerous, both from the risk of falls from the unsupported sides of the pits, and from noxious gases building up in certain formations, but the only serious accident I recall was when a burly fellow named Sam, ex-Kings' African Rifles, almost severed a toe whilst working in the cramped conditions of the bottom of the pit. This courageous fellow never even mentioned his wound until I came across him resting at camp rather than out at work one day, and by then his whole foot was bloated and a mass of green pus: at the hospital he refused the medical advice of amputating to save his foot, and by some miracle and careful nursing he recovered completely and didn't even lose the toe. But I will always remember the stoic way in which Sam merely accepted the pain without complaint, and my anger with Doughnut who had failed to report the accident when it happened.

Pits provided many experiences, none of them pleasant. The labourers dig footholds into the side of the pit in order to climb in and out, but the geologist logging the pit would be lowered on a seat and rope over a pulley, with a lamp, as he needed both hands for writing, measuring and to use a clinometer and compass. Thus one examined the walls of the pit and would call out to the team above to stop lowering at each point of interest: small snakes, and occasionally not so small ones, sometimes tumbled into the open pits and managed to lodge in the footholds. I well remember noticing a tapping on my boot as it dangled below the seat and looking down to see a snake repeated striking at it. Even more alarmingly was to find a snake at eye level, only a foot or so away. Fortunately this only happened to me once when my team above were awarded a bonus for their speedy response to my instant yell of *'pa mulu!'*, literally meaning 'upstairs'! Other encounters, all unpleasant, were with rats, soldier termites, bats and driver ants, apart from stifling gas accumulations, crumbling walls and cramped wet conditions. If these indignities and discomforts accompanied the gleaning of invaluable geological data they were bearable, but a frustrating day did nothing to improve my humour. It was only the thought of the labourers toiling to actually dig those pits, day after day, year in year out, that made me realise that a few hours once a week to inspect them was a comparatively small effort. Each dead rat, or frantic bat clattering past me up the pit, was always a time of great amusement to my crew on the rope at the surface, and it often crossed my mind that all the boisterous uproar and side-splitting above me might one day be accompanied by a loss of grip and a consequent drop into the revolting morass at the bottom, perhaps 40 feet below. But it never happened, either to me or anyone else, and this primitive but effective method of exploration is still as useful today as it was at the start of the 20th century.

My pitting excursions were the source of a number of our household pets, as the Africans quickly learned of my interest in wildlife of every sort. Anne loved the bush-babies and night apes of every sort and especially a baby vervet monkey which I acquired during the first four years, but we soon realised that the supply caused suffering as the animals were cruelly trapped and kept, and by buying them one merely created a demand and more and more were caught and others injured or killed. Appealing bush-babies and night-apes, furry and with long tails and huge eyes, were a common sight being hawked by the roadside, dangling on bark twine tied tightly around their hindquarters, and many a European has been tempted to barter and buy one for a small sum. At one time we would buy them out of pity, and release them elsewhere, but this merely ensured that more were caught and sold, so that eventually we hardened our hearts and passed them by. But in our early days our fascination for these creatures got the better of us and we gave homes to a number of them, for better or for worse.

Our night-apes were adorable, but developed some less than appealing habits such as peeing on their hands, probably to give a better grip; but clammy and malodorous fingers in one's hair and ears lost its appeal and we released them. Next we kept a pair of the larger and fluffier bush-babies, but again captivity was not their metier and even when given a large outdoor enclosure, which they shared with a pair of laughing doves named Powder and Puff, they were sickly and sad. They returned our affection and interest by eating Powder and Puff, leaving just a pile of feathers, and that was our first indication that bush-babies were carnivorous. We should have known, but accidents will happen.

Our longest-standing domestic pet of the non-conventional type was a young vervet monkey whom we called Humphrey, and who succeeded a pair of love birds which not unexpectedly took off for the bush with a shriek of derision as soon as we released them. Humphrey proved a most affectionate pet, attentive and faithful, and although allowed almost complete freedom, always confined his activities to our house and garden except when voluntarily accompanying us and our dogs for walks. The dogs were most long-suffering and tolerated many indignities at the hands of Humphrey, even to allowing him ride on their backs like a jockey, but Humphrey unfortunately had a jealous streak and a temper to match. If he wished to show his displeasure he would shriek and yell. A favourite trick, which he knew exasperated Anne, was to rub a peeled banana backwards and forwards on the wire mosquito netting on the windows, thus making a truly unspeakable mess which was almost impossible to clean. But his jealousy led to his undoing after our first baby arrived, and when we saw him jumping up and down on Guy's pram, chattering with rage, we realised we could not risk keeping him longer and sadly gave him to a friend with a less complicated household. From then on we limited our pets, with the exception of a short-lived and rather dozy white rabbit called Bunny, and an occasional tortoise, to our faithful and delightful dogs and cats and their various puppies and kittens. Though we did once engage a chameleon called Charlie as a self-propelled fly-swat during one brief shortage of aerosol insect sprays: he was efficient, but hardly affectionate.

Creatures of various sorts were not all that I brought home from my regular forays and spells in the bush. My teams of labourers soon learned to expect curious requests, or instructions, as to what I required them to collect or search for before my next visit, whether it be wild honey, tree ferns, orchids, river sand, lucky bean seeds, bamboo poles or even more items which could be added to our diet, curio collection or garden. Consequently, anything out of the ordinary which appeared would be brought along for inspection, in the hope of purchase, and from time to time I would be offered anything from fish to diamonds. 'Grade four diamonds' was a popular offering since the high value of genuine diamonds was well known due the extensive diamond fields in neighbouring Zaire's Kivu Province, and at the Williamson Mine in Tanzania, but never once was I offered a real diamond as the 'grade four' versions were always in fact quartz crystals of no value whatsoever. In some ways it was a relief not to have to make the decision as to what to do if offered the genuine article, since of course trafficking in diamonds was illegal and there are many informers. Of course from time to time one was also offered rubies, emeralds and sapphires, normally in the form of bits of reflector glass, bottles and so on, but one had to be equally careful since emeralds are mined at Miku south of Kalulushi and more reach illicit outlets than legal ones; and rubies and sapphires have been mined from Malawi further east. But one wonders how many Africans, and for that matter Europeans, are swindled in this way, as the proportion inadvertently offered to qualified geologist must be extremely small. However, it's the same the world over, as my experience in western Ireland, where I was once offered a 'Kerry diamond' in a pub, bears witness. In arguing with a well-oiled Irishman that his diamond was in fact a quartz crystal, and therefore would not scratch a mark on his glass of Guinness, the glass slipped to the floor and shattered due to his strenuous attempts to prove me wrong. There was more dismay at the waste of Guinness that at the disappointment in failing to make a sale to a young English geology student.

When unable, for various reasons, to reach camp for a week or two it was sometimes necessary to send a colleague or assistant to collect samples, deliver rations, or otherwise check on work progress and the state of the project. Frequently we were in radio contact with the more remote camps, but in routine work in more accessible areas we relied on regular vehicle trips for supply and communication, and on Doughnut or his equivalent crew-bosses for information. In this way we had a delightful series of written reports or letters in often curious English and these gave us continued amusement. Considering the lack of any expatriate's knowledge of any of the local dialects, and disinterest in using them, it was remarkable that the uneducated Africans were able to learn the smattering of English they did; and the written language even for semi-educated helpers was a remarkable achievement. Thus our amusement was in no way derogatory but thoroughly enjoyable nonetheless. In fact many of these missives reminded me of part of a speech by Gerrard Hoffnung to the Oxford Union, in which he referred to replies from Tyrolean landlords in answer to his holiday enquiries; and especially the prospect conjured up by the assurance that 'there are French widows in every bedroom, affording stupendous revelations'! The letters I have from Zambia are perhaps less erotic, but I liked the one asking for leave starting 'Dear Sir, I am sick, suffering from madness'. One delightful and stern missive, an official circular from the Kalulushi District Secretary's office, addressed to the committee members of various sports and social clubs in the town, included the following sentence: 'It is the utmost wish of this office that this ruling is accorded the seriousness and the contempt it deserves in conformity with its requirements'. Another exhortation, from the same source, stated that 'It should be noted that late submissions will not be entertained, otherwise you will be made to pass through the valley of humiliation'. Strong stuff, and I'm sure there were no late submissions.

Chapter 3
TRAVELS AND TRACKS

In recent historical terms many of the countries of Africa have now passed through two major and protracted convulsions, both relating to the aspirations of alien, expatriate cultures, and separating the pre-colonial from colonial, and latterly, colonial from post-colonial eras: and however sanguine one's viewpoint it is hard to avoid the conclusion that the colonial phase was essentially, if not exclusively, an exploitative episode. Consequently, the expatriates' role in Africa today is one of being needed but not wanted, a sad reflection on our record especially since many individuals, and some administrations, have genuinely strived for honest progress. But commercial pressures, in the form of national, corporate or personal greed, sometimes assisted or condoned by evangelical zeal, served to strengthen and crystallise the wave of emergent nationalism.

Whilst it is certainly melodramatic to speak of the indigenous peoples of Northern Rhodesia as being collectively oppressed on our arrival in 1959, there were equally certainly many legally supported inequalities of opportunity, and indignities, and much offensive legislation. Consequently, a good-natured acceptance of an inferior lot in life gradually gave way to a powerful resentment that what was preached was not practiced, a fact which could not be ignored for ever. The troubles for the white man in Central Africa erupted tragically in 1960 and 1961 in the rich mining province of Katanga in the southern Belgian Congo, now Zaire, when streams of terrified whites poured over the border into Northern Rhodesia with horrendous stories of pillage, harassment and murder. I personally saw pictures of a butchered Belgian farmer's body, reputedly cannibalised, with joints hacked from buttocks, legs and arms.

In pre-colonial days much savagery and brutality existed in Africa, but that continent has no exclusive claim to a barbaric past, and in viewing our personal safety in Northern Rhodesia and after 1964 in Zambia, it was necessary to remain unemotional and keep matters in perspective. Despite a few atrocities, publicised and otherwise, we never really considered ourselves at risk to a larger measure than we had been elsewhere; and although I was signed up as a Special Constable in 1961, my sole duty was to attend a lecture on how to wield a truncheon and blow a whistle. I well remember being told by the police lecturer that truncheon blows must only be aimed at the limbs of an attacker, but that head blows might be unavoidable if the assailant moved unexpectedly, or accidentally fell against the officer's truncheon! And so we went our way without regards to the probability of hazards, other than petty theft, though taking common-sense precautions to avoid political rallies or other potential flash points.

Life on the Copperbelt in the early 60's was most enjoyable and we revelled in the new sights and sounds all around us and took little interest in the political machinations there or elsewhere. We travelled extensively and enjoyed a lot of leisure, as even on my starting salary of under £90 per month as an inexperienced geologist we were able to live comfortably and employ two full-time servants, one in the house and one in the garden. During our first five years we had many servants, some leaving to return to remote villages, others dismissed for dishonesty or idleness, but with experience it became easier to select reliable and pleasant personalities who later became almost part of the family. Indeed it is easy to recall both the strength and weaknesses of many of these Africans, who rejoiced in marvellous names like Ignatius, Pelekamoyo, Simon Wellington, and finally our loyal, likeable and long-serving James Melek Kalukuluku, and Dickson Kamanga, the last from Malawi where since he has returned. But more of them later.

In order to enjoy to the full all that the country had to offer, it was, and still is, essential to own some form of transport and consequently our first aim was to save sufficient cash to purchase a second-hand car. Within a year we had acquired an old but sturdy Humber Hawk, not a common car in those parts but rugged and very comfortable, and we lavished a lot of attention on polishing and smartening the non-mechanical bits: these latter we left to garage mechanics, as car maintenance has never been one of my skills or interests. Petrol was no problem in those days although distances between supplies were often such that a spare jerrycan or two was essential luggage if one was travelling away from the Copperbelt. The major roads throughout the Federation were in fair shape by the early 60s but a number of key links were still most uncomfortable; if not downright hazardous. The road classification system varied from dirt at one extreme to full-width tar, at the other, with all-weather laterite – or murram as it was known in East Africa; strips, and single-width tar, as progressive steps of improvement in between. The dirt roads were unsurfaced and normally impassable to light vehicles in the rainy season, and frequently also in the dry season in very sandy areas where it was easy to spend hours moving only yards: fortunately none of the trunk roads were still of this standard by the time of our arrival, but some were still surfaced with laterite. These rapidly became pot-holed and corrugated as the rains set in, and all-weather became something of a euphemism. But perhaps the nastiest to drive on for any distance were the so-called strips, which consisted of two parallel ribs of tarmac each about 18 inches wide and laid to correspond with the normal width between the vehicle wheels. Between the tar strips, and also on both sides, was a laterite surface. Consequently when vehicles had to pass each other, travelling in either the same of opposite directions, each vehicle had to traverse the central laterite and align one wheel on one tar strip and the other on the laterite verge. This manoeuvre, even at moderate speeds, was distinctly hairy, even where the laterite strips were in good repair, which was frequently not the case. Coupled with the fact that drivers of larger vehicles tended to give way only grudgingly, and then at the last moment, these strip roads had to be travelled with great caution by the inexperienced driver.

Precisely a year after our arrival in Africa, Anne and I decided to have a holiday. We selected a favourite Copperbelters' resort, high in the Inyanga mountains of north-eastern Southern Rhodesia, at a spot nostalgically called Troutbeck by early British settlers familiar with the similar but less imposing scenery of the English Lake District. Friends assured us that it was a comfortable two-day journey with a night-stop in Salisbury. We were also particularly keen to ensure that the roads were not too rough as Anne was now six months pregnant and already cumbersomely large. Our friends reassured us on all counts, however, and we set off in the cool of early morning on the first leg of the 700-mile journey in mid-October, the hottest time of the year. We reached the northern escarpment of the Zambezi in reasonable time, with only one unscheduled stop to clean the dust out of the carburettor, but were then dismayed to find extensive roadworks and diversions on dirt tracks for mile after mile. The car ploughed gamely on, and Anne and I got more and more dishevelled and hot in the searing sun, enveloped in clouds of red-brown dust which penetrated everything, but we eventually reached the quite impressive Chirundu bridge and the Zambezi River itself. Brief formalities completed we drove on, over continuous diversions and by now in the furnace-like heat of midday, across the flat and low-lying valley floor with gaunt and sinister baobab trees squatting grotesquely by the roadside, and grey louries, the go-away birds, shrieking their advice which we were striving to take. We struggled on, slowly and almost imperceptibly winding our way up to the baked roads of the southern escarpment, until we eventually crested a slope that left the valley behind us; we felt a fresh evening breeze, which seemed like pure wine after the dust-laden hot air we'd been inhaling for so many hours. The view back was quite spectacular, and we were so elated on resuming our journey that we drove past the first motel, at Makuti, and made another 50 miles before stopping at a pleasant hotel at Karoi. A good night's sleep repaired most of our tiredness and cramp and we headed on next morning for Salisbury and the big city, then the capital of the Federation of Rhodesia and Nyasaland where we decided to add a day to our trip in order to get the carburettor attended to. Salisbury was looking beautiful, well-cared for and immaculate, with streets and parks lined with jacarandas and flamboyants, a mass of purple and orange blossom, and seas of colourful bougainvillea and hibiscus bushes even more splendid than those we had left behind in the Copperbelt. But we had not come for a city holiday, happy place though it seemed, and so we drove on towards Umtali and the Inyanga Mountains.

The all-weather roads to the north of Umtali proved exhausting for Anne, as they appeared to be endlessly corrugated and potholed. We began to worry about the effect on Anne's pregnancy as we drove deeper and deeper into the mountains, and the roads got progressively worse, but at least the air became crisper and fresher the higher we went. On arrival at the hotel, a splendidly sited resort with its own trout-stocked dam and nine-hole golf course, Anne was feeling decidedly unwell and felt occasional twinges, like contractions:

we then got a somewhat unimpressed management to crank away at the field telephone to speak to a district nurse some 20 miles away. We put Anne to bed, beside a blazing log fire and with a hot water bottle against the chill mountain air, and she awoke next morning tired but otherwise none the worse for the experience: and there were still only two of us, much to our relief! We had a wonderful week's holiday, wandering through the local hills and valleys and beside the lake, through the resin-scented coniferous forests, and enjoying the unusual flora, with tree ferns and aloes alike, and the air as clean and pure as anywhere in the world. The hotel flew the Union flag at its masthead and had tubs of yellow and pink standard roses at the entrance; the food was elegantly served and included many imported cheeses and wines; the atmosphere was relaxed and comfortable. The whole ambience of the place was redolent of the best of Old England, right down to the skittle alley and golf course, and tea on the terrace overlooking the lake. Everywhere there were African servants, attentive but unobtrusive and courteous, in their crisp white uniforms and little white gloves; the only concession to Africa being the beating of a drum, not a gong, to summon guests to dinner. But even with the studied British surroundings, and the evening rise of trout in the lake, one could never forget that this was Africa with its unique blend of scents, sounds and scale.

The journey home was less arduous and exacting than we expected, not because of any instant improvement in the tracks and roads, but because the route was known. Familiarity had in some way reduced the depth of the pot-holes and the height of the corrugations. Even so, compared to our later journey between the Copperbelt and Salisbury, after the entire route consisted of good double-width tarmac, the experience was quite memorable. Anne was also better prepared, both mentally and practically, and she was able to stuff cubes of ice down her bra, and my shirt, at frequent intervals whilst we ground down the Zambezi escarpment, lurched across the valley floor and up the far side, a luxury we could not enjoy on our outward trip as we had then barely enough cold water to drink, let alone squander. Our education in the needs of African travel continued.

Reflecting on our first conventional holiday in Africa the most significant aspect is that in those days (early 1960s), the only people one met were fellow white Europeans. Not only were the whites the only people who appeared to actually get holiday, or have enough money to afford one, the Africans were just not allowed into the hotels or resorts. Some white expatriates actually travelled with a nanny or personal servant, only to despatch them to a one-roomed hut, discretely sited out of the gaze of hotel guests, on arrival at the destination. Of course, this bears close comparison with the European era of 'upstairs, downstairs' and numerous servants of the titled or wealthy, but in the case of the African situation it was based not on a well-established system of wealth or class, however incongruous, but on the decidedly degrading distinction of race and colour alone. Nowadays it is common to meet Africans on holiday in hotels, both in their own countries and elsewhere, but the African staff of such tourist hotels will still instinctively serve first the white person before attending to the needs of his compatriot. In fact it is not unheard of for such staff to scorn the custom of the most cultured and courteous African in favour of a white skinned customer however rude or arrogant. The opposite may sometimes be true but normally only at times of political extremes or upheaval.

Returning, 20 years on, to the formative years of Zambian nationalism, it is interesting to recall my surprise, on remarking to Doughnut and his labourers that their records showed that they did not appear to have been absent on leave for several years, to find that leave, or holidays, were not really an experience they understood. The all received 'pay in lieu of leave' but appeared to have no appreciation that they were entitled to so many days of paid leave each year, normally two weeks, or that they always merely accepted an extra fortnight's pay and considered it as a sort of bonus whilst they continued working for six days a week, every week of every year. The concept of holidays for their own sake, to relieve the monotony of a working existence, seemed quite incomprehensible in a society where to work for wages was considered a privilege.

Leave for an expatriate in the Copperbelt mining industry was, and still is, the opportunity to travel to exotic places. In the early Sixties we had to save hard to pay for our fares to return to Europe or elsewhere, to visit our families, and these journeys were minutely planned in order to call at all sorts of weird and wonderful destinations *en route* to London. But in addition to our annual leave, which could be accumulated over several years in order to make the huge outlay on fares worthwhile, we were given casual leave of five days a year, which, added to a weekend or a long public holiday, enabled up to nine or ten consecutive days' leave to be taken. This casual leave could neither be accumulated nor added to a period of annual leave, thus ensuring that everyone took a good week's leave each year, even if one just stayed at home. But most of us were only too enthusiastic to use these short leaves to get as far as possible away from the Copperbelt, often to beauty spots in Zambia, but also further afield. The most popular time for these excursions was in early July, the most beautiful time in the Zambian bush with guaranteed sun and no rain, and relatively cool days with chilly nights. This is idyllic holiday weather and coincides with what used to be the Rhodes and Founders holiday weekend, the Monday and Tuesday following the first Sunday in July; since independence this was renamed Heroes and Unity weekend. Oddly enough the mining industry only enjoys the Heroes Day holiday, whereas everyone else in Zambia also enjoys a holiday on Unity Day!

Modern contract leave is on an annual entitlement basis only and fares are paid, by the employers, to the expatriate's country of recruitment. Consequently, and sadly, many expatriates fail to take advantage of the travel opportunities in Zambia and its neighbouring countries and save all their leave, and cash, to spend on their return to Europe, from where the large majority are still recruited despite an increasing number of Asian technicians and professionals. Even allowing for the difficulty of travelling by car in the sixties and seventies, due to increased police and military activity, as a result of both armed urban crime and the presence in the country of many thousands of Zimbabwe freedom fighters or guerrillas, nationalists or terrorists depending upon your viewpoint, it was still surprising that more expatriates did not travel more within the country when and where permitted. There have of course been tragic cases of expatriate families being robbed, raped or even murdered, and these occurrences quite rightly resulted in outcry, but similar incidences affecting Zambians received far less publicity, and in any case one suspects that the frequency of such tragedies was less than in Britain. Be that as it may, my family and I enjoyed many journeys through various parts of the country over the years, both in good times and bad, and we were fortunate to have been involved in no nasty incidents, though many amusing ones, and received abundant politeness and nothing worse than occasional misunderstanding and consequent inconvenience. Friends of ours proved less lucky from time to time but generally speaking it is true to say that courtesy breeds courtesy. The greatest hazard by far of any journey in Zambia remains that of an accident caused by undisciplined drivers or excess speed on indifferent road surfaces. In fact the country has the unenviable, but well-earned, reputation as having the worst road accident record in the world. Many is the tragedy caused by a driver crashing into the rear of a lorry parked on the road with no lights. However, enough of the dark side and more of the lighter aspects with which our journeys seemed, particularly in retrospect, to have been liberally sprinkled, although far funnier things did happen to others than to ourselves.

Perhaps our favourite story was of the motorist who was stopped by armed police on the main thoroughfare of the Copperbelt, the road linking Kitwe and Ndola, on one of the many occasions following an armed incident in one of these towns. The driver was told to get out of his car which was then searched inside and within the boot: nothing suspicious was found and the driver was politely informed that he could proceed. Some 15 miles further on he arrived at a second police checkpoint and again he stopped at the barricade and was asked to get out of the car, which was searched. However, imagine his horror on opening the boot to see that lying there, large as life, was a rifle. The innocent motorist was totally amazed, whilst the Zambian policeman quite naturally became highly excited, but knowing the unpredictability of local policemen whom he knew to have a tendency to walk about with live ammunition up the spout and the safety off, he remained as calm and rational as he could. After a quite incoherent and volatile gabbling between the proud discoverer of the rifle and his police colleague, during which the motorist half expected to be shot at any moment as one of Iain Smith's dastardly Rhodesian spies, it occurred to him that the rifle must have been left in the car's boot by the policeman at the last checkpoint. Some half an hour later this line of thought had been accepted by the disappointed police, who were then faced with the problem of what to do with the offending rifle. The solution, however, was obvious, and the amazed motorist was instructed to drive back the 15 miles and deliver the rifle to its rightful owner; and rather than risk upsetting the police he obliged. The wretched policeman, who had by this time realised he had lost his weapon, was disconsolately picking his nose and reflecting on his probable fate when the driver stopped and informed him that if he would care to search the car again he would no longer need to look so miserable, and so the incident ended happily for all concerned.

Stories of road checks for safety purposes abounded, and although it was not always possible to authenticate all of these, a couple do make amusing anecdotes. One such concerned a motorist with faulty windscreen wipers, and his heart sank when the policeman checking his car told him to switch them on: strictly with tongue in cheek and with great presence of mind, the driver replied that his were the new automatic type which would only work if it was raining! Half-expecting the policeman to jump on the bonnet and pee on his windscreen, this motorist was delighted to be told by this gullible soul that he could proceed. Another incident, which I can vouch for, involved a motorist who was in fact genuinely driving to town for the express purpose of having two bald tyres replaced, and hoping that he would choose a day when there was no police road block for safety checks. However, he chose badly, and sure enough he was stopped and his car inspected in great detail. Finally he was told to switch on his side lights, then dipped beam and full beam, all of which were in good order. He was then told to proceed, with the caustic remark that he was lucky, as today their instructions were to check lights, but that if it had been tyres he would have been in deep trouble. I remember on one occasion travelling in our Austin Maxi which had the rear seats folded down in order to provide a nice flat space for our champion Irish Wolfhound, Rory, to stretch out in comfort. Nothing would induce the policeman to approach Rory in the back of the car as part of his search, but he was clearly mystified that there was no boot for him to search and didn't know how to proceed. However, an elegant yawn from our vast and well-toothed hound finally convinced him that this unconventional motor-car was not worth further inspection, and he waved us on with a frustrated and fatuous grin, trying to imply that he had known all along that hatchbacks didn't have secret compartments. Rory was in fact our greatest asset in ensuring speedy progress through police checks.

After independence in 1964, and before the start of the unhappiest phase of Rhodesia's UDI in the early seventies, Zambia was still a relatively safe place to travel by road, and in fact saw great advances in communications in large part specifically as a result of the closure of the Zambia-Rhodesia border. The silver lining for Zambia of the UDI situation saw the reconstruction and tarring of both the Great North Road, right through to the Tanzanian border, and the Great East Road to Malawi: many bridges were built and other roads upgraded, and the Chinese built a new railway enabling rail traffic to reach Dar-es-Salaam port on the Indian Ocean in Tanzania. Whatever the short-comings of these projects, and there were many, they undoubtedly improved accessibility of many previously remote areas, and despite considerable deterioration of these lines of communication since their construction, the immediate benefits were immediately very substantial. The greatest crisis for Zambia's economy at this time was the threat to its previously reliable export-import routes through Rhodesia to Beira port in Mozambique in the east, and to South Africa in the south, and the most critical single item in short supply became oil. In 1966, all oil and petrol had to be imported by road from the north along what became known as the Hell Run from Dar-es-Salaam: additional petrol and diesel fuel was also air-lifted in by a fleet of four Hercules aircraft operating almost non-stop and taking out some 20 to 40 tons of vital copper exports per trip to provide the country's foreign exchange and life-blood. Consequently petrol became in very short supply and was rationed, so curtailing many individuals' excursions both locally and on holiday. We all scrimped and saved as best we could and many Copperbelt homes harboured illegally acquired and hoarded petrol for private motoring. But petrol problems were not all due to rationing and there were frequent periods of shortages, some genuine, others due to inefficient distribution, and some due to a combination of these and other factors such as was the case on one of our trips through and out of Zambia in, 1970.

On that occasion we had planned a circular route, first on the Great North Road to the Tanzania border, then east across country to the Nyika plateau in Malawi, and then returning via Chipata and the Great East Road to Lusaka and the Copperbelt, thus retracing our steps for only about 100 miles out of a total journey of rather over 2,000 miles. The first day's journey was easy and we motored comfortably on full-width tar all day, arriving in mid-afternoon at Mpika which is where our problems began, halfway between the Copperbelt and the Zambian border with Tanzania. No petrol. We tried the Tanzania truck depot; Indian traders; a White Father's mission station; and finally the police, all to no avail. We spent an uncomfortable night at the Crested Crane Hotel, which had deteriorated drastically since my previous visit some years before, and it was clear that they were now unused to having visitors. Anne and I shared one room, Guy and Barry aged nine and seven shared another, but both rooms were grimy with dirty sheets, greasy chipboard bedside tables containing fragments of cigarette ends, spent matches and antique potato crips; there was no hot water, and one needed to sneak up on the cold tap and take it by surprises to coax out a decaying trickle of bright red ooze which represented cold water. And the flush lavatory appeared to have no plumbing to connect it to the source of the bright red ooze. Supper consisted of sweet potatoes, rice, well-charred leather of dubious origin, and some almost crystalline material which was described on the menu in childish handwriting as 'jelly pudding'. We spent an almost sleepless night whilst Anne and I considered the merits of trying to go on, versus attempting to cancel our trip and return ignominiously home but we were both agreed that whatever we did, we couldn't risk staying another night at the Crested Crane. We had ample food with us, as we had planned several days at rest huts in Malawi, and a precious four-gallon jerrycan of reserve petrol: but unfortunately this was inadequate, even at an optimum speed, to take us either to Tunduma on the Tanzania border, or back to Kapiri Mposhi, 'Hill of the Ants', where we had last been able to obtain petrol. So it was that we resolved to take our problem to the District Governor the next morning even though it would be Sunday.

The morning dawned and we paid our ridiculously expensive bill, including ten per cent 'in lioo *(sic)* of tips', and drove over rutted dirt tracks to the *boma* of the district headquarters, where we found a dreamy and offhand messenger who directed us to the Governor's pleasant but run-down bungalow. We knocked on the door, feeling extremely foolish and expecting short shrift, only to be greeted by a polite Zambian in a dressing-gown stifling a yawn and rubbing his eyes. This kindly official, disturbed early on Sunday morning, promptly agreed to help us and asked us to wait while he dressed when he would find us some petrol. He neither questioned our story nor told us what he must have felt, and when dressed instructed us to follow his car which we did. At the depot of ZESCO, the Zambian Electricity Supply Company in Mpika, he merely sent messages for an official to be brought and then ordered him to supply us with sufficient petrol to get us to Tunduma. Now this may seem unremarkable in itself, as no doubt the Governor acted quite properly and in a thoroughly humanistic way, 'humanism' being the philosophy of Zambia, but Anne and I were unable to avoid reflecting on the outcome should the roles have been reversed and the incident happened in similar circumstances ten years earlier. A Zambian motorist running out of petrol in a rural area, even supposing he had had the temerity to try, would almost certainly have been faced with an enraged white District Commissioner, apoplectic at the cheek of being woken early on a Sunday morning by a black African who had himself to blame for being so careless. That episode remained a comforting memory on subsequent occasions when Zambian bureaucracy and petty officialdom reached its most aggravating and intransigent extremes.

Perhaps the most exasperating of such occasions followed the theft of Anne's handbag whilst she was shopping in Kitwe, and the loss of her driving licence. The saga of attempting to obtain a duplicate extended over our final three and a half years in Zambia, and remained unresolved on our departure and presumably is so to this day. The most complicated aspect, apart from dealing with a plethora of diverse and obscurely involved Ministry departments, resulted from a helpful comment by Anne, on one of the many quadruplicated forms, stating that the number of her lost licence was either one above or one below mine, since our licences were both issued by the same office on the same occasion. Therefore, Anne stated, her licence must be either No. 2251D or 2253D. This constructive remark attracted a scornful and suspicious reply to the effect that Anne could not possibly have held either two licences or one licence with two numbers, and at least a year's correspondence elapsed before that particular red herring had been exorcised. Judging by amusing stories of achievements by the Swansea licencing computer in this country since our return, we perhaps should not have been quite so cynical about its Lusaka equivalent, but the inconvenience was no doubt greater in Zambia since one was quite likely to be stopped at road blocks and asked to produce one's driving licence at least once in almost every journey. On these occasions Anne had to produce sheafs of affidavits and correspondence to illustrate and substantiate her predicament, and these resulted in long delays and awkward moments such as when one policeman insisted that Audrey, Anne's first name, was a man's name. Anne was sorely tempted to shorten the protracted interview by saying that, yes, she was really a man, but happily refrained from such a contentious comment, and common-sense, combined with by that time a long and impatient queue of other motorists, eventually prevailed and she was waved reluctantly on.

Chapter 4
CAMPS AND KAIYAS

My first work assignment was to join a reconnaissance party at a remote camp deep in the bush, a long day's drive from headquarters at Kalulushi and over dirt roads and bush tracks that proved particularly uncomfortable to my unaccustomed frame. The country we traversed was unexpectedly featureless and dull and did not fit my expectation of darkest Africa at all. The dust was there all right, and in fact was impossible to escape; and so was the heat in no small measure; but instead of the expected majestic vista of plains and hills, lush valleys and rivers we drove on and on through a monotonous landscape packed right up to the roadside with an endless array of rather undistinguished trees, so that only rarely could we see further than a few hundred yards to the side or in front of us. As for the billowing clouds of dusty fall-out in our wake, and the similar clouds which enveloped us on the rare occasions that we met oncoming vehicles, events always preceded by a frantic winding up of windows and closing of air vents, these had coated everything in range with a drab reddish-brown shroud so that even the new foliage on the trees looked tired and sad. Little of interest was seen on this journey, apart from a few scruffy villages, a guinea-fowl or two, and the occasional family of baboons or monkeys. I was never able to sleep on journeys of any sort and I was only able to relieve the tedium by such absorbing calculations as how many cubic yards constituted the larger termitaries; or how many trees there were per acre, or in a square mile, or in the Northwestern Province; and so on. Even this African variation on the theme of counting sheep failed to induce anything other than a headache, however, and since my boss who was doing all the driving clearly intended to stay at the wheel, rather than risk an inexperienced driver turning us over on the rutted road, it proved a thoroughly uninspiring journey.

There was little time on arrival for other than a brief introduction to my future colleagues, as all were in some way or other involved in the doomed attempt to save the pitifully dying Dalmatian I mentioned earlier (see Chapter One). After a gloomy meal and a few desultory scraps of conversation, those of us who could not help just grabbed the Tilley lamps provided by the camp servants and drifted off to our tents for the night. The following morning, with the dog dead and the snake found and killed, I got to know the pleasant and mixed assortment of people with whom I was camping. The senior man, Ernie, had recently returned to the company after studying sulphur isotopes for a doctorate degree in an American university, and he was the only other professional geologist in the camp. Mike and John, helicopter pilot and engineer respectively, were both well-seasoned in the ways of the bush and were an interestingly dissimilar but compatible pair. The remainder of the party consisted of three instrument observers. Two youngsters, Ken and Arthur and Chick, the eldest and most-experienced bush-boy of them all, with many years in the country, his father having served in the colonial Provincial Administration. Chick, a qualified engineer who had served in India during the war, was a confirmed bachelor and had never felt the need to put down roots; and he thrived on the varied and unconventional challenge of working with an exploration team. It was Chick who had been the owner of the Dalmatian, and that sad incident had made him more withdrawn than usual: he sought consolation with his own company and a bottle of Scotch in the privacy of his own tent, and no one attempted to disturb his genuine grief. I was to get to know Chick better in the years ahead, but right until his stoic death from cancer some 18 years later, he was a person who chose to keep his private affairs very much to himself.

Those first few weeks in the bush proved happy days. We rose early, before the sun got up, and returned around midday, leaving the afternoon free for writing up notes, plotting our maps and preparing for the next day's work. My own first task was to map blocks of ground and collect soil samples for geological analysis, and so each day I set off with a gang of six Africans, driving to my starting point on a pre-surveyed grid. I don't think my crew appreciated the inexpert way in which I attempted to control the truck as it slipped and roared through deep sand and rutted tracks. I had passed my driving test only very shortly before leaving England, in a small car on the edge of London, and this new environment was totally unfamiliar. So we jerked and bumped our way between and into trees, sometimes sideways but usually forwards, and miraculously did serious damage only to the vegetation, little to the vehicle, and none to ourselves. But I soon got the knack, and then found it rather exhilarating, although I suspect my enthusiasm was not shared by my passengers in the back for several weeks at least.

The monotonous bush I had seen on my long journey to the camp was now all around me, but I was amazed and delighted to find it alive, vibrant, colourful and exciting. Now that I was away from the dust and the noise of the truck there was interest all around, with constantly changing detail and a host of new plants, birds and insects in every direction. My enthusiasm for the most mundane item clearly amused my crew of Africans, mostly Kaonde tribesman from neighbouring villages, and my mapping progress was initially slow as I stopped to look at and examine these new surroundings.

Our method of mapping, established long before, was to advance in line abreast, with the geologist and crew-boss in the centre with a chola-boy or bag carrier, and two other men on either side at distances such that any rocks traversed on the line would be seen, at which point the geologist would be called to examine them and note their characteristics and location. This proved most effective, but since rocks were very scarce in the deeply weathered environment it was also necessary to record soil colours and textures. Additionally we noted details of the vegetation, at regular intervals, so compiling a map of soil and vegetation types as well as topography and rock distribution. In fact, though, such was the poverty of outcrop, that most of the geology was inferred from the maps of tree types and soils, a point I initially found both baffling and irritating, especially as even the tree names had to be recited to me by my crew-boss. My sturdy crew-boss also collected samples of soil at regular intervals, putting them in special waterproof packets for later analysis to determine concentrations of metals which might lead to a source area of mineralisation. All this was very new to me, but the method was well-proven and even after a whole day of recording nothing but trees and soils it was comforting to know that an overall pattern was emerging nonetheless.

My crew-boss at this first camp was called Sine, but whether he had been christened from a book of logarithmic tables, or his name was abbreviated from something else I never discovered. He was a likeable enough young man, quite slight but nonetheless well built, with a prodigious ability for walking at great speed over any terrain without changing his stride; and he could also keep a compass bearing with far greater accuracy that I could myself. His English was rough and ready but we were at least mutually intelligible and he was always keen to please. I was unused to such attention and found it strange not to have to carry anything, as Sine would never permit me to carry even my own compass or geological pick unless I was actually using them, so that I strode unencumbered through the bush with just a notebook and pencil to hold: Sine carried the important items such as pick, compass and snake-bite kit, whilst the chola-boy brought along the rear with the water-bag and the ever-increasing load of soil samples. If we were making good time we used to stop for the occasional rest, when the men would either lie about and talk and smoke, or else disappear on a search for honey and mushrooms. Much excitement followed a honey discovery, and even if it meant felling a huge tree to get at it, a honey halt was then mandatory.

Occasionally a buck or rabbit was sighted and pandemonium reigned whilst everyone streamed off into the distance with wild shrieks of expectation, but none of these impromptu hunts was ever successful. This pleased me, although it undoubtedly frustrated the men, especially on occasions when work was slow and I forbade them to chase away, and then the day became gloomy and the men sulked. I think I was considered rather odd by the Africans in not only disliking killing but in not carrying a rifle or shotgun as many of the other bwanas did. Shooting for the pot was quite commonplace in those days, and I dare say that if I had needed meat I would have been prepared to do the same, but since our meat ration, and quantities for the men, were sent out regularly from headquarters shooting was more usually a sport rather than a necessity. As far as self-protection was concerned there was little need for firearms, though wild animals were in fact plentiful, but to see then it was generally necessary to track them. Snakes too were common, although normally they will disappear at the slightest sound of an approaching man.

One early morning on a day's mapping we did come across a large black mamba in a tree. The snake posed no threat to us and could easily have been left alone, but Africans have an instinctive loathing of all snakes and feel they must destroy all that they find. It was impossible to prevent the men hurling sticks at the inoffensive mamba, which slithered elegantly through the branches until it was obliged to drop to the ground. I shall always remember the speed with which this slate grey snake surged through the long grass, standing on its tail with its head some four feet above the ground like a periscope, dodging and swerving in its attempt to escape. But the men cornered it and beat it to death. We measured it as eight feet nine inches long, and its fangs were most impressive. Other snakes, mambas, boomslangs or tree snakes, puff adders and gaboon vipers, were occasionally found in camp, a favourite place being by the bath-house. This consisted of a raised platform of bamboo poles, with a thatched roof and open at one side: the tin bath tubs were placed on the bamboo floor and a bath-boy filled them with hot water from a fuel drum which was heated by a vigorous log fire. The bath-house ritual was part of life in the bush, and to soak in the hot water, liberally laced with Dettol, drinking one's ice-cold beer after a hot day's trek, was a truly memorable bliss. Most bath-houses were sited on the edge of a grassy open space, known as a *dambo*, and the siting was always critically supervised to ensure the best view. The bath-boy's job was not only to fetch and heat the water but also to provide a smoke-free bath-house!

On one occasion the bath-boy, during the course of the morning, had found and destroyed a large and lissom boomslang which uncharacteristically had been little damaged. We therefore decided to use it as the basis of a joke, unkindly, on Chick. That day Chick had been out on a helicopter sortie and would be the last of us returning to the camp. We therefore rigged up a life-like pose for our dead boomslang, draped convincingly across a small bough just beside the path along which Chick would be returning to the mess from the helicopter pad. As the helicopter landed, we were all ranged along the front of the mess hut, lounging in camp chairs with beers in hand, and we watched Chick alight and start the short walk up to camp. Chick, who was a small man, was as usual positively hung over with knives, panga and shotgun, as he was wisely always well-prepared, and as he drew abreast of the snake we all shouted in a panic-stricken way, pointing at the wretched decoy. Chick's reactions were quite splendid and spontaneous as he swung his gun up and blasted a couple of cartridges at the coiled corpse nearby. But he was decidedly not amused at our juvenile prank, particularly when we stopped laughing, momentarily, only to discover that not a single pellet had struck the snake. It was of course a silly and potentially dangerous joke, and Chick was right not to be amused, but in those days we were perhaps still young enough to enjoy a prank which later seemed irresponsible.

A position in every camp chosen with equal care and skill to that of the bath-house was the camp lavatory, the traditional place for such thrones being on the top of the largest ant-hill within a few minutes stroll of the line of tents or huts. For a while the derivation of the title for these establishments, which were known as PK's, escaped me, but I discovered that this simply stood for *pikinini kaiya* which in fact translates as 'little house'. Little houses they were, being thatched and with a small hessian-hung doorway, and normally a strategic view of the camp and its surroundings more befitting a machine-gun post than a thunder-box. The internal construction was simple, a vertical shaft dug some 20 feet deep and covered with a hollow frame and crowned by a wooden, and later and more contemporarily plastic, loo seat. The shafts were regularly and frequently sprinkled with lime and consequently quite hygienic and fly-free. Snakes and PKs would appear to have little in common on the face of it, but since these bush PKs were so often located on ant-hills, or more usually termitaries, and these latter were riddled with tunnels and holes made by the termites, a good sized ant-hill might well be the home for several snakes, which loved the labyrinthine intestinal structure of these huge mounds. It was therefore usually with caution that one took up occupancy of the PK so as not to infringe any prior rights, established by a family of cobras, or a python or two.

One luckless geologist, exhausted after a long day of misfortunes during which his helicopter transport had failed, forcing him to trek 12 miles back to camp, crossing a river and a swamp in the process, was careless enough to approach the camp PK without due care and attention and received a jet of venom in his eye from a spitting cobra as his reward. The eye was quickly washed out and the man was evacuated to headquarters without delay to receive medical attention. He was lucky to escape with temporary blindness, and several days' pain, but suffered no lasting damage. A number of the cobras in Africa have this ability to spit venom at their enemies or prey, hitting their target from distances of six up to as much as ten feet away. In fact I remember only too vividly facing such a stream of venom from a black-necked spitting cobra at our home in Kalulushi one night many years later.

We were sitting on the enclosed verandah reading one evening, enjoying the peace of the house after our baby daughter Beccy had been tucked up for the night, when one of our dogs started barking frantically just under our window. Since the shouted orders to be quiet made no effect on the excited dog we went out with a torch to investigate and saw some movement at the base of one of the bushes. On more careful, but not closer inspection, we identified a few sinister grey coils and realised that a fair-sized snake was hiding next to our front door. Since it was dark and we couldn't see the head of the snake I decided to fetch a ten-foot bamboo pole, which we normally used for knocking down our enormous avocado-pears, and prod the beast into the open. This only resulted in persuading the snake to take refuge in the drain under our front door step, and there he stayed until the combination of the hosepipe and bamboo pole forced him to make a run for it when he shot out of the drain and into the Virginia creeper clinging to the side of the house. To our dismay we saw the sinuous creature was at least six feet long, and quite thick, and it proceeded to entwine itself into the burglar-bars of Beccy's open bedroom window. Anne rushed inside to remove Beccy from the room and we were mightily thankful that the wire mosquito screens were sound and in place, as there could otherwise have been a tragic ending. At this stage we imagined that the intruder was a black mamba because of the ease with which it climbed, and consequently it never occurred to me that it would spit: but having rescued Beccy we realised that we would still have to try and kill the snake as it could easily attack one of our dogs, and in any case we couldn't possibly leave it to roam through Kalulushi. I therefore chivvied it with the pole from as discrete a distance as possible, to try to dislodge it from the bars at the window; and as luck would have it, the open window was between me and the snake as it spat, so that I merely saw a pool of venom suddenly appear on the glass as if by magic and in direct line with my eyes. A lucky escape, and eventually I managed to knock the snake down and kill it with the pole, finally decapitating it with a spade, relieved to have ended the episode but sad at destroying a creature which had only retaliated when attacked. Strangely enough I saw more snakes in the gardens of Kalulushi than in the bush itself, perhaps as they were attracted to the warmth of the compost heaps, the vermin and eggs in the chicken runs, or the water from hoses and swimming pools.

But to return to the bush and my first camp where there were many other entertainments and encounters to be had. Our supplies arrived at regular intervals, and one of our number took it in turns to calculate the quantities and instruct the cooks on each days' menu. We lived well but paid for our food out of a meagre field allowance, such that we invariably spent more than our allowances, and depending on the efficiency of our monthly mess officer had months of luxury or mundane meals, but always augmented by ample supplies, bought personally, of beer. In those days there was a choice between Castle lager, Lion lager or Export ale, all thoroughly excellent and each with its own devotees. Of course the spirits were not neglected either, but these were usually saved for special occasions which were chosen as the whim took us. Other brews, which we were occasionally tempted to try, were local products either from our own compound or workers' encampment or from the local villages, and included maize or honey beer, and more rarely some more powerful concoction such as one well-known elixir made from a small wild fruit, *mupundu*, which could make a passable wine with skill. But its smell was not attractive and could easily put one off, as could the general opacity of all these potions; the nickname for the mupundu was 'drain tree', due to the awful smell of the rotting fruit found beneath the tree.

Eggs were of course not an easy item to transport by road and we usually were able to purchase these from the villages, all of which had swarms of scraggy chickens. Usually cash was the item of exchange but we did on occasions resort to a form of barter, using nails or paraffin or some other scarce commodity. But the most memorable transaction was for a short helicopter ride for the local chief, Chief Chizera, in exchange for a few dozen eggs. The occasion was no doubt remembered with great glee by this notable character.

In our time we tended to amuse ourselves in varying ways; Ernie mostly puzzling out some geological problem; Chick reading, and cleaning his weapons; Arthur I remember as being preoccupied with a body-building course, much to all our amusement; Ken tinkering with the vehicles; John reading, writing letters and playing and beating all of us at Scrabble; and myself soaking up the natural history and wandering around with my binoculars, and practising very inexpertly with a small throwing knife. Mike, the helicopter pilot, I remember as essentially associated with lurid magazines, and boasting of past exploits of both the sexual and aeronautical varieties. He was a good pilot but was most anxious that we should all be very well aware of it.

Another character who was a frequent visitor to our camp, and whom most of us visited once or twice a week, was our diamond driller; a really earthy

Afrikaner named Jan, who seemed to be a thoroughly wild and independent character quite capable of surviving for ever on his own resources unless murdered in bed by one of his workers, all of whom appeared to fear and hate him, and whom he despised. He hunted often, both for the pot and for pleasure, and his camp, some miles from ours, was always strewn with skins, stretched and salted, and with strips of biltong drying in the bright hot sunlight. In many ways I quite genuinely admired his self-sufficiency and his tracking skills, and enjoyed listening to his much-exaggerated hunting stories, but I later discovered that his methods were unscrupulous and devious. His usual source of meat was from night-hunting, an illegal and despicable form of shooting in which the hunter drove or walked with a powerfully beamed lantern, a *bulala lamp* or a 'killing lamp', which dazzled and dazed the hunted animal which was then shot at close range. Jan narrowly missed a sticky end on one of his night hunting excursions when he had shot at an unidentified pair of eyes, shining in his beam, to be greeted by a snarl and charging leopard. The animal was, fortunately for Jan, grievously wounded and unable to carry through the charge, and was killed with a second shot. Jan was proud to display the beautiful pelt to all his visitors. Of course it takes all sorts to make the world and Jan and others like him undoubtedly contributed to the legends of the bush and the characters of the time, however distasteful his exploits may appear to others.

Of course, if one is hungry, killing at night is morally no different from killing by day, and to kill for one's own subsistence cannot really be condemned as it is no worse than buying meat that you have expected someone else to kill and prepare for you. But killing for sport is another matter, and one that I have always abhorred ever since my only first-hand experience of wild-fowling whilst on a working vacation in the Swedish forests. I was one of a party of international undergraduates from all over Europe, and one of our employers had arranged an evening's duck-shooting for us, as one of the many courteous gestures made to us during our six-week vacation job attached to a large paper-producing industry. Just before dusk we rowed out from the edge of one of the many lakes and secreted ourselves in various hides on some of the small sandbanks and islands: as it grew progressively darker several flights of duck came skimming in over the lake to be met by a barrage of multidirectional shot from some six double-barrelled guns, one of which was mine. The net result of this unskilled fusillade was that one small bird came fluttering down into the water where it squawked and flapped pathetically but since it was one that I had aimed at, however badly, I felt personally to blame for its agony. Being on a small island I was unable to reach the bird, and was forced to listen to its desperate struggles. It was still feebly quacking and fluttering some half an hour later when the boatman came to collect us. Oddly enough that single scrawny duckling was the entire bag for the evening, and although no less than two others claimed it to have been their shot which had winged it, I knew in my heart of hearts it had been mine. I vowed never to hunt again, a vow I have kept, however irrational or odd this may seem. It was perhaps a marginal relief to be able to publicly disclaim responsibility for the duck's death, quickly ensured as soon as it was retrieved, since others were only too anxious to acquire what was to them the accolade of success. To me, however, it was strangely upsetting, a small incident but one which I shall always remember. But I digress.

To the indigenous peoples of Africa hunting is instinctive and based on their need for survival, and so it was not only difficult, but unnatural, to apply my criteria to their activities. Nonetheless, I would always destroy or dismantle their snares, and release any unharmed animals should I come across such in the bush. Some snared animals were of course found dead, or so horribly maimed that they had to be killed, but the most loathsome custom that I came across was the sale of wounded animals. A buck which had been caught would be kept alive, sometimes for days, and its flesh therefore fresh, by breaking its legs so that it couldn't struggle or escape on its way to be sold as meat or *nyama*. Even this extreme cruelty was not seen as such by the rural African people, since they did not feel the need to justify the means to the end. The needs of the European, who appeared to demand fresh meat, without requiring to know how it was procured, illustrates the double standards which the African found it hard to understand and accept, let alone adopt.

Another incident I still remember quite vividly was my first encounter with a monitor lizard, or iguana as I still prefer to call them ever since my first sight of one, stuffed and on a tall bookshelf in my grandfather's study in England, one of numerous mementos the doctor returned with after his service in South Africa during Boer War. This stuffed and curiously dragon-like reptile was no more than three feet long but looked positively mythical to me as a small boy. However, the first live iguana I was to see was when mapping some ten miles from my first camp in Zambia, the more strange to me since I had always assumed that these lizards were water dwellers as in fact, I later discovered, some species are. But there we were, a string of six Africans and myself stretched out line abreast as we advanced slowly through an uncharacteristically rocky patch of dry bush country, miles from the nearest water, when this large crocodile-type beast erupted practically from beneath my feet and scuttled rapidly into the rocks. We were all thoroughly startled by this totally unexpected encounter, the Africans volubly alarmed whilst I was extremely puzzled, since I could not think what the creature was, especially since we had only received a fleeting glimpse of it. We were in plenty of time to reach our rendezvous with a Land Rover and so I ordered my crew to find the animal and flush it out, which they most reluctantly did, making very sure that they kept well clear as it rushed and slithered, hissed, and slashed its enormous tail in all directions. The lizard was certainly larger and much more powerful than I had expected, but I was determined now to capture it so that I could take it to camp for identification by my colleagues, half-imagining that it was a rare discovery. With much difficulty, and a certain amount of bribery, I eventually persuaded my men to cut sticks and bark twine for the capture and we at last cornered the exhausted animal sufficient for me to hold down its head whilst others, fortified by my tight grip, managed to immobilise the thrashing and dangerous tail. It was between five and six feet long, and looked very evil with its flickering tongue, but we had not injured it in any way despite its undignified capture and we managed to carry it for the short distance to the vehicle where it was carefully and securely tied on to the bonnet: there was no way that I could persuade the Africans to allow it in the back of the Land Rover as they were very decidedly afraid of it. This was understandable, as if the lashing tail had come loose it could very probably have broken one of their legs, and anyone rash enough to get bitten could easily, I suspect, have lost a finger or two. But their main fear was its evil looks and sinister reputation as it was believed, as were smaller lizards and chameleons, to have poisonous fangs and supernatural attributes.

I was a little disappointed on my return to camp to find that my prize was a land monitor, in no way a rarity although it was unquestionably a fine and large specimen, and we released it to wander off in an arrogant and offended way into the bush. A small dog, belonging to the camp, had a frantic fit of barking and yapping as it tried to harry the monster, but this ended abruptly as it collected a mighty whack from the tip of the lizard's tail, when the anguished hound squealed in fright and pain and ran for the protection of the amused bwanas. It was lucky that the dog was not caught by the full force of the monitor's fury as it would have undoubtedly been badly injured. I later saw other monitors, both on land and in the water, but only one that was approaching the size and ferocity of the one I had first encountered.

Less exciting but more threatening hazards of the bush were the common and insidious diseases of malaria, sleeping sickness, and bilharzia but it was quite possible with care to avoid all of these dangers. Perhaps the most repulsive though was the *putsi* fly. These common flies lay their eggs in damp clothing or fur, and when the tiny grubs hatch they penetrate the skin and slowly grow in size forming horribly painful and itchy swellings like boils, eventually bursting out leaving festering and infected craters. We were all very careful to ensure that all washed clothing was thoroughly ironed, this being especially important in the bush where the washing was left to dry outside on the grass in the open air. But even with all our precautions, each of us as well as our pets suffered from these loathsome putsis. Anne spent long hours squeezing the grubs out of infected animals, ours and others, from time to time, and on one occasion she removed over 50 from a single guinea pig owned by our neighbour's children. Some careless mothers found their babies, whose nappies had been dried in the fresh air and then not ironed, in great pain and discomfort due to the dreaded grubs.

Not only did the bush pose natural hazards, particularly to the unwary and inexperienced, but it also provided notable cures and potions which the indigenous peoples have discovered and exploited over the centuries. Quite a number of these remedies, known to layman and witch-doctor alike, and others the specific preserve of the latter, undoubtedly are effective and are still little understood by modern doctors and scientists. Others of course are quite obscure, and probably only of psychological importance, but many certainly have splendid theoretical, if not practical, attributes. Most of these preparations are derived from vegetation, leaves, bark or roots, whereas others combine these materials with such exotic additives as eagles' claws; part of a goat's penis; or even the flesh of a goblin, or an armadillo's scale. One curious recipe, including roots from a small perennial herb, together with a leech, and other roots from a place where animals have been grubbing, provides a powder after ingredients have been dried and pounded: this powder, rubbed into cuts on the hands and arms, will supposedly improve a woman's porridge-making abilities. Other, less frivolous concoctions, are available as treatment of cure for virtually every ailment from tuberculosis to swollen testicles; from earache to wounds from lion, leopard or witch; as aphrodisiacs and fertility mixtures; or just to bring luck or keep one out of prison. I never tried any of these remedies or prophylactics as I was quite happy to make use of the normal services provided by the company's own hospitals, but many of the local people would rely solely, and from choice, on the traditional medicines and spells, even though these could be expensive while the white man's were free. Anne once had great difficulty persuading the wife of one of our houseboys to take her young baby to the clinic. The wretched child was a sad sight with the top of its head encrusted in what appeared to be resin or gum, which in fact it proved to be. On checking with the local sorcerer's apprentice we discovered it had been applied as a sticky glue, which had subsequently hardened, since the child's mother had feared that the child's fontanel was not closing. The same mixture or medicine also served as an agent for tightening the skins of village drums in order to achieve the desired tone.

Chapter 5

DRUMS AND DREAMS

Drums, perhaps tuned with some of the said mysterious tree gum, are very much an integral part of the warp and weft of Africa, their throb and rumble being as essential as the noises of cricket or tree frog to the sounds of the night. The rhythm of drums, since time immemorial, evoked every emotion from terror to ecstasy, and no other musical instrument, with the possible exception of the bagpipe, is so capable of stirring the soul. But it is the drum, not the pipe, which dominates the African musical, recreational and ceremonial scene, either as the trivial cacophonous accompaniment to a night at the urban beerhall, or the solemn and awesome beat at some chieftain's funeral deep in the bush. We initially found the repetitive evening concerts rather oppressive, and even a trifle menacing, as there was no way of avoiding the noise short of producing one's own; but the feeling of foreboding as we first experienced the abstract and ominous echoes of the drum from the compound soon gave way to an acceptance of the noise as part of the inherent background of the dark continent. Occasionally, at times of particularly racial tension, the rhythm of the unseen drums in the darkness did seem to take on a sinister and threatening significance, but we learned to ignore even the wildest and most agitated thundering which would often reach crescendo after crescendo throughout the entire night. Our frequent response was to draw the curtains, switch off the lamps, and envelop ourselves in splendid stereophonic waves of Sibelius or Rachmaninov, so obliterating primitive magic with its imported technological counterpart. We wondered if the sounds of Finlandia were to the African ear as the sounds of Zambia were to our own, though I found the haunting music of Sibelius, in particular, equally at home in Africa as in Europe and marvellously evocative of all wild places irrespective of continent or climate: whereas recordings of African drums played in Europe, though certainly stimulating seem incongruous.

Probably the earliest use of the drum was as a means of communication, and the annual movement of thousands of the Lozi peoples of the Western province of Zambia is still to this day heralded by a beating of drums. This signal informs the people that their *Litunga*, chief of the Lozi, is preparing to move to higher ground due to the flooding of their homes on the vast Zambezi plains in February or March each year. The swollen river encroaches on the low ground, earlier or later depending on the rainfall, and at a given signal the Litunga and all his family and villagers and their possessions are moved, in a ragged flotilla of traditional barges and canoes, to higher ground some one day's paddling away. The occasion is a memorable one, full of African pomp and pageantry and not a little chaos, and now features high on the tourist menu, but the gradual transition from a cultural symbol to an international spectacle is bound to degrade the occasion. To have seen it only 50 years ago must be to have seen the real Africa, whereas now, whilst the huge black and white Royal Barge, the *Nalikwanda*, and its 30 colourful paddlers no doubt appear the same, as do the dust and sweat with the myriad ululating people, the setting has changed irrevocably. The blue and white Mercedes coaches with their air-conditioned comfort, and the presence of uniformed and armed police and slick-suited politicians amongst the rural and unsophisticated crowds, as well as the inevitable camera-toting tourists destroy in fair measure the magic of the occasion and its significance to the participants; but the shallow immediate visual and aural excitement remain nonetheless. However, it is interesting to reflect whether such essentially tribal ceremonies will survive for long, in a country which is striving to replace tribalism with Zambianism in the interests of political stability. Ironic indeed if the craving for foreign exchange and the tourist's currency perpetuates the tribal customs, whilst the government's philosophy urges nationalism as a replacement for the traditional tribalism. There is of course no reason why nationalism and pride in one's tribal heritage should not go hand in hand, the one a part of the other, but it may take several generations to achieve the unquestioning confidence needed to allow, for example, a Lozi to accept without question a Bemba leader in the interests of Zambia as a whole. At the time of writing, the present President, Kenneth Kaunda, has made remarkable progress towards such unity and is widely admired for this achievement, but it is undoubtedly a slow process.

Whilst the traditional entertainment of the Zambian peoples remains their music, essentially the rhythms of drums both large and small, augmented by gourd xylophone and thumb pianos, with other local variations on these basic types, the expatriate demands a greater variety of amusement and recreation. Before independence much of the itinerant skills of the international world of theatre, music and entertainment, were channelled through the main centres of Northern Rhodesia whilst on tour throughout the African continent, so that although audiences were perhaps small they were always appreciative and enthusiastic, and guest artists and troupes were always well received. Nowadays, with a smaller expatriate element, combined with political and financial constraints, it is largely necessary to create one's own amusements. A greater emphasis is now, partly due to necessity, centred on improving and enlarging the already excellent facilities which exist for almost every conceivable sporting activity from bowls to power-boat racing, golf to horse-riding, and badminton to fishing. But many still bewail the good times in the fifties and sixties when all sorts of cultural and imported events took place.

The most exciting family event in the early sixties was the visit of a well-known circus from South Africa, complete with clowns, tigers, acrobats and candyfloss. The big top was probably not big by world standards but it certainly housed all the thrills and charisma of larger circuses, and provided a highlight to look forward to with great excitement for the children. In those days the audience was almost exclusively expatriate, as of course were the performers, but the throngs of youths and *picannins* who were roughly dismissed by the hired hands when caught hanging around the cages and caravans, were no doubt unable to believe their eyes at the sight of strange beasts and jugglers, and all the glitter of exotic costumes and harnesses. The cost of a ticket in the early days was beyond the means of all but a handful of the local people, but I recall well our last visit to the circus, in June 1967, when several hundred Zambians were in the audience. Clearly the favourite set was that of a midget clown, Tickey he was called, who had the Africans in complete rapture with his antics and slapstick humour. But the performing tigers were something quite different, so that whereas I found the act degrading for these magnificent, muscle-rippling creatures, which were admittedly in fine health and condition, the Zambians were very frightened indeed and were clearly most relieved when the snarling beasts made their exit through the arching tunnel of steel. The tinsel-clad animal tamer was applauded with reverence as well as relief.

The most curious exhibition that I recall seeing in Zambia was heralded as 'Jonas, the Largest Animal in the World!' You would be right in guessing that this improbable exhibit was the refrigerated carcass of a whale, which I believe had considerable difficulty in negotiating the Zambezi valley and escarpments on entering the country. Not that it had managed the journey on its own of course, as not even a live Jonas could have swum up the Zambezi, but the colossal transporters needed for this leviathan and its mobile refrigeration plant were more suitable to the world's motorways than the euphemistically notated N1 of Zambia. But arrive it did, in January 1968, and my one regret was that it was virtually impossible to judge the size of it because of the need for massive hoardings to prevent people viewing it for free. In 1968 it was still essentially an expatriate's privilege to be able to afford entry to such a spectacle, but although there was plenty of interest from the local population they surely believed the whole performance was a hoax: not only had the inhabitants of this land-locked country no true concept of the sea, but they also, even in mythology, could not conceive of anything swimming which could exceed in size the admittedly huge Nile perch of the great rift lakes to the north of their country. My family and I queued for admission and were ushered into the cavernous creature's jaws, around the throat and back on the other side of the mouth, to be metaphorically spat out into the dust of the African continent in about five minutes flat. The entrepreneur who engineered this absurd show-business epic no doubt deserved every penny he earned from such an improbable exhibit: a pity he didn't direct his skills in mobile refrigeration to more practical propositions. Many are the embryo Zambian businessmen who have rapidly become bankrupt in attempting to sell fresh fish on the Copperbelt by buying a lorryload at Mpulungu, on the southern shores of Lake Tanganyika, and driving hell-for-leather back to their market with a rapidly melting pack of ice dripping over their increasingly putrid cargo. Admittedly, the vicissitudes of broken-down ferries and corrupt officials as they journeyed across the narrow Zairean pedicle did little to improve the chances of arriving on the Copperbelt with fresh fish, but a little extra planning for such predictable eventualities would have been amply rewarded. Perhaps someone has now got it right, but it was still a most unlikely event a year or two ago, when Birds Eye fishfingers, though a rare commodity, were still a more easily acquired item than fresh fish from a nearby lake. Jonas' journey, since being caught off Norway weighing in at 106,000lbs and 66 feet long, via Japan where he was apparently viewed by over two million people, to Kitwe where we saw him for a three-shilling entrance fee, should remain an example to the frozen food industry. Come to that, perhaps hydraulic engineers should take note that Jonas' heart was reputed to pump 8,000 litres of blood through his body 13 times a minute according to the exhibition of his carcass: personally, I'd far rather remain unaware of these awesome statistics, and marvel at the grace, efficiency and peacefulness of these superb creatures in the freedom of the oceans of the world.

Various exhibitions and occasions continued from colonial times have struggled against the odds to maintain standards, passing through very low times in the mid- seventies when some failed to withstand the pressures of sadly accelerated and misguided Zambianisation. But some have survived and there are even signs that the excellence of past decades may one day be emulated, if not surpassed, provided continuity can be maintained through the stringencies of present cash shortages. Many societies and associations are managing to stay alive and with a little commercial assistance are even expanding. One such is the Photographic Association of Zambia, which through the sheer hard work and enthusiasm of its committee members turned its traditional annual exhibition into an international exhibition of some standing as recently as 1977. In order to achieve this it was necessary to seek the cooperation and support   of foreign embassies and it is perhaps significant that this was most readily, though not exclusively, available from the Soviet Union. The Russians made marginal political capital out of the affair by staging an official photographic exhibition of their own alongside the Zambian exhibits, and by providing refreshments to officials and exhibitors after the award ceremonies: but few who attended the occasion were naïve enough to consider other than the pictorial and photographic merit of huge murals depicting 'the glorious struggle of the revolution' and various aspects of heroic comrades overcoming adversity. The evening became less cultural and more social as the vodka dripped home and a good time was no doubt had by all whether or not any brain-washing occurred. In Zambia, as elsewhere in a free society, one can still accept aid without strings, even if it's only a glass of vodka and a chicken vol-au-vent.

The Copperbelt Agricultural Society's annual show has also survived, though few would disagree that as a family occasion it has deteriorated drastically since its heyday in the early sixties. In those years it was a must, three days over a public holiday in the dry season, and attractions then varied from a South African fun-fair complete with carousels, toffee-apples and hoop-las stalls, to lavish exhibits by the copper industry and motor vehicle distributors, and prestigious contests for the nation's farmers and sportsmen. The site in Kitwe was a big one, overlooked by the mountainous heaps of slag disgorged periodically in blazing trails of red-hot silica from the Rokana smelter nearby and the well-watered gardens and red laterite paths and roads provided a vivid and festive spectacle.

The Show was a family occasion, when Dad could look at the latest motorcars on demonstration; Mum could examine the row upon row of beautifully presented lemon curd and fairy cake entries in the home produce section; whilst the children would occupy themselves in the fun-fair. Later, after a picnic lunch in the shade of the grandstand or clump of trees or flowering shrubs, followed by a leisurely ice-cream cone or two, the whole family might watch the show-jumping in the main arena followed by a military band march-past or perhaps a free fall parachute display, or police dog demonstration. But over the years the standards dropped and the flavour changed such that the occasion no longer held the same interest for the whole family. The South African fun-fair could no longer tour the country for political reasons. The motorcar distributors could not continue their stands as it became impossible to import other than Ministerial Mercedes, and the Livingstone-produced Fiats were all too familiar to everyone to bother to advertise them. The WI and other worthy bodies found it increasingly difficult to support sections for home produce due to prolonged periods of shortages of flour, butter and sugar. A near riot took place one year when imported cheese was shown by the major state retailer after many months of cheese unavailability. The farm animals still competed but the style of the Show changed for the worse with the demise of the supporting attractions. The Show authorities have made valiant efforts to replace the imported element with cultural interest, craft and local dance group, raucous pop music competitions and the like, but our final visit was a failure with a vengeance. The crowds of ill-disciplined Zambian youths and children jostled and pushed in the dust and the heat, sprawling everywhere, many drunk, and littering the site with bottles and paper rubbish. It was impossible to peacefully view the exhibits, dull though they were, and Anne had the contents of her handbag stolen early in the day. But the final indignity occurred in a vice-like crush of sweating and yelling people trying to force themselves out of a small arena, when a distressed and pregnant Zambian woman was unable to control herself and let rip a stream of steaming pee on the spot; which happened to be a spot she was sharing with my family. Finally extricating ourselves, and reeking of urine, we headed for car and home, and never attended a future Show, though friends reported that times had improved. Enough was enough!

One of our favourite weekend outings in the sixties was to the colourfully named Monkey Fountain Park and Zoo near to Ndola, about an hour's drive from our home in Kalulushi. The park had been unimaginatively laid out to broad sweeps of grass, flower-beds and rockeries, situated on the side of a valley and with a permanent stream trickling down through lush, jungly vegetation, and cascading into pools from small waterfalls edged by round boulders. It was a most refreshing spot, especially in the middle of the hottest month, October, when just the sound of tumbling water was a blessing. There were many interesting and unusual shrubs and trees to see, and goldfish to watch dozing amidst the water-lilies. Whilst the children rushed and tumbled on the grass, breaking off at frequent intervals to empty yet more bottles of Coke or Fanta, the adults would doze quietly whilst waiting for the heat of the day to ease into the lesser heat of the early evening, the best time to visit the zoo. In the early days, the animals were all fit and well. A curious assortment of imported animals, wallabies and fallow deer, with a cross-section of birds and smaller African mammals, monkeys, porcupines, jackal and ostrich. We enjoyed showing the children the animals they later saw in the vast game parks of the continent, as well as the posturing peacocks and mucky Muscovy's that thronged around at the merest suggestion of the rustle of a paper bag. After the arrogant but harmless nudging of these opportunists it was easy to forget that the caged animals, though without malicious intent, were always interested in tit-bits too and more determined in their procurement policies. It was in this way that Guy suffered the undignified distinction of being bitten by a bush-pig, a ferocious creature as ugly as sin, which luckily only tore one finger rather than the whole hand which was rashly offering scraps through the wire mesh. The scar remains to this day and early on served as a useful reminder to Guy in determining which was his right and left hand, the one with or without the scar: in fact he will still to this day subconsciously glance at his hand in a reflex action when referring to right or left.

Anne's particular favourite at Monkey Fountain was a mountainous black bird with a striking red wattle and bare skin around the prolifically lashed eyes, a Ground Hornbill affectionately known to all as Oscar. This turkey-sized bird is a ground-dweller, living naturally off small mammals, snakes and lizards as well as insects and frogs and has a marvellous and penetrating deep booming voice: it is said that the female calls 'I'm' going, I'm going, I'm going home to my relations', and the male replies, 'You can go, you can go, you can go home to your relations'. Oscar had his wings clipped each year to restrain him, but every so often he would avoid capture and attention for long enough to disappear from the zoo, but he always seemed to be there with a welcome for Anne and would come and clamber on her lap and bat his huge eyelashes at her. He loved attention almost as much as food, and he knew that Anne would readily provide both.

Alas, Oscar and many other of the animals soon knew less happy days when the charity of expatriates who voluntarily cared for them became less readily available and funds for the few local staff and all the feedstuffs ran dry. The zoo closed for a time until the local council was persuaded to help, yet one feels that its future is at best insecure. The fate of the park itself is little better and on our last visit we were sad to see the obvious neglect and the use of this peaceful place being changed to a venue of truant and transistor radios for the youth of the nearby townships. Even the goldfish were missing, and it was not hard to imagine them having become a meal for some hungry or just plain loutish lads.

But near to the Monkey Fountain Park was a place of continuing fascination and solitude, once introduced to us by Colin Duff, who spent much of his lifetime in the country as a forester and who became a distinguished Chief Conservator of Forests. A walk in the bush with Colin was worth days of reading, in learning about the life of the countryside. The spot he once showed us was a comparatively small experimental plot composed of surveyed blocks of forest which had for years received similar treatment to demonstrate the effects of planned or random forestry activity. Our favourite plot was one where the forest had received total protection from fire for many years, and here the trees were massive, jungly, overgrown with leaves and huge mahogany timber reaching clear to the sky. Adjacent was a plot where no protection had been offered, permitting random burning by natural causes, such that it represented the natural development of the Zambian woodland. Another plot had been deliberately burned annually early in the dry season, thus clearing the debris of the forest floor but not harming either the sappy resistant timber or the ungerminated and fire-resistant seeds. The most dramatic plot of all, perhaps, was that where the stand had been subjected to fire late in the dry season. At this time the forest is tinder dry and burns like a torch, so that even if the mature trees survive, the freshly germinated regenerative growth is destroyed, year after year, and the forest rapidly gives way to desert with ever-accelerating erosion. A startling demonstration, with near-desert next to lush jungle resulting from 30 years of varied forest management. Despite the thriving insect population of the stand of jungle it provided a splendid picnic site in the heat of October, with soft moss to lie on and cool leafy shade above.

Of course the evenings are short throughout the year in central Africa and the sudden arrival of darkness precludes most outdoor activities after seven pm or earlier. It is then that the worst affliction of the Zambian entertainment world takes over, namely the television service. This was inaugurated by Sir Roy Welensky during the dying years of the Federation of Rhodesia and Nyasaland, in December 1961, and was heralded as a great cultural leap forward, with endless educational potential; but by 1978 the Zambian TV output was little better than a poor joke, not simply because of financial constraints and consequent increasing unreliability and obsolescence of equipment, but also because of the moral absurdity of the service's government-dictated policies. It was inevitable that the medium be used for political propaganda, as it extensively was, but it was also subject to a whimsical and astoundingly naïve censorship which became both exasperating and hugely amusing. Thus it was decided in a fit of obsessive and zealous moralising, that kissing was decadent and all kissing must be excised from TV programmes. We then saw erratically-slashed films where mothers' goodnight kisses to their children were mysteriously deleted, leaving curious-looking sequences reminiscent of the silent movie era. Full-bodied embraces and other libidinous scenes were of course treated to the same censorial knife, as were any sequences showing violence of any kind other than on news reportage films. It was therefore quite possible to view the macabre and cold-blooded execution of bound and blind-folded Ugandans by Idi Amin's butchers, whilst a swash-buckling pirate comedy leapt from one picture of, say, a swordsman about to commence battle, to another of some previously unidentified marauder, or hero, sheathing their sword, in a bewilderingly comic episode quite impossible to follow. The enforced TV diet thus became a series of news bulletins, unintentional comedies and political broadcasts, in a sandwich of commercial charades. Our set eventually died a natural death, prematurely exhausted but having lived through exciting times. We were delighted to refrain from replacing it, even though we at first missed the perplexing visual jigsaws to which we had grown accustomed. No doubt the local population were better satisfied than the undoubtedly cynical expatriates: though, to be fair, it was on Zambian TV that we saw The Forsythe Saga, one of BBC Television's most notable productions.

Much of Zambia's evening entertainment these days takes place in the country's private clubs, theoretically all multi-racial but effectively still very much the preserve of expatriates. It is easy to make political capital out of this, but in fact the continued segregation seems to be largely a matter of personal preference, and occasions of racial disharmony are few, and more often than not are contrived by either Zambians with a colonial chip on their shoulders or else by drunk, insensitive Europeans; or, and now much rarer than in the past, by frankly anti-black Afrikaaners who have managed to survive the sorting out process which has dramatically and thankfully thinned their ranks since the country's independence in 1964. Most of these clubs are sporting organisations, supported by bar profits and self-financing social functions, and none can exclude non-white members by law. Some have unrealistically high entrance fees and annual subscriptions, but most will genuinely welcome allcomers, and many tread a deliberately astute line by inviting local Zambian dignitaries or politicians to join as honorary members, so that their lack of racial bias can be observed at first hand. Of course there have been occasions when pompous officials of either European, Asian or Zambian extraction have attempted to discredit suspect organisations by deliberately provoking a row for political or other reasons, but in the main the life of the clubs in Zambia is harmonious and well-ordered. Many such clubs are at least in part supported by large employers, such as the great mining companies, and facilities are frequently every bit as good as, and in some cases far superior to equivalent British organisations.

In the fifties and sixties the hub of the social life in the mining towns of the Copperbelt was the Mine Recreation Club, which provided everything from restaurants and bars to swimming pools, libraries and cinemas. In those days membership was restricted to expatriates, or more specifically whites, but for many years now they have of course been open to all mine workers and the atmosphere is quite different. The bars have become monopolised by Zambian workmen, the swimming pools by their children, and the organising committees by financially unaware members so that facilities, whilst maintained after a fashion, are no longer the same. But of course they now cater more specifically for the majority of their members who must therefore accept responsibility for the way these clubs are managed and for the facilities they provide. Expatriates still use the Mine Clubs, of course, but they no longer have the same objectives as in the past and so do not provide the desired atmosphere of relaxation still catered for by the sporting clubs which consequently have large non-playing memberships. But clubs are the same the world over, and if exclusivity is demanded it must be paid for.

The cinemas in Zambia have gone, to some extent, the same way as the Mine Clubs. Kitwe, our nearest big centre, still has the same two cinemas as it did on our arrival in 1959, though the same prurient censorship has affected their future as it has the fare shown on television. The Astra cinema, in the centre of town, is quite a large building with both stalls and balcony, and in the early days provided a pleasant venue for a family night out: with a bar and restaurant below, and a good selection of sweets and chocolates, it was much like an English cinema in a medium-sized English provincial town. The Rokana cinema, on the edge of town, is the other establishment, adjacent to, and originally part of the local Mine Club: a smaller, one-level cinema. An interesting series of changes took place affecting these cinemas and reflecting the changing social patterns in a newly independent state.

The first noticeable change was the gradually increasing numbers of Zambians who attended the cinema, and the slightly ribald and rough atmosphere of a child's Saturday afternoon matinée in post-war England began to prevail. Beer bottles appeared in the stalls, love scenes were laughed down and baddies were howled on to worse extremes. Slowly, the expatriate audience no longer patronised the stalls and the Astra acquired a whites upstairs and blacks downstairs clientele. The restaurant and bar became the haunt of unemployed youths and layabouts, drunkenness increased, and the expatriates appeared only for the film and not for an earlier meal or sundowner as before. Likewise the smaller Rokana cinema started to provide films appealing more directly to the expatriates, so that in time the Astra became the cinema for Zambians and the Rokana for the whites. The availability of sweets and chocolates at either establishment disappeared along with the increasingly problematical supply shortages linked to Zambia's more general economic and foreign exchange hardships. A natural corollary of the migration of the white cinema-goers to the Rokana was that after a while it became the elite thing to do for the higher-ranking Zambians to attend there rather than at the Astra as this implied a coveted form of sophistication. Kung-fu and cowboy films at the Astra, but classical cinema at the Rokana.

But most curious of all, though perhaps predictable, was the latest situation of both cinemas showing the same film, on the same days, but out of phase by about half an hour. In this way it became of course necessary for the cans of film to be rapidly conveyed between the two cinemas, and this is what actually took place. Occasionally, a reel would be delayed and one sat patiently, or otherwise as the case may be, whilst messages flew backwards and forwards by phone, or cleft stick, as the problem was resolved. By and large the system worked well, but it was usually reserved for the James Bond epics suitably clipped, of course, which were judged, quite correctly to be appealing to the anticipated audiences at both the Astra and the Rokana. It must have proved a little hair-raising for the cinema managers but no doubt delighted their accountants. However, easy though it is to be cynical about such hazardous enterprises it is to the credit of all involved that we were able to see, over the years, many of the great films of our time as well as some appallingly censored rubbish thrown in for good measure and which undoubtedly helped us appreciate the good ones.

Chapter 6
MINES AND MANSIONS

My livelihood, like that of the majority of expatriates on the Copperbelt, and indirectly that of much of the population of Zambia, was derived from one of the two giant copper-mining companies which between them dominated the economy of the country and set the standards by which we all lived and worked. It was sobering to reflect that the area of the Copperbelt, including both Zambia and the adjacent Katangan province of Zaire, was according to earliest known records a source of the metal at least 360 years before my own arrival on the scene. In those days the metal was smelted from the green oxidised ores exposed at surface, primarily malachite, and which formed a weathered cap to a richer ore which is now mined profitably, as copper sulphides, from thousands of feet below the surface.

Written accounts of the earliest mines and their methods are extremely rare, and the locations of their workings obscure or imprecise, but we do have information from the last century and the days of Dr Livingstone's fabled and well-documented expeditions. The site of one of the early workings, at Kansanshi, was until recently well-preserved and accessible, but the latest of a series of attempts to revive the ill-fated Kansanshi mine has now probably destroyed the amazing system of shafts and trenches which were undoubtedly being worked over a century and a half ago. Kansanshi lies well to the west of the main Zambian Copperbelt and the ore consists of a different type of copper mineralisation to the latter, providing a more complex, lower grade and metallurgically awkward source of the metal. The deposit at surface is represented by an elliptical *kopje*, or hillock, standing about 100 feet above the surrounding woodland and almost bare of vegetation itself due to the poisonous effect of the excessive copper in the sparse soil. Thus it is a natural landmark, added to which the *kopje* has an overall greenish colour due to the malachite staining on the rocks. Copper-bearing veins extend erratically and some would say randomly, although this is a dangerous word for a geologist to use, throughout the shaly rock, and the primitive miners dug deeply down into the hill, cutting trenches to follow these veins. Records indicate that the hapless miners were local Africans working under the whips of Arab slavers, although Portuguese slavers were also known to have operated in nearby parts of central Africa. There have been no smelting sites discovered near Kansanshi and it is generally supposed that it was the broken malachite ore, rather than the crudely smelted copper items such as the well-known Katangese crosses, which were then carried by manacled slaves to the trade centre at Ndola where the Slave Tree is reputed to mark the focal point of these caravans. This tree, still standing to this day, is now a national monument and part of the country's heritage of oppression over the ages. Zambian or Katangan copper articles have been found widely scattered throughout central and southern Africa, and as far as the trading ports on the Indian and Atlantic Oceans in Mozambique and Angola, carried there respectively by the Arab and Portuguese slavers and traders of past centuries.

Standing on Kansanshi hill some years ago I re-lived in my mind the scene of a century past, with naked sweating Africans labouring 20 feet below in a rough slit, little wider than the blades of their crude picks or shovels, loading fragments of green-stained rock into the baskets to be handed to the surface by other exhausted men. Any slackening of the pace would be rewarded by yells and blows from white-robed Arabs who strode across the hillside maintaining the efforts of the struggling slaves. A cruel and ruthless scene indeed, and one forgotten, but the Zambia of today would, with some justification, maintain that he and his ancestors were still exploited in one way or another right up until independence was achieved in 1964. Black tribes also of course enslaved each other.

The great years of discovery, and re-discovery since the old workings were of course well-known to the local natives, began at the end of the 19th century, and many of the vast mines of today were in fact the result of the pioneering Europeans being led to these sites by the people of the district. George Grey, a brother of Earl Grey of Fallodon and a friend of Rhodes, set foot on Kansanshi towards the end of the dry season of 1899, and was no doubt amazed to see the size and extent of the early mining activity which had clearly been responsible for removing thousands of tons of ore. Shortly afterwards, in 1902, there followed the location of the Bwana Mkubwa or 'Big Chief' mine, a scene of even greater mining activity; and Roan Antelope, where Collier discovered malachite-stained shale, outcropping at the spot where he slew the buck he had been hunting and from where the natives were reputed to obtain malachite for use in the cure of ulcers. In 1903 the old workings at Chambeshi were found and claims were pegged. It is unclear when, or by whom, the great Nkana discovery was made, but it was certainly later than Chambeshi and earlier than the next spate of discoveries in the early 1920s. The last of the major discoveries made by the formidable prospectors of the early 20th century were those of the mightiest deposits of all, at Nchanga and Mufulira in 1923; and finally the somewhat smaller, but still by world standards a very large deposit, namely Bancroft in 1924. Mining on all these sites is still currently progressing, though not without disruptions during, for example, the recessions of the 1930s which affected both production and development work, and at other mines at various times. Only one entirely new mine on the Copperbelt, namely Chibuluma, located at Kalulushi and discovered by then advanced exploration techniques in 1939, has since been opened.

But it is the Bancroft discovery, by Williams and Babb that interests me most, as J.E.G. Williams was the only one of the old prospectors that I ever met, and in fact we worked for the same organisation for the first five years of my time in Zambia. 'Pop' Williams, as we affectionately called him, was an old man of 74 when he died in 1965, but he had already lived a full life by the time he came to central Africa, and his stories of West African and South American mining camps in the early 20th century were certainly exotic. He worked at Bwana Mkubwa as an assayer in 1921, and subsequently held various jobs as prospector, overseer and general factotum until his disenchantment with the Anglo-American Corporation, the later owners of the Bancroft, Nchanga, Nkana and Bwana Mkubwa mines. He then joined Rhodesian Selection Trust Ltd for the final decade or so of his lifetime. Although 'Pop' would talk bitterly of his treatment, it was never clear what was his real grievance, though it certainly did appear that his contribution to the early pioneering days of the great copper mining industry had neither been well-recognised nor well-rewarded. The records are all agreed that 'Pop' Williams, or 'Bugs' as he was earlier called because of his interest in and knowledge of insects, discovered the malachite-stained outcrop at Bancroft whilst his partner Babb was in camp and he himself was out shooting guinea fowl for the pot. When he talked of Bancroft mine he would talk derogatively of Dr J Austen Bancroft after whom the mine was named when it was eventually opened in 1957, but it was Bancroft who had initiated and supervised the full and scientific exploration of the claims in 1928. But I feel it would nevertheless have pleased 'Pop' to know that Bancroft town was renamed Chililabombwe, 'the place of croaking frogs', during a period of intense nationalism some years after his death. In his last few years, 'Pop' presented a sad picture, though he was always appreciative of RST's consideration and thoughtfulness in keeping him on the payroll and in a nominally useful job right up until his death, and long after normal retirement age. He aged rapidly since I first knew him and most around him were unaware of his past and fascinating career. His final job was to operate, or supervise, a diamond saw which was used for slicing samples of rock from drill cores which were to be assayed. He would also sit for hours, polishing slices of ore by hand, grinding them down with increasingly fine-grained corundum powders on a sheet of plate glass. Even to the end he took pride in his work, though he lost all interest in his personal appearance and became something of a figure of fun to some of the junior staff and young African employees who would hide his glasses, deliberately misplace pieces of rock he had polished, and generally take advantage of his fading mobility and eyesight.

Pop's pride and joy has always been his well-tended garden next to his single quarters in Kalulushi, and towards the end this also became somewhat unkept and the myriad picannins delighted in stealing mangoes and pawpaws from the old man's garden, knowing full well that he could do nothing to prevent them. He tottered about his flowers and vegetables, unshaven and shaky, wearing the familiar knee-length baggy khaki shorts of the colonial days, and we hoped his memories blanked out the irritations of the day. The solitude of an ageing white bachelor in a newly-independent black nation was an unhappy one, though many of us who liked and respected him would have given much to have shared some of the challenges and adventures of

Pop's youth. As it was, Anne and I contented ourselves with enjoying his rambling reminiscences on the occasions when he walked across to visit us for a sundowner: in typically generous fashion he would always bring along with him a gift of fruit or vegetables from his own garden, and he enjoyed pottering in ours, and giving us his advice on our efforts. Like many of the whites who had experienced years of colonial rule, Pop was scathing about the potential of the Zambians to manage the affairs of state of a developing and independent African nation, but although he outwardly had no time for the blacks, or Kaffirs as he preferred to call them, his bark was considerably worse than his bite. In fact he was genuinely liked by many of the workers who knew him best, and whilst the youngsters might mock him, though always from a safe distance and never to his face, the long-serving and mature Africans respected him and I feel had rather a soft spot for this slightly eccentric old man. We were quite touched to see a number of these Africans attend Pop's funeral, and I feel he will be at peace in his grave, at the Kitwe cemetery where he was laid to rest, in the country he knew and loved so well.

On joining RST in 1959, not only had I an extremely sketchy and vague knowledge of the historical past of the Copperbelt mining industry, but I had no concept of the vast scale of the enterprise and its incredibly autocratic system of operation. In those days the General Manager of one of the vast copper mines was literally lord of all he surveyed, and he was something of a godlike personage to the community. Not only did the mine's productivity support the mineworkers themselves, but the entire towns had been built by, and were owned by, the mining companies, complete with mine schools, mine hospitals, mine houses, mine clubs and playing fields, and even a large and powerful mine police force answerable to the mine management. The town councils were staffed by mine officials, the power and water supplies provided and serviced by mine engineers, bus services were owned and operated by the mines specifically to enable the African employees to get to and from their place of work. Of course the housing provided for the African employees was of a far lower standard than the European houses, but was functional and was more permanent than the accommodation most of them would otherwise have dwelt in: it was more the siting of these multitudinous rows of two- and three-roomed buildings, huddled squalidly close together, that provided the dramatic contrast between living standards for blacks and whites. The African townships, or compounds as they were known, are all sited on the edges of the towns and extend for miles around. The European houses were usually grouped in categories, according to the status of the staff who were eligible for each increasingly lavish type, and the street names became a symbol such that one's address indicated instantly one's rank in the community. Different towns had different systems of street names, from the alphabetical and orderly pattern of roads in Luanshya which are named after trees or shrubs, like Hibiscus or Eucalyptus, to the commemorative names of Kalulushi honouring the great mining engineers and officials of the past, many of whom became Directors of the companies. Our first bungalow was in Albert Bennett Road, and our second and third homes were in Irwin Drive as I crept up the social ladder. Sad to say, our fourth home was in Siankandobo Lane since the move took place after the Zambianisation of the old names which were no longer to the liking of the nationalist government officials who took over the town councils and infrastructure of the mining towns; but we could console ourselves that a few years earlier our address would have been No 2, Park Lane. This was rather an unfortunate and inappropriate change of names as Park Lane was in fact a park-like area, and Siankandobo is the name of a harsh coal-mining district in the Zambezi valley region. Our final move in Kalulushi was to the traditionally most elite part of town, inevitably named 'Snob's Row', where the palatial houses were enormous and well-appointed, set in huge gardens and each with its own large private swimming pool. By the time we were installed the street renaming was complete, but we rather liked the sound of Mwaiseni Close, which not only has a pleasant and happy sound but *mwaiseni* means 'you are welcome'; a nice word.

Since independence in 1964 Zambia has made great progress towards its goal as a multi-racial society, and the mines have been thoroughly integrated racially, sometimes setting the pace and at other times dragging along behind the rest of the country. One area in which the mines were slow to move, understandably, was in the question of housing, as the expatriates tended to resent the intrusion of Zambians into their previously exclusive streets and avenues. This was not essentially a racial reason, but more of a cultural problem in the African way of life unquestionably differs from the Europeans'; but of course it nonetheless created quite a lot of friction. But what an enormous social change it was from our days of arrival, when blacks lived in compounds and whites in towns, to the time of our departure when Zambians and Europeans lived side by side in houses of all types, from the mansions of Mwaiseni to the small bungalows of Albert Bennett Road, which had long-since been renamed Mosi-oa-Tunya Road.

There are many stories associated with the first moves of Africans into the previously exclusive European houses. Like the Zambian who called the mine's Estates Department, who were responsible for all house maintenance and service, because each time his wife washed his clothes they disappeared. In due course it transpired that she had been washing them in the lavatory bowl, and 'each time she pulled the chain to change the water, the clothes washed away as well'. Perhaps it should be explained that in the African compounds the lavatories were of the squat-hole type, an elliptical porcelain hole in the ground with nothing to sit on, so that one is forced to squat in what to most people is an uncomfortable position but which presents no problem when adopted of necessity. A study of lavatories of the world might be interesting, although my own knowledge is rather limited. I do though, recall a squat-hole type in Italy, where imprints of a person's feet were preserved in the concrete, astride, as it were, the hole. Whether these represented a guide as to the optimum spacing and locations for one's feet to ensure a stress-free squat, or whether they resulted from the urgent needs of a workman caught short whilst he was installing the item and before the concrete set, I am not sure. Another variety, no doubt due to a paper shortage, was the installation I once was obliged to use in Suez, where the hygiene after one's performance was provided by a rather inadequate jet of water: quite a shock to the system of the inexperienced user, and alas, from my own recollection, most inefficient. However, I digress, and I'm pleased to say that I never came across a 'Suez-loo' in Kalulushi or even Zambia.

Another frequent problem to the weary Estates Departments of the mining towns, was the habit of the unsophisticated Zambian housewife scorning the use of electric stoves and continuing to use small charcoal fires and braziers for their cooking. Unfortunately, this was not really advisable in the European-type housing as no provision existed for ventilating the smoke, and since these charcoal fires were often merely lit in the middle of the concrete floors in one or other of the rooms in the house, the paints and decorations deteriorated rapidly. Combined with the usually large numbers of children in a Zambian family, together with the many non-paying guests and relations of the African extended family system, the housing tended to deteriorate rapidly. There are still instances of African families being unable to maintain these unfamiliar houses to a decent standard, either through ignorance or unwillingness to spend money on what we would consider to be normal domestic items like polish and cleaners, but the majority are careful and house-proud and very conscious of the increased status they gain by living in what are still considered to be expatriate areas of the town. One should add though that the standards of housekeeping of some of the new expatriates also leaves a lot to be desired, and many have allowed previously colourful and well-maintained gardens to fall into neglect and become scruffy dust-bowls and backyards.

A few years ago a tendency developed for newly-arrived expatriates to use the Copperbelt as a profitable jumping-off place for reaching jobs in South Africa. A number of cases occurred of young men from England or elsewhere signing a contract with the mines, collecting all the perks of an expatriate mineworker and vanishing within a week or even days. With an allowance to help buy a car and furnish a house, and with their fares paid, it was an easy matter for an unscrupulous employee to hop over the border into Rhodesia, and thence South Africa; several cases even occurred of such employees first negotiating the sale of the mine house which they had been allocated, complete with furnishings, to some naïve and gullible Zambian, so swelling their pickings by several thousand pounds. It proved almost impossible to recover any part of these fraudulently-acquired sums, which proved both embarrassing and exasperating for the mining companies, and so regulations were quickly tightened up to make such activities far less easy and attractive, though probably not impossible. To completely eradicate such practices would probably be too complicated without seriously affecting the situation of the vast majority of expatriates who need these perks to attract them to work on the Copperbelt: and the mines will still need, and need badly, the skills of expatriates for many years to come.

One of the items I was handed during the initial and formal signing-on interview in Kalulushi, together with such bumf as pension rules, details of sickness benefits and the medical specialist fund, a copy of the constitution of the now long defunct Mine Officials and Salaried Staff Association, and of course my contract, was a little cloth-covered green book called simply *Glossary of Chikabanga*. This proved a most interesting little book as Chikabanga was the highly functional lingua-franca of the mines, used to provide a common language of essential words for communication between the employees of many races and tribes who ran and staffed the mines. The words have a wide range of sources, including English, Afrikaans and Portuguese, as well as the local languages and dialects, particularly Bemba, the language of the largest tribal group of the Copperbelt. Sadly, this much-used and most useful language of the mines is now falling into disuse, since the official language of the land is English and nearly all the local mine employees have now had formal education of one sort or another, including the use of English, since an early age. It is therefore only the older Zambian or expatriate official who uses Chikabanga, and many of the now plentiful and politically aware Zambian mine officials now actively discourage its use as they consider it a distasteful part of their colonial heritage, and degrading. A pity, as Chikabanga is splendid, and although I never became proficient in its use, nor that of any of the truly local languages such as Bemba or Nyanja, my family and I still use a few of the lovely descriptive and euphonious words instead of the English language. The lingua-franca used in South Africa was essentially the same as Chikabanga, but known as Kitchen-Kaffir, and was needed particularly in the mining districts of Johannesburg and Kimberley where many different European and Bantu languages were intermingled with, predominantly, the local Zulu.

Chikabanga uses English characters, an alphabet of 24 letters excluding our letters *g* and *x*, and for all practical purposes is written phonetically. The numerals are as in English. Kitchen-Kaffir has a number of differences to Chikabanga, but principally in the way *c* is pronounced, like a click produced by a sudden withdrawal of the tongue from the palate, and having one fewer letter in the alphabet. This is the letter R, but that letter and the letter L are generally interchangeable in Chikabanga. And so, to our family and other favourites from our Glossary of Chikabanga:

Absentee	*Lofa*
Aid	*Helpa*
Annoy	*Shupa*
Bad	*Mubi*
Best	*Mooshle*
Bottle (acetylene)	*Botolo ka lo brown* (brown bottle)
Bottle (oxygen)	*Botolo ka lo black* (black bottle)
Canvas	*Tenti*
Electric motor	*Moto ka lo lite*
Engine	*Lo stima*
Fever	*Sick*
Gas	*Smoko*

Letter	*Brif*
Machine	*Machini*
Many	*Maningi*
Medicine	*Muti*
Overtime	*Ova*
Recruit	*New one*
Red lights	*Danger lite*
Shovel	*Fosholo*
Thief	*Skelem*
Wheelbarrow	*Bara*

We still talk about *mubi muti* instead of rotten medicine, and use fosholos and baras in the garden: Chikabanga is such a useful language that odd words frequently pop out at the most unexpected moments; as when I once dazzled both my family and a French woman who had driven into the back of our brand-new Fiat in the south of France, by bursting into a fluent and frenzied combination of schoolboy French and Chikabanga. The English are reputed to be poor linguists, and I am no exception, but the simplicity and naivety of Chikabanga appeal to me. What nicer than to describe the vast complex mine concentrator as *sillo* and its concentrates as *black stof*!

I mentioned earlier that the great copper mining companies of the Copperbelt maintained their own police force, originally in order to ensure law and order in the heavy industrial plant areas and to control pilfering and take care of loafers and scroungers in the compounds. They still fulfil these functions but additionally in more recent years have taken on a major security role in the mine towns in order to safeguard property and deter elements of major crime which have been proliferating all over Zambia. In towns without mines, and therefore without mine police, the commercial security firms have moved in, and many of the business premises and privately-owned houses are now patrolled by uniformed guards on either a 24-hour or night-time basis. But even with these precautions the spate of house break-ins and car-thefts periodically reached alarming proportions, sufficient to upset many expatriates to the point of packing their bags and leaving the country. Burglars nowadays are frequently armed, and several of our friends underwent most unpleasant and traumatic experiences, including being roughed-up and threatened at gun point. Others less fortunate have been wounded or even killed, but it's more often that the wretched and ill-trained security guards are found murdered or badly injured. Since their sole means of defence, let alone attack, is a pickaxe handle and a whistle, and almost all the burglaries are the work of well-organised gangs, it is scarcely surprising that the numbers of thieves caught is very low. The national police force, though armed, is too ill-equipped and under strength to make a serious impact on crime in the country, and with actual or recent nationalist wars on several frontiers, and armed guerrillas within the country, there is no shortage of automatic weapons available to the unscrupulous criminals. But even crime has its lighter moments, and although we never suffered a successful burglary in all our 18 years in Zambia, we were lucky enough to be protected by our mine police force in Kalulushi.

Our mine policemen were smart, courteous and quite efficient. They operated very effective dog patrols within the town, and along tracks around the perimeter, and certain areas had fixed guards and 24-hour patrols. These areas included, naturally enough, the General Manager's residence and also the Director's Lodge, a palatial establishment which was the social centre of the universe of Kalulushi, and used for entertaining and accommodating the company's Directors, the most senior employees and official visitors. This elegant and tranquil place, with its own swimming pool, tennis court and impeccably maintained grounds and gardens, was originally called the Guest House, until it became embarrassing for the mine management to be continually turning down bookings by highly insulted local politicians who expected to be given free accommodation as and when they wished. However, back to the mine police and their duties, one of which was to provide certain high-ranking officials of the company with a permanent watchman at their houses during periods of leave.

On one short absence with my family, for a week or so, whilst we visited a game park on holiday, we had asked Nora, a very good friend of ours, to keep an eye on our two cats which were to be fed in our absence by one of our two servants. This she did, and on the evening of our return she had left a basket, suitably cat-proofed, on a table in the open verandah at the back of our house: in the basket were some home-made chicken pies for our supper. Our return was delayed for several hours for some reason and we eventually arrived home, very tired, at about midnight, much later than we predicted. The watchman hastily appeared and unlocked our gates, rather startled we thought, and we checked that all was well and then dismissed him so that he could return home now that we were back once again. Several days later Nora enquired if we had enjoyed the six chicken pies, which of course was a surprise, as although we had found the basket it was very definitely empty. When the mine police sergeant visited us to check that his watchman had proved satisfactory we casually mentioned that we hoped he enjoyed the six chicken pies. The wretched watchman was summoned to explain this dreadful deed, admittedly very foolish of him, but he had wrongly assumed that we would not be returning that night and the temptation had been too much. And so the mystery was solved, and the culprit duly reprimanded, but that amazing incident was the only loss we suffered from 'burglars' in all those years. We were certainly very lucky.

It is hard to describe briefly the vast complex of activities that constitutes the mining industry, as not only are the installations on a massive scale but they have become increasingly technical and of limited interest to the layman. But several impressions will remain with anyone visiting the Copperbelt mines, whether it be the cathedral-like caverns and huge tunnels of the underground mines with their integral road and railway systems, or the enormous vistas from the brim of one of the larger opencast mines with colossal machines looking like toys on the floor of the pit. The massive machinery workshops, huge fleets of mammoth earth-moving equipment, and the noise and hum of concentrator, smelter and refinery with their smoke and fumes, all leave lasting impressions. An aerial view of one of the Copperbelt towns puts these in perspective, as from a height of a few thousand feet it is possible to unscramble what, on the ground, looks like disorganised chaos. The mine itself, either open pit crater or series of interlinked headframes at the shaft sites of an underground mine, is surrounded by its supporting services of workshops, offices and stores which merge into the adjacent suburbs of the so-called low-density housing areas of the expatriates. These latter are now more tactfully referred to as the high-cost areas, whereas the high-density African compounds have become the low-cost areas! These compounds stretch for miles around the edges of the towns, neat geometrical patterns of tiny permanent houses and blocks of buildings with their own shops and markets and sports fields, quite separate from the originally white towns. On the far edges of the towns, and normally away from any permanent housing are the huge barren wastes of slimes, the fine mud and clay pumped out from the concentrators after the metals have been extracted, and used to build dams for both recreation and water supply. These vast white expanses can look attractive to the local children but can equally well prove treacherous: tragedies are common despite notices warning of the dangers. In addition to the slimes dams, a few of which are now the scenes of reclamation programmes by planting grasses and trees, are the waste rock dumps and the far smaller slag heaps, the latter from the smelter and the former the natural product of the mining. The waste rock dumps are of course largest at the mines operated as open pits, where huge quantities of waste must be excavated to reach the valuable ores, and these man-made mountains typify the scale of operations on the Copperbelt, rather like the gleaming white conical heaps of china clay which form the so-called Cornish Alps near my present home, at the time of writing, in Cornwall.

Whether one calls them high-density housing areas or low-cost housing areas, the compounds of the Copperbelt, as elsewhere, no longer form the natural limits of these towns and cities, as Zambia has an increasing squatter problem which seems impossible to solve despite crude attempts by councils and governments to persuade the occupants of these areas to return to their villages. And so it is that beyond the compounds and around the rock dumps and slimes dams, has mushroomed a proliferating sore of squalid shacks and hovels occupied by unfortunate families trying to survive in these desperate surroundings. The shacks are mostly made of salvaged packing cases, bent and broken corrugated iron sheets and dismembered cardboard boxes. A few are constituted in the traditional way with mud and wattle walls and thatched roofs, but all are sadly inadequate to provide proper shelter for the large families who live in these and none have any water supply or sewage provision so that health risks are severe. From time to time the local governor will order the demolition of these large and squalid squatter compounds and angry scenes result, but any cure affected is only transitory and the problem returns and magnifies, a perpetual thorn in the sides of the administrators and the police, as these rabbit warrens are the source of much petty crime of the Copperbelt. Money is not available to provide a permanent cure, and although most of the squatters would be able to live a healthier and happier life by returning to their rural houses, the lights and the cash economy of the big towns and cities will always prove an attraction which is hard for them to resist, as they all hope for the lucky break which will provide them with a job and a regular wage.

It would perhaps be wrong to leave the reader with the impression that all of Zambia's mines are vast complexes with integral infrastructures surviving from colonial days and with apparently limitless resources. On the contrary, there have also been small mining operations in the country which survive to this day, others which have been periodically revived, and yet others resulting from modern exploration. Many metals and minerals apart from copper occur in Zambia, including excellent gemstones and semi-precious stones, gold and less exotic ores, as well as large coalfields which provide some of the energy needs of Zambian industry. Near to Kalulushi is a source of small but good quality emeralds, and many are the interests who have attempted to work these deposits profitably: but the area is easily accessible and it is probable that less than a third of the stones mined are legally marketed. The Zambian amethysts mined in the Kalomo district of southern Zambia are more professionally managed and are of a high quality, so forming the basis of a small but successful enterprise. Other small mines and alluvial deposits, for tin for example, are worked by co-operative ventures and provide, if not fortunes, at least a reasonable living for groups of Zambians who need only a minor element of management and expertise to operate these deposits. There is undoubtedly a future for small-scale mining in Zambia, and it is well to remember that the massive deposits of the Copperbelt are finite, and without great advances in technology at least some of these huge ore bodies will be either exhausted or economically non-viable within a decade, and others by the end of the century. Considerable thought must be given now to the means of supporting the huge population of the Copperbelt with its schools and hospitals when the goose has flown which laid the copper egg.

Energy is undoubtedly the key to successful industrial development, and Zambia is fortunate in this respect with ample hydro-electrical sources, from the great Kariba dam and the impressive Kafue dam, as well as uranium resources which are currently being explored and studied in detail in both the north-western province and in the Zambezi valley. The Zambezi region is already the source of hydro-electric power, and fossil fuel, and with the addition of uranium resources it could perhaps become the Energybelt of central Africa, while the Copperbelt slowly dies. But the real potential of Zambia, which perhaps will not be fully realised until the 21st century, lies in agriculture; and there is every reason to suppose that one day this huge country will be a net exporter of both energy and foodstuffs on a huge scale. But these enterprises must be financed by the efficient management of the copper industry whilst this survives, and so the Copperbelt of the present still holds the key to the country's future as it has done throughout the whole of this century.

Chapter 7
KASABA BAY

I have already mentioned how the expatriates on the Copperbelt attached great importance to their holidays. This was largely because of the opportunities for travel presented by contract terms, and the idiosyncrasies of IATA regulations which encouraged air passengers to include stop-overs at fascinating places, whilst *en route* to their final destinations, without incurring extra travel costs. At one time it was equally permissible to use these contract passages on a combination of air and sea travel, thus opening up almost limitless possibilities for the adventurous traveller. It was therefore hardly surprising that the mine employees were amongst the most widely-travelled people you could meet anywhere, and the subject of the next holiday was always a favourite one, whether it be to Beira and up the East African coast, through the Suez Canal to Italy and the Mediterranean; or by air to London via Cyprus or Rome; or via Kinshasa and Douala to Paris. Later, holiday destinations which became popular included Mauritius and the Seychelles, whilst others saved passage entitlements and combined them to provide tours of the Far East, thus bringing Japan and Hong Kong within reach, whilst others headed for Australia or the Americas. All these destinations were of course in addition to the more straightforward but nonetheless exciting and popular holiday resorts of South Africa and East Africa. Little wonder therefore, that a great many expatriates, living and working in Zambia, chose to leave that country out of their holiday plans until they had sampled the delights of at least some of these enticing alternatives, and we were no exception to the rule.

By the time that we had become less adventurous with our own holiday plans we had been living in Zambia for over nine years and my family had seen little of the country outside the Copperbelt and its weekend picnic sites. Occasionally Anne and the boys would accompany me on a day's expedition to one of my exploration basecamps, but this provided them with little relaxation as most of those trips involved several hours in a small aircraft, frequently in the rather turbulent air conditions of the hot dry season, and although different, was not a substitute for a holiday. And so it was that in 1968 that we planned a visit to Kasaba Bay, nicknamed Zambia-by-the-Sea, a holiday resort situated within the Sumbu National Park at the extreme southern tip of Lake Tanganyika. It was technically possible, though hazardous, to reach the resort by road during the dry season but this would have involved a minimum of two days driving in each direction, and as we only planned a week's holiday anyway, we opted to fly by Zambia Airways on one of the package tours offered by the Tourist Board. The price of our all-inclusive holiday was remarkable, even for those days, the whole trip including return air fares for the 350-mile journey from Ndola to Kasaba, and full board and lodging for two adults and two children for seven days, costing the equivalent of £112. It was a lovely holiday and worth every penny despite the few shortcomings of the facilities and occasional unscheduled dramas.

Our flight, including a stop at Mansa, previously known as Fort Rosebery, took approximately three hours in a splendid old Zambia Airways DC3 or Dakota, surely the most faithful and reliable aircraft ever built. I recall the lessening of tension after leaving Ndola where I had been admonished by the Zambian police for trying to photograph 'our' 'plane. The Zambians at the time were already highly excitable and suspicious at the slightest security risk, as most whites by then were regarded as potential *agents provocateurs*, and spies of Rhodesia's Ian Smith. I always like to record our journeys and I was pleased to find no objections to my photographing the 'plane as it stood on the runway at Mansa. The 'plane's arrival at the grass runway at Kasaba Bay was uneventful, though we had to buzz the airfield once both to clear it of the grazing antelope and to summon the transport from the nearby hotel. The site was idyllic, and we looked with delight at the view of the lake and its sandy beach as the aircraft banked steeply before making a perfect landing.

A Volkswagen minibus had by that time arrived and the dozen of us and our bags were shuttled to the main hotel building, a small bungalow with a restaurant, bar and shady verandah dominated by a huge winterthorn tree. Our accommodation was in thatched huts, each comprising a porch, two twin-bedded rooms, and a bathroom with hot and cold water and a flush lavatory. Camp generators provided electric lighting during the evenings. Our hut faced across a stretch of rough grass to the lakeside, where reeds and clumps of papyrus grew, the sandy bathing beach being several hundred yards away on the other side of a narrow isthmus; but the view was superb, right across to the distant western rim of the lake where the hills were visible as a purple haze, and in the heat of midday the water looked thoroughly enticing. In fact Guy and Barry were so excited that no sooner had we dumped our cases in our rooms than they had burst open their own bags, strewn their clothes everywhere, and changed into swimming trunks practically before we had flopped onto our beds. They then rushed outside, across the grass, and ran headlong into the reeds at the water's edge, splashing and yelling in their excitement for a full minute before their play was rudely shattered by the white proprietress, who came rushing across in a fury from the main building and sent them packing back to our rondavel. We were at first slightly put out by this apparently high-handed attack on our children, but quickly responded to her information that there were plenty of small crocodiles which inhabited the reeds along the edge of the lake, and we felt somewhat chastened in accepting the lady's advice to read the hotel rules before we did anything else. The rules were simple but included the provision that bathing was only permitted from the beach on the other side of the isthmus, and then only if accompanied by an armed game guard. Likewise, we were reminded that all the game animals were wild, and that we should be extremely cautious when leaving our rondavel on foot, even if only walking the 50 yards to the hotel building. It was difficult to see how there could be any risks in this tranquil setting especially as there was not an elephant, or even a hippo in sight, but during the week ahead we had every reason to appreciate that the rules were not only well-intended but should also be strictly observed.

After an adequate if uninspired lunch, featuring a high proportion of pasta and dried vegetables but prefaced by a delicious piece of freshly caught fish known as *nkupi* or yellow-belly, we quickly drank our coffee, which had the thoroughly familiar and distinctive taste of the powdered milk which is of course ubiquitous throughout the camps of Africa, and then headed to our hut for a brief pre-prandial snooze. The boys were somewhat rebellious at this enforced reaction, and although we had come well-prepared with puzzles, books, games and crayons they were not interested in anything but swimming. After about half an hour of attempting to read our own paperbacks but being interrupted at five-minute intervals to be asked how much longer before we were going to the beach, Anne and I gave up the unequal struggle to digest our lunches and decided to make the move in the interests of peace. We changed, collected our towels, binoculars and camera, and strolled over to the hotel to ask about a lift to the beach and a guard to accompany us. This was quickly arranged and the four of us, plus uniformed game guard, were driven some quarter of a mile across the isthmus in a minibus. After leaving the last of the rondavels behind us the track wandered through a patch of open grassland and thickets, past a huge sand dune with clumps of trees which were inhabited by swarms of monkeys, and round behind the dune to a glorious empty beach of yellow sand. In the middle of the beach was a thatched sunshade stuck in an old oil drum and providing a broad patch of shade, and some 30 yards back from the water's edge the shore was lined by large thorn trees. The water in front of us stretched away endlessly, rippled by a light breeze, towards the faintest smudge of hills which formed the far distant edge of the lake. Before departing, the driver asked us when we would like him to bring our tea, and after giving him our instructions we reflected on what a thoroughly civilised way this was to take a holiday, with the peace and wildness of a remote and beautiful part of Africa, and yet the service one would expect of a European seaside resort. We knew we were going to enjoy ourselves.

One of the greatest joys of bathing in the great freshwater lakes of Africa is the absence of salt, and the water always leaves one feeling fresh rather than sticky. Likewise, Lake Tanganyika has no currents to betray the unwary swimmer, and although reaching depths of close to a mile in parts, many of the beaches, as was the one at Kasaba Bay are gently sloping with shallow water extending out some way from the shore. Even the risk of bilharzia, a most unpleasant disease transmitted through a small freshwater snail and prevalent in Africa, was absent, and so we could all relax and enjoy the pure and crystal-clear water at our leisure. Guy could swim after a fashion, but Barry, although able to stay afloat, was only five years old and it was a relief not to have to worry about him being washed out to sea or caught in some undercurrent. We were wary of the possible threat of crocodiles, but although we once saw what looked like a largish one floating off the shore some quarter of a mile away, there was no threat of these creatures in our stretch of the bay, and in any case we were watched over by a vigilant armed guard whose presence we quickly took for granted and put from our minds. His job really was to gather us in, in the unlikely event that one of the plentiful elephants in the area should decide that the piece of beach that we were using was the piece that he wanted, in which case discretion was the operative word. In our week we saw several elephants in the vicinity of that beach, and their footprints, like impressions from some huge fossilised leathery pancake in the sand, were frequently all over the place, but we never had to surrender our patch and our guard never had to so much as lift a finger although it was certainly reassuring to know that he was there. The guards were provided by the Game Department, not the Tourist Board, and we found them always most efficient, smart and courteous. Our particular guard was called John, and he had the curious distinction of having five fingers and a thumb on each hand: apart from one lapse of concentration John proved a most pleasant and helpful guide, but more of that later.

Whilst Guy and Barry splashed and played endlessly in the water and on the sand, Anne and I relaxed in the shade taking turns with the binoculars. At first we concentrated on nervously scanning the lake for crocs, and the shoreline patches of shade for elephants and buffalo, but after the first day we were more at ease and left John to do that for us so that we could watch the prolific bird life. Our favourite noise, and the most redolent of the wilds of Africa, was then and remains the haunting and eerie cry of the majestic fish eagle and these birds were plentiful all around Lake Tanganyika. It is difficult to describe the marvellous cry but to us it evokes the very spirit of this vast and impressive continent. The fish eagle emblem is also, fittingly, part of the national flag of Zambia and is an important symbol on many crests and designs of Africa. We never found it easy to approach close to a fish eagle but although they are handsome birds it was more their dramatic call than their looks which we enjoyed so much and will never forget. Another favourite of ours was the ubiquitous pied kingfisher, found wherever water occurs, and we never tired of watching them as they hovered, motionless apart from a blur of wings, before dropping like a stone and snatching some small fish from the water. The egrets and herons were also beautiful as they stalked and fished, and flew gracefully to roost as dusk descended each day. The birds and scenes all around us were thoroughly photogenic and I never moved far without my camera bag.

After a leisurely tea on the sand, feeling relaxed although tired from all our swimming and all the fresh air and hot sun, we returned to the hotel in the minibus and strolled to our cool and clean hut to change, and to attend to the inevitable patches of sunburn which we had all acquired, despite our precautions and being well used to the heat of the African sun. Nothing painful, though, and none of us were more than a little sore. The final hour before darkness is an enchanting time in the bush, cool and refreshing after the glare of the day, and we decided to explore the camp before our traditional sundowners. We strolled over to the thatched shade of the *nsakka*, or shelter, in front of the main building and speculated on how old was the huge winterthorn tree which had been used as the living central pole of the structure. It was certainly impressively large, and one of the huge family of Acacias which are so widespread throughout Africa. The word acacia comes from the Greek word *akantha*, meaning thorn and all acacias possess thorns: the winterthorn loses its leaves in the rainy season and develops its flowers in the cold dry weather which follows, and so hence its name. It is also a useful tree, with a straight strong trunk standing to a height of 20 feet or more before branching, on a mature tree, thus providing timber for canoes. The fruit, in the form of seed pods looking rather like dried apple ring, is a favourite food of elephants who will shake the tree violently in order to dislodge the pods from the upper branches of the tree which may be beyond even their prodigious reach.

Stretching out from the shore in front of this wonderful old tree was a jetty about 50 yards long, beside which were moored a collection of small boats and one ancient old tub that reminded us of the African Queen. This was the workhorse of this southern end of the lake and plied between the Zambian port of Mpulungu and the various lodges and camps maintained in the area by the Tourist Board and Game Department, bringing in supplies and transporting staff. On most evenings during our stay this boat, the Sea Worker, was used to tow vast clumps of floating papyrus away from the general area of the jetty and lakeshore by the hotel, as the papyrus was another favourite food of the elephants and there was always a risk that these ponderous creatures would damage the boats during their feeding forays. Having strolled the length of the jetty, and casually examined the motley craft assembled alongside, we turned and walked back to the shore just as the sky in the west was turning to a dull golden glow as the sun sank behind the clouds rimming the distant hills. Simultaneously the camp generator spluttered into life and lights sprang on in the huts and buildings all along the shore. It was time for a quick wash and to grab sweaters from our rooms, and so we headed for our nearby rondavel. As Guy and Barry were ready first they waited for us on the grass outside, where they discovered the delights of the resident fireflies which danced and teased in the semi-darkness: the boys were fascinated and followed the pulsating little fluorescent insects as they drifted from place to place. Then the tiny sticky red and white tree frogs appeared and the boys' attention was so fixed on these little creatures that they failed to hear the amazingly soft approach of a vast grey shape, as an elephant materialised, less than five yards away from our hut, ghostlike in the gloom. Sensing, rather than seeing the beast, Guy and Barry suddenly froze solid close to the wall of our hut and Guy called quietly to us to come and see what was there. By that time the elephant had moved casually on towards the hotel, quite disinterested in any of us and peacefully going about its business, but it was some considerable time before our hearts stopped pounding. We had learned our second lesson at Kasaba Bay, and in future we never failed to look in every direction before moving about the camp, either by day or night.

After our sundowners and supper that night we were a little nervous about walking the 50 yards back to our hut, despite the lights and our exhaustive stares into every area of shadow within sight. It is incredible how silently an elephant can move, and we have never ceased to marvel at the delicacy with which these four- or five-ton animals can feed and travel, and how they pose no threat to any other living creature unless they are in some way themselves threatened. After that first encounter with the Kasaba Bay regulars we got to know them quite well, Anne in particular as she has always had a close empathy with all animals of any shape or size.

Of course the elephants at Kasaba Bay have become well known on the tourist safari circuit and so the staff at the camp have tended to encourage them to pay regular visits for the benefit of the two-legged visitors. On most days, one or more elephants will wander through the camp and up to the hotel, where they will lean against the strongly-constructed rock parapets around the verandah and extend their rubbery trunks inquisitively towards the tables, and to the hotel guests or staff. The waiters normally have a supply of raw potatoes or other acceptable offerings ready, so as not to offend the elephants, and Anne used to love popping a potato into the extended tip of a sensitive trunk. Guy and Barry were a little too young to make solo offerings but were allowed to go closer than most children will ever get to a truly wild elephant and they have always remembered their encounters at Kasaba Bay. Needless to say, these mammoth inhabitants of the area provided a feast of photographic opportunities for myself and I shot reel after reel of colour film in the first day or two until I realised that I would have to conserve my stock for it to last the full week. One irritating habit of the bull elephants was for them to thoughtlessly unsheathe their giant penises, so that an apparent fifth leg appeared, a massive grey scimitar of mind-boggling proportions, and which could subsequently prove embarrassing to over-sensitive audiences at slide shows, when someone might inadvertently ask an instantly-regretted question. I later learned to keep an eye on the rear end of elephants when photographing them, as a strategically-placed leg would often hide a potentially embarrassing, though impressive, statistic. Guy and Barry, like most small boys, found anything vaguely rude to be quite hilariously funny and once realising what the fifth leg really was, they took every opportunity of pointing out any bull advertising his wares in this way.

The day following our arrival dawned to the noise of much grunting and snuffling behind our hut as the night-feeding hippos cropped the sweet grass short before returning to the lake for the day. We were only ever able to see, at night, the vague outline of these monstrous round beasts, which seemed more shy than the elephants, though it was possible with a torch to get a better idea of their bulk. Like the cry of the fish eagle, the grunting of hippos is a wonderfully African noise, and was a lovely sound as a prelude to the dawn chorus on the lakeside. Our visit was in early January, in the middle of the rainy season, but the rains were less heavy and persistent that we were used to from the Copperbelt further south, and so we knew that although it was raining and misty when we woke, the day would still provide plenty of sunshine later on. Meanwhile it was exhilarating to watch a mist-shrouded elephant disembowel a tuft of papyrus reeds right in front of our bedroom window before we even dressed for breakfast: the huge creatures seemed to be particularly partial to the roots of papyrus.

Sure enough the mist soon lifted and the rain ceased, giving way at first to rather watery sunshine but later turning into a full-blooded African day. We had planned a morning trip on the Sea Worker which was to take visitors and supplies some miles down the lake to a second, smaller resort, known as Nkamba Bay., but there were plenty of storm clouds around as the ancient launch chugged out into the lake towing a small skiff behind it, and so we took sweaters and raincoats with us as a precaution. The skipper of the Sea Worker was a mountainous and swarthy European employed by the government Public Works Department, and he was clearly a handyman-cum-mechanic well-used to the vicissitudes of his unique craft. The oily and smelly diesel engine clattered gallantly away but we soon realised that the pleasure trip was going to be less pleasurable than we had anticipated. Not only did the waves out on the lake become impressively large as the wind rose and the first squall hit us, but the boat appeared to be reluctant to make any progress and rolled and wallowed in a stomach-churning way, so that we had gone barely five miles before we were all feeling quite sick, the feeling worsened by the smell of the all-pervading diesel fumes. Finally, with a despairing last clatter, the engine died and silence prevailed, broken only by the now quite fierce noise of the wind and the spray and the slap of the waves on the sides of the wallowing boat. Our captain appeared to be quite used to such a hazardous situation and casually set about tinkering with the antediluvian and evil engine to attempt a repair, but after about half an hour and raising no more than a dispirited splutter he decided to try to seek some assistance. There were about a dozen visitors on the boat, together with the skipper, a couple of African spanner-boys, an armed game guard, and another P.W.D worker, who now hauled in the skiff and with considerable skill fixed an outboard motor to its stern and set off for what was going to be a decidedly risky journey to reach Nkamba Lodge. The skiff's little engine coughed and spat as it was thrown about by the heavy waves, but we crossed our fingers and felt rather safer left in the drifting Sea Worker. This may sound over-dramatic but one should remember that the lake is some 500 miles long and up to 75 miles wide: the prospect of being shipwrecked on the shore in due course appealed to us more than the prospect of being drowned in the little skiff. Perhaps the sailors amongst us were less affected, but certainly my family and I were all feeling decidedly green and the boys were gallantly trying not to look frightened and were concentrating on holding the contents of their stomachs down.

In due course the crippled Sea Worker drifted close enough to a wave-drenched shingle shore for our enormous skipper to leap ashore and fix a line. We carried ashore the ladies, or those who needed a strong arm, whilst the rest of us jumped into the water and waded ashore: we were already soaked to the skin and only too thankful to reach firm ground. Safely ashore the situation looked better. Soon after we beached, a light aircraft flew overhead, summoned by radio from Nkamba Lodge by the courageous skipper of the skiff, and signalled that he'd seen us by rolling his wings of his aircraft. We were then told to follow the game guard as we trekked away from the lake to reach the nearest track. Guy and Barry had by now started to enjoy the experience, and we were soon all thoroughly dry again as the sun had returned to warm us up rapidly once more. Within an hour, during which the boys had found a clutch of porcupine quills to add to their collection of odds and ends, we were on to the rough dirt track which encircled the lake, and half an hour later had been collected by a minibus sent to complete the rescue. We have often reflected on that ill-fated boat trip and are all agreed that our passage on the heaving Sea Worker, drifting out of control on really heavy seas, was a most unpleasant experience that we would not wish ever to repeat, though perhaps it was all in a day's work to the P.W.D. crew and their stalwart skipper. Of course any danger involving one's family and children always seems much more vivid than one's own solo adventure of any kind.

Following a late lunch, and a beer or two to celebrate our rescue, we decided to settle for a doze on the beach and a swim to relax us all, and since the sun had kindly returned we spent the afternoon peacefully forgetting our exciting boat trip. The Sea Worker was eventually rescued and continued to ply its trade along the lake for several years until it was replaced by an elegant catamaran cruiser, complete with bar, which took over the duties of the tired old launch. I suspect that even that catamaran may by now have become retired or unserviceable, as the tourist trade to Kasaba suffered quite a blow as soon as the expatriate staff were withdrawn when their contracts were not renewed. Perhaps that is cynical, but a flair is definitely needed in the remote areas in order to provide the facilities required by today's sophisticated tourists, and Zambians so far have not acquired that flair. Apart from the family holiday, Kasaba Bay provided an important venue for the many fishermen of the Copperbelt, and at any time of the year at least half of the visitors were likely to be the latter. The best time for fishing though is between November and March when the larger fish follow the migrating smaller fish to the shallower inshore waters. There are commercial fishermen based at Mpulungu and these operate particularly to catch the small freshwater sardine known as *kapenta* and which forms a valuable source of protein, either as the fresh fish or dried and salted. Much of this fishing is done from quite small boats and the boatmen fish at night with huge nets, attracting the kapenta to the surface by the use of lamps or flares mounted on the bows of their canoes. But the expatriate fishermen of course are after the game fish which abound in Lake Tanganyika, and which vary from the Tiger fish of five to ten pounds, to the Goliath Tiger which may weigh up to 70lbs. There are also the Giant Catfish, or *sampa*, which can weigh anything up to 100lbs, but perhaps the most sought-after by the angler are the Nile Perch which weigh anything from a few pounds to 100lbs. The Nile Perch will take a spoon, or live bait, but usually lie in deep water and it requires both expert skill and patience to land one of the really large specimens.

On our visit to Kasaba Bay there was a handful of fishermen as usual, and one in particular, a tough and vociferous Afrikaans mine captain from Mufulira, was full of the usual fisherman's tales of his skill and past achievements. He was quite amusing company, but a number of us were sceptical of his assurance that he would undoubtedly catch the largest fish of the day and we watched him load his impressive and sophisticated tackle on to a small boat and disappear off up the lake for his day's sport, followed by several other less confident but equally well-equipped fishermen. Shortly before dusk the boats started returning, and with all of them in, sure enough, it was our Mufulira hero who had the largest fish, a 23lb Nile Perch together with three smaller Perch and a dozen nice *nkupi* each weighing between three and five pounds. This was undoubtedly a good day's catch but whilst weighing in at the back of the hotel, with our Mufulira man glowing and bragging, along came one of the kitchen staff who had just returned from a few hours in his canoe with a hand-line and casually handed in a huge Nile Perch which tipped the scales at 33½lb. We felt a little sorry for the Mufulira champion, who had his thunder stolen so dramatically, but were secretly delighted that a humble Zambian waiter had delivered such a splendid and unintentional *coup-de-grace* to our boastful friend.

It was just after the weigh-in, as darkness finally descended, that the cook fell through the kitchen window. At least that was the explanation we were given, and whether he had slipped, or merely went out of control with laughter at the expense of the undone Afrikaaner fisherman on hearing the story, we never discovered. But we were attracted to the kitchen by the hubbub and bedlam which arose and were horrified at the disarray and pools of blood. The wretched cook had a vicious gash on his arm which clearly needed multiple stitches, and practically the only first aid available seemed to be a couple of bandages and some cotton wool. Anne quickly fetched the few things we always travel with, Dettol, antiseptic cream and plasters, and between half a dozen of us we did the best we could for the poor cook who had lost a lot of blood and was looking quite ashen. He was then bundled, in a blanket, into one of the P.W.D. vehicles and was driven off into the night for a journey of some 30 miles over appalling tracks to the nearest clinic run by a mission deep in the bush. It was certainly a salutary reminder of the remoteness of the hotel and we were not a little disgusted at the European proprietors who had clearly provided thoroughly inadequately for such eventualities. At least the diversion took the heat off the humiliated Mufulira fisherman who was no doubt relieved to escape his fellow guests' amusement.

Guy was the only member of our family with any particular interest in fishing and so one day we hired a boat and two small rods, with an African to row us, and spent an hour or two drifting on the lake inside the Bay. Both Guy and Barry dutifully hung their rods over the side whilst the totally bored African waited patiently for us all to give up. It was tiringly hot, with not a breath of wind that morning, and after an entirely unproductive session we headed back to the jetty and abandoned all prospects of catching a fish. After dumping our clobber on the jetty, and paying off our helper, Guy hung his line over the edge and almost instantly felt a bite. Rapidly hauling in his line, he discovered the smallest fish you've ever seen, dangling pathetically on the line and after unhooking it and posing for a quick portrait with this gasping tiddler in the palm of his hand, he quickly returned his prize to the water. It was the first fish he had ever caught, and although he was near to tears at the time Guy has since become quite interested in fishing, if still rather inexpert, and no longer shares his parents' soft-hearted allergy to killing even a fish. I personally still draw the line at threading a worm on a hook, let along hitting a fish on the head.

One of the almost unique features of Kasaba Bay is that it is still permissible to take safaris on foot into the surrounding Sumbu National Park, and viewing big game in this way is a most exhilarating experience. Of course one must be accompanied by an armed guard but this is a most essential and comforting requirement. We twice went for these escorted walks from the camp during our stay and on one of these, an early morning stroll, we saw what looked like a dead hippo washed up on the shore and lying half-submerged in the reeds. Our guard advanced in front of us in a most confident way, and when only about 30 yards away proclaimed that the pinkish-brown hulk must in fact be dead. It was at that precise moment that the passive and motionless beast exploded into action with staggering effect, sending reeds and rushes in all directions and a tidal wave surging back into the lake, as well as freezing us to the spot in utter shock and amazement. It was thoroughly foolhardy of our guard, the many-fingered John, to have been so careless in his approach, but he had been excited at the prospect of all the free meat the carcase would have provided that he had allowed his training to be forgotten. A disturbed and enraged hippo is one of the most dangerous animals in all Africa, and stories abound of these beasts maiming and killing the unwary: they are well able to slice a person in two with their massive scissor-like teeth. Luckily for us we were not between it and the lake, as a hippo's first instinct on being disturbed is to run straight for the water scything anything down in its way but in this case the startled brute surged backwards, fixing us with its little piggy eyes, swinging its great head in defiance, and eventually submerging into the depths of the bay. I remember, at the back of my mind during the first shock of the encounter, considering the rather absurd question of which of his many fingers John would have used to pull the trigger, and practically, whether he even had a bullet up the spout. John was clearly a little shattered himself, most uncharacteristically as the Zambian game guards we have met are unquestionably courageous and well-trained, and so we decided that his slight distress was due to his recrimination at his own poor judgement combined with disappointment at the loss of a huge pile of meat. We didn't ask about the bullet.

On our other safari at Kasaba we went in search of the ruins of an Arab fort which we had been told existed some couple of miles from the camp. I suspect that I was the only member of the family who was interested in this expedition and so I was the only one of us disappointed when we failed to find it. On this occasion John was again our guide, and we were never able to establish whether he genuinely did not know where the ruins were, or whether he was superstitious of the site and deliberately led us astray. Either way, we wandered through thick scrub, thorny and unpleasant to walk in, with my family becoming increasingly disenchanted with the idea of searching so uncomfortably for a pile of old rocks. I eventually succumbed to their pleas to head back to the beach for a swim, and we had to content ourselves with a good look at a most impressive sausage tree, *Kigelia Africana*, and its enormous, pendulous fruit. These occur quite widely throughout Zambia but Guy and Barry had never seen one before and they were already at their young ages most interested in the flora as well as the fauna of the African bush.

By now, and nearing the end of our short but action-packed holiday, we were becoming quite familiar with the silent but swift appearance of the elephants right in the middle of camp, and we were suitably careful about wandering about ourselves. We had also got to know the more regular visitors by name, like Broken Tusk and Old Faithful, and were quite used to seeing a leathery and bristly trunk rubbing up and down on the outside of the wire gauze door to our rondavel. Old Faithful in particular had an irritating habit of appearing out of nowhere after we had returned to our hut to collect something, and lounging obstructively in the doorway with his trunk nonchalantly slung over one tusk, preventing our exit. This could be exasperating if, as often happened, we forgot to take the binoculars with us when going for a drink or a cup of morning coffee or afternoon tea in the *nsakka*, and suddenly saw something in the distance which we wanted to watch and by the time we were released from our hut the object had disappeared. But we always forgave these delightful animals their casual irritations and will always remember them with affection. Sipping our beer under the winterthorn tree on our last evening at Kasaba Bay, watching the last of the canoes returning from an evening's fishing, silhouetted against the silvery grey lake, and with a blaze of red and yellow as the sun disappeared over the distant hills, it seemed a far cry from the industrial Copperbelt and truly fitted our mental image of what Africa was really all about. A wonderful life and a splendid holiday.

Chapter 8
PETS AND PESTS

One of the worst aspects of going on holiday was the effect one's departure had on the family pets, which seemed to be aware, for weeks beforehand, that they were about to be abandoned and confined for an indefinite period. Long before the suitcases were brought out and dusted, our dogs and cats always became particularly attentive, and we couldn't help being a little more conscious of them than usual. It was probably our concern which in fact was transmitted to the animals and induced their actions, reproachful eyes and the familiar hang-dog expressions, but we were of course always careful to ensure their wellbeing in our absence. And the welcome we received on our returns, whether from a week's holiday or four months leave, always more than repaid the considerable cost of kennelling the animals. But our return from Kasaba Bay was a little sadder than our earlier homecomings as we had lost dear Wattles, our first dog, in a road accident shortly before our holiday had started.

Wattles, a black and white patchwork hound looking rather like a cross between a spaniel and a beagle, with lovely silky fur, had been acquired as a tiny puppy by Anne during our first weeks in Zambia whilst I was away in the bush. We had named her Wattles because of her lovely drooping jowls, and although she had a questionable heritage she had come from a distinguished home as she was given to Anne by Peggy Garlick, the wife of our Consulting

Geologist. Peggy was one of the great characters of Kalulushi, with a strong farming family background and having spent most of her life in Africa. Both Peggy and her husband Bill were a fund of information on the ways of the people and the country in which they had brought up their large family. They were both sad to leave Zambia on Bill's retirement, but felt that they had seen the best times, and having lived in company houses for so many years they were looking forward to making their own home in the Eastern Transvaal. Peggy and Bill were both known for plain speaking, and calling a spade a spade, but Anne was not aware of the Garlick reputation or idiosyncrasies on her first visit to their home, where she had kindly been invited to dinner a week after she had been left on her own following my despatch to the bush on my first assignment. Anne expected a formal dinner and was a little nervous on arrival at my ultimate boss's house, but she was very soon put at ease. The house and garden appeared to be overrun by birds and animals, which were allowed an astonishing element of freedom, so that ducks were occasionally found to be waddling through the enormous kitchen, and one particular parrot, an opportunist, apparently had the run of the place. Cats and dogs abounded and appeared to occupy most of the chairs, and Peggy frequently chucked chicken scraps over her shoulder, during the course of dinner, to be collected by the nearest of the horde of pets. Anne was very quickly completely relaxed, even despite the repeated attempts of a small parrot to tweak off all the buttons of her dress, and it was on this first meeting that she was promised the puppy which became our beloved Wattles, a particular favourite of mine for many years.

Within a few months of acquiring Wattles we experienced one of the worst outbreaks of rabies which we were to witness on the Copperbelt. This truly horrifying disease, due to a virus to which all warm-blooded animals are susceptible, is endemic in Africa, and since dogs, and to a lesser extent cats, are the most frequent transmitters of the disease to humans, these domestic animals were required by law to be inoculated against rabies. But of course it was impossible to physically enforce this law, and whilst Europeans were mostly familiar with the requirement, many of the dogs owned by the Africans, in the towns as well as the rural areas, were not inoculated. A reservoir of infection is maintained in the wild animals of the region, and although such animals as wild dogs and jackals may be the most susceptible, it is also possible for such widely diverse creatures as rats, cattle and chickens to be killed by the disease. Bats also are so widespread throughout Africa that they may well provide a constant pool of the virus. Elsewhere, in South America, the vampire bat is a well-known vector of the virus, and the human dread of this creature may well be due at least as much as the hideous symptoms of rabies resulting from the bite of an infected bat, as it is to the more recognised and loathed habit of blood-sucking itself. Treatment of the disease in humans can in fact only be successful if it's started before the symptoms appear, as only a very few authenticated cases exist of victims surviving after contracting the disease, and then only with massive intensive care. Several friends of ours were obliged to endure long and painful series of injections after bites from animals which had been suspected of being rabid; in each case the suspected animal had to be destroyed and its brain tissues carefully analysed to determine whether or not the suspicions were substantiated. The rabies virus is transmitted in the saliva of the animal and so it is not always necessary to be bitten to contract the disease, as a lick, on skin with a cut or graze, could prove equally fatal. Little wonder that the British laws to prevent the disease entering this country from Europe are so conscientiously observed, and the penalties for breaking these laws enforced with such vigour. I have fortunately never seen the tragic and appalling pain and terror of a human rabies victim, but the pack of rabid dogs outside our Kalulushi home in 1960 will remain a vivid memory for both Anne and I.

As soon as a confirmed case of rabies was notified a tie-up order was declared in the towns, and all owners were required to physically tie their dogs up out of reach of any other animals. It was not sufficient to merely restrain the animals within wire fences, which many expatriates held to be acceptable, as it was still possible for the virus to be transmitted through the fence from an infected animal, either in its saliva by mouth-to-mouth contact, or on scratches or bites on muzzles poked through the wire. Unfortunately in Kalulushi, as in every other town and village in the land, the tie-up orders were never wholly successful in execution, and many stray dogs, whether or not infected, were shot out of hand due to carelessness or disinterest of their owners. Our Wattles was kept strictly indoors except for brief excursions on a tight lead for essential purposes, and she had also had the required injection of anti-rabies serum; so we were relatively happy with our precautions. But one evening, just as it was becoming dark, we noticed a number of stray dogs roaming about in the bush behind our garden and they appeared to be acting strangely. We watched for a while and with the aid of a torch noticed that they were salivating and had staring eyes, and we at once suspected the worst and telephoned the Honorary Game Warden to advise him of the rabid pack's presence. The leader of the pack was clearly not an Africa's dog, being a large and very handsome Alsatian bitch, which periodically sat on its haunches, put its head in the air and howled in a curiously unnatural way. Dogs, unlike humans, do not appear to contract the hydrophobic phase of the disease so distressful to the sufferer, when the sight, smell or even mention of water produce spasms and even violent reactions. This pack appeared to have the dumb, or paralytic phase, rather than the furious rabies which manifests itself in manic attacks and ferocious bites, and even swallowing of anything and everything in sight. This we felt to be even more upsetting as the ten or so dogs prowled about, howling, and some obviously already having lost some muscular control. The guard arrived with an assistant and a rifle and told us how he abhorred having to destroy these wretched animals, but he explained he would have to kill every single one. This proved a difficult task at night and some inevitably escaped the gun, but the hunt went on next day, and the next, until eventually all the strays infected or otherwise had been either destroyed or disappeared into the bush to die of the disease.

In this first rabies scare that we experienced, the tie-up lasted several months and spread to nearby towns as well. Other tie-ups occurred every few years but we never saw another rabid animal to our knowledge, and hope never to do so again. The treatment of a mad dog's bite, painful and uncertain, and the virtual inevitability of an agonising death if the disease is contracted, is a sobering thought, especially when one considers that according to expert estimates, probably in excess of 10,000 people are killed worldwide by this ghastly virus. The inoculations against rabies were provided free as a government service, and the queue of pet owners formed once a month at the local police station where a government official from the Veterinary Department administered the injections and provided certificates stating the dog's name and sex and the owner's name and address. Cats also were inoculated but fewer people were aware of this advisability, and since no licence was needed to keep a cat, the majority of cat owners didn't bother. One friend of ours, a fellow animal lover, once kept a genet as a pet, a small wild member of the African cat family looking rather like a stretched domestic cat with short legs and a long bushy tail. This particular genet was a melanic or dark strain so that the spots were barely visible. It was in fact illegal to own such an animal without special dispensation, but Iain nevertheless took it to the police station for its rabies jab and successfully explained that it was a Special Cat, thus getting the appropriate injection and certificate. It is surprising how few of the new generations of urban Africans can recognise the wild animals of their own country, although upon reflection it's probably also true of many of today's city-dwellers of whatever nation.

At about the same time as we acquired Wattles we also took on an elegant black and white cat which made something of a matched pair of cat and dog. The cat was exceptionally inscrutable and we named him Ming, but like many cats he was a great explorer and this soon proved to be his undoing as he returned one day, after a short absence, with a rear leg dragging a wire snare behind him. He disappeared again some weeks later, never to return, and we presume he met his death at the hands of a cruel hunter in a similar way. We still have a picture of Ming, stretched elegantly and luxuriously on a comfortable couch, but he never had time to become a real part of the family. We soon replaced Ming with a silvery-grey little cat which we named Piwacket, from Bell, Book and Candle as his favourite resting place was beside a besom broom in our garage. Piwacket became something of a mystery to us, and although affectionate and well-loved he never seemed to need our company and preferred instead to live and hunt on the anthill and adjoining patches of bush. After our first house move, about three years after getting Piwacket as a tiny kitten, he never accepted us again despite our doing all the age-old and recommended things like buttering his paws and keeping him for days in our new home. Time and again we had to return to our first home and garden and entice him to come to us, but eventually he too disappeared. A full year later we were told that a friend was sure they had seen Piwacket in the bush a few hundred yards from our old house, and we rushed there in an attempt to lure him back. We were sure it was him, although he was lean and thin, and although we actually got near enough to touch him, he was entirely wild and would not accept us. We sadly left him to his chosen life in the wild and it was several years before we owned a cat again, and then we had much better luck. Meanwhile we had added another dog to our family, this a lion-coloured cross between a Great Dane and an Alsatian. We named her Zara, for no special reason other than that it sounded both fitting and feminine for the potentially large bitch, and like Wattles she became a faithful member of the family and stayed with us for her natural life. Wattles, sadly, survived only nine years, and it was ironic that whilst Zara seemed accident-prone and survived endless hair-raising dramas, poor Wattles was fatally injured in the one and only accident that she ever had.

Although being the smaller of the two dogs, Wattles was unquestionably the Top Dog and also usually the team leader in any mischievousness which she and Zara perpetrated: she was also the more energetic and enterprising and was quite capable of being thoroughly bossy and inquisitive. It was this latter characteristic of Wattle's that led to a happy ending to what could have been a dreadful accident. Beside our first garden was a patch of indifferent bush bordering our embryo hedge of Napier fodder, a sort of razor-sharp grass which grew to a height of over ten feet and provided a rapid screen, and behind a large termitary in this patch of bush we had established a huge compost heap for all our garden rubbish. Guy was still a toddler, still less than two years old, and Barry had not been born, when one afternoon there was a terrific rumpus from the direction of the compost heap. Both Anne and I thought the other was watching Guy, but in fact he had followed the dogs on one of their garden expeditions and we arrived to see Wattles dashing about like a deranged mongoose whilst a fat puff adder hissed at her from the centre of the heap of dry leaves, and Guy yelled ecstatic encouragement. Zara was also on the scene, but at a safer distance than Wattles, and was adding her deep bark to the alarming situation as we scooped Guy up out of harm's way. I had to kill the snake of course as it posed a very real danger: it had obviously spent the winter curled up in the warmth of the compost heap and we were far more careful in future in ensuring that such heaps were well fenced off.

Occasionally, for reasons both of economy and to avoid their tedious confinement in kennels, we would arrange for a friend to look after one or other of our dogs during our leave absences. On one long leave we loaned Zara to one of my expatriate staff who was working in a field camp deep in the bush, and for a period of three months Zara was living a very different life to her accustomed domesticity. We hoped she would enjoy the freedom this provided, but on her return we noticed that she had become extremely nervous and in particular became terrified in the thunderstorms which were so frequent during the rainy season. At the first clap of thunder the poor dog quivered like a jelly and could not be comforted, and as the crashing continued throughout the storm she would become quite frenzied and struggled to escape from her torment, squeezing under tables and behind chairs and quite unable to be calmed. We later learned that this tendency had developed during a hunting expedition when a shotgun had been, unintentionally, fired directly above her head. On another leave we loaned our house to a friend and thought it would be ideal for her to look after Zara which she was quite willing to do. Regrettably, since the girl was working normal office hours, Zara was allowed to roam free during the day and got into bad habits, raiding dustbins and wandering off into the bush. When we returned from leave we discovered at once that Zara had become infested with fleas and ticks, in particular, and we subsequently found that these revolting pests had inhabited every tiny nook and cranny in the house, and the minute young could barely be seen with the naked eye: these repulsive insects can live for several years without a feed and it was essential for pet owners to regularly check their dogs and cats to keep them clean. An easy job if done routinely but a long and unpleasant chore if left for long. Like some other Zambian pests, ticks became worse at the end of the rainy season in March each year, this also being the worst time for mosquitoes, or mozzies as they are universally known.

The malarial mosquito, *Anopheles gambiae*, is a major scourge in Africa and Zambia was no exception. Ever since our arrival, whether we were in town or in the bush, we took a regular Daraprim or Maloprim tablet once a week as protection against malaria, and although Anne suffered one bout, whilst in hospital in Johannesburg oddly enough, the rest of my family escaped this unpleasant disease. Malaria had long been officially eradicated from the Copperbelt towns, a major achievement by the early mine doctors and medical staff, and prevention schemes were maintained effectively whilst responsibility remained with the mining companies rather that the town councils. Great ditches had been built around the town and the water sprayed with insecticides regularly to kill the mosquito larvae, and in the addition all the windows and insect gauzes in the houses were regularly sprayed with a residual mixture. We were therefore little bothered by the mosquitos in Kalulushi until the latter part of the 1970s when the spraying programmes became sporadic and inefficiently supervised.

Other seasons became a nuisance to us, and those were the few weeks twice each year that each of our bitches came into season. Wattles and Zara became the targets at these times of what seemed like every randy dog in the entire Copperbelt, and wherever we kept them, the packs of dogs ranging from our neighbours' to those from miles away came in droves to pay court, and it became a nightmare to keep them at bay. We tried wire enclosures with double fences, but eventually had to keep our dogs inside the house and established elaborate systems of door opening and closing, like the escape hatch on a submarine, in order to ensure that neither Zara nor Wattles got out and that none of the invaders penetrated our defences. Inevitably it was Wattles who became the most devious, and she managed to produce two litters of adorable puppies as a result of her love life before we had her spayed. Zara was a great house-mother for Wattles' puppies but never had any of her own as we had her attended to in the interests of our sanity. Not only were the male dogs of Kalulushi a noisy nuisance but they were also tearing holes in the mosquito gauze at our windows. There were of course far too many dogs in Kalulushi, owned both by the expatriates and their Africans, and it is sad to say that the Europeans set a generally poor example in looking after their own dogs. Our dogs were far from trouble-free, but at least we attempted to keep them on our property and fed them well, whilst many others kept dogs solely to scare off unwelcome Africans and their fruit-thieving picannins, and treated them as yard-dogs rather than as pets.

I have already mentioned Wattles' sad and early demise under the wheels of a van, and it was a miracle that Zara didn't suffer the same fate several times over as she had an exasperating habit of taking a spontaneous dislike to certain vehicles, leaping our four-feet high fence and pursuing an offending lorry or car down the road. She once was badly hit and her whole flank ripped open and one back leg smashed, but the excellent vet in Kitwe managed to patch her up after an operation lasting several hours, and she mended almost as good as new. We tried all sorts of recommended remedies to clear her of her very bad habit, but even her near fatal accident didn't teach her the required lesson and she still hated some vehicles, mostly noisy lorries, until she became too old and feeble to do anything about it. Zara was a lovely pet, a great favourite with our and others' children, and so we were terribly sad to see her decline at the age of 13 years. We decided reluctantly that the kindest thing would be to put her to sleep and Anne gallantly took her for a final visit to the vet: tears were shed by us all but we still have her memory.

Another much-adored family pet was our Simpkin, named after the Tailor of Gloucester's cat since Anne had met and known Beatrix Potter as a child in the Lake District. Simpkin, like Zara, survived many dramas including once being caught and half-killed by a stray dog, and it needed all Anne's patience and the vet's skill to save her on that occasion when she undoubtedly used up a large share of her nine lives. We had other cats also, one being the product of one of Simpkin's amorous adventures with an enormous and handsome

Burmese, and we were often hard-pressed to explain to incredulous visitors that the huge, creamy-coloured Bonny was in fact the son of our tiny grey Simpkin. Bonny's brothers and sisters were also most impressively beautiful, and whilst that could never be truthfully said of Simpkin she certainly made up in intelligence and affection for anything she may have lacked in beauty or stature. Another cat we had for a very short time was blind, and despite our love and attention it was killed by the same stray dog which almost certainly accounted for Simpkin. There were times when we felt so sad at losing one of our much-loved animals that we determined never to own a pet again, but our family seems incomplete without at least one dog or cat in the house and preferably several.

I have already mentioned our encounters with ants and other insects, like fleas and mosquitos, which from time to time irritated or plagued us or our pets. But one should not omit mention of other pests like scorpions and spiders as these also provided us with occasional excitement. We had actually expected to meet plenty of scorpions but although these are not actually uncommon they are essentially nocturnal and I only ever saw very few. The first that any of us saw was in fact not until we had been in Zambia for several years, and it appeared out of nowhere and was first spotted by Barry as a youngster of five when he came to tell us that there was 'an electric crab!' in the dining room. This interesting phenomenon turned out to be a small brown scorpion about an inch long and it was rapidly flattened before it could demonstrate its electric or other capabilities. Its curious movements did in fact resemble the action of an electrically operated toy, and the claws were certainly crab-like, and so in retrospect we felt that Barry's description was quite apt. I later saw a few other scorpions in the bush, including one monster of several inches in the Eastern Province near Chipata, but the only other to invade our home life was found floating dead in our swimming pool one Sunday morning. Wanting to keep it, I opted for the nearest available preservative, and we still have what is surely the only scorpion pickled in vodka. Spiders were much more plentiful, from the ubiquitous wall spiders of all sizes and which were so flat as to appear two-dimensional, to the huge and hairy baboon spiders, evil-looking but harmless garden spiders and the crafty trap-door and hunting spiders. But whatever the shape or size of such creatures, whether insect, spider or centipede, there was always a host of interesting life to be seen and found by the most casual observer.

One of the most bizarre animals we ever saw in our garden was one brought to us at our suggestion, by a friend of ours, who had seen the brown furry shape slowly moving along the grass outside his office window one day. None of us could identify the creature and none had seen one before. It was about a foot long, smelled horrible, was totally blind with merely vestigial eyes on the side of its head, and possessed impressively large, curved incisors: the fur was a dull brown and quite thick. This thoroughly slothful and halitotic bundle was eventually identified as a mole rat, but not before I had foolishly agreed that it could be released in our garden so as to prevent it being hit on the head and eaten by any of the most interested African observers. And so we deposited it gently on our lawn, taking care to stay well away from its huge teeth which had already sunk into a nearby boot, and watched it open its mouth and hiss blindly at where it thought we were. In due course it moved off, inexorably slowly, and started to burrow into a patch of earth as we watched from a distance so as not to alarm it; and in due course it disappeared underground never to be seen again. Unfortunately we were only too soon to become acquainted with its diet, as clump after clump of our plants and shrubs mysteriously died, to be given funeral mounds of loose rich soil in the remembrance, and it was then that we realised that the curious mole rat enjoyed succulent and well-nourished roots as a major part of its diet. The mole heaps proclaimed the rat's steady progress through our garden, and we hoped that when it had eaten all it fancied it would go away, and leave us to reconstruct our shrubbery: it was many months before this ungrateful beast disappeared as dramatically as it had arrived.

It was some years or so after Zara's sad departure that we realised we would have to get another dog, and both Anne and I were determined to pander to our preference for a large dog, despite the increasing difficulties in obtaining food supplies for our own consumption let alone another large addition to the family. However, difficulties exist to be overcome, and since we never do things by halves we decided to search for an Irish Wolfhound, the tallest breed of dog in the world and one which we had both long admired. These dogs are notoriously difficult to raise, partly due to the bitches inadvertently smothering their small pups with their enormous bulk whilst sleeping at night, but we knew of one or two in Zambia and had also got to know one in Cornwall on a recent leave. However, without importing one, which we felt to be prohibitively expensive as well as slightly risky, we thought we would have a long wait since the pair which a friend had imported, and from which we hoped to buy a puppy from the first litter had been stillborn, another only lived for a few days and the remaining pup had been smothered. Some months later the owner of the wolfhounds phoned us to say that she had permitted her dog to mate with her purebred Rhodesian Ridgeback bitch, that the puppies were strong and adorable, and would we like one. My own feeling was that to see them would be fatal as we didn't really want a cross-bred wolf-back or ridge-hound, and I knew only too well that once Anne saw them we would be committed to having one. What we really wanted was a pure wolfhound, like the massively impressive Rory, father of this litter, but sure enough we set off to visit the pups and came back the same day with Fingal, as we named him, a galumphing wolf-back puppy with an engaging nature and feet the size of saucers.

Fingal was a real extrovert from the word go, phenomenally strong and bumptious as well as lovable, and a potential giant of whom his namesake Finn MacCool would have been proud. He grew rapidly and we began to worry over his boisterousness, as we had by then produced little Beccy, our daughter, into the world; and as she tottered about she was frequently getting flattened and sent sprawling by Fingal's endearing but uncontrolled attentions. It was also at this time that we had the totally unexpected opportunity of acquiring Rory, Fingal's father, as his owner was regrettably leaving Zambia and was unable to take Rory with her. After much deliberation we decided that we had to have Rory, who was still a young dog, and much as we loved Fingal we knew that we could not manage to keep both of these huge dogs. We were also not a little anxious about a possible accident to Beccy, however careful we were, because of Fingal's exuberance. Dear Fingal had many admirers by this time, and as we had a wonderful opportunity to give him to a good home we tearfully let him go, and devoted all our attention to Rory who had so far had a rather difficult life.

Rory was a huge success, in every sense of the word, with all of the family and quite rightly became known as our gentle giant. He had the most lovable and devoted nature, gentle as a lamb with Beccy, our cats, or anything smaller than himself, but massively strong and impressive when there was no risk of hurting anyone or anything. Rory would never have bitten anyone, but his sheer bulk and height were sufficient to keep all but the most courageous visitors outside our gate, quite useful in the days of burglaries and daylight theft. Word soon spread that a huge dog like a lion lived at No.2 Mwaiseni Close. Rory was a grey brindle and a real champion of the breed. Anne showed him at many of the Copperbelt Kennel Club shows before international judges and he always did well, gaining a championship certificate under the South African Kennel Club rules, and almost reaching the same status under the Zambian Kennel Club rules which were adopted shortly before we left the country. He would certainly have achieved the latter status which automatically would have gained him an International Championship, much-coveted in the doggy world. But although Anne enjoyed showing him Rory was first and foremost a family pet, and without a doubt was the most lovable, handsome and rewarding animal which we have ever been fortunate enough to own.

Owning such a dog, and he was 36.5" high at the shoulder and could comfortably tower over me whilst standing on his hind legs with his front paws resting on my shoulders, did of course present some problems. He had a prodigious appetite and required a great deal of expensive meat, but we were lucky in having almost two acres of garden and so he could rapidly get enough exercise by rushing around like a mad whirlwind on his own. He was frequently quiet during the day, liking nothing better than to curl up in a surprisingly small bundle as near to where Anne was as he could get, but in the cool of dusk, or in the evenings, he would often go quite crazy and circle around us at great speed so that we feared he might slip and injure himself. Wolfhounds are so heavy, yet with such long legs, that it is not unusual for them to break a bone on falling: several times Rory did fall, and on these occasions he invariably pulled a muscle and squealed pitifully, but always healed up in a few days' time. He adored attention and could manage any amount of petting and patting, and we sometimes wondered whether he didn't make a bit much of his temporary injuries in order to capitalise on all the extra loving that this entailed.

Of course Rory was not always being praised and admired, as he had his share of mischievousness like any other dog. One particularly exasperating bad habit of his was to dig the most colossal holes in the garden, and lie and roll in the resulting damp earth in order to cool himself down. If you know the size of hole a normal terrier-type dog might dig, and Wattles was a culprit in this respect often in the past, then multiply it at least tenfold in order to get an idea of the sort of cavernous hollow which Rory could produce. Another of Rory's bad habits was to bark at the African children who used to pass along a footpath in the bush just outside our six-foot-high back fence and hedge. If the children had never seen Rory before they would scatter, screaming with terror, in complete pandemonium: but those who were used to the sight of this monstrous and shaggy grey thing prancing about, barking at them, would retaliate by pinging their catapults at him, and sometimes hurling quite large rocks over the fence. This of course only made Rory more excited and furious, but since the children knew that the dog was effectively captive within our fence there was always a risk he could get a serious injury from the miscellaneous projectiles. We therefore discouraged these barking forays both to avoid terrifying the children who might be first-comers, and to minimise the risk to Rory caused by his own silly antics.

The end to our tale of Rory is a tragic one. When we left Zambia we had to face the agonising choice of either taking him with us, and risk his dying in the enforced six months of quarantine kennelling where we knew that this sensitive dog might well pine desperately, for Anne in particular; or giving him to good friends of ours who were staying in Africa and who had hopes of breeding from Rory and their own wolfhound bitch who had so far failed to breed despite Rory's earlier attentions at stud. We felt that Rory would have a better chance, and we knew a good home, with our friends, and so we gave him to them. The first tragedy was that Rory's girlfriend, the wolfhound bitch, died unexpectedly from cancer just before we left the country. We still felt that it was fairest and kindest for Rory to stay in Africa so avoiding both the nerve-wracking flight and undignified crating required, and also the terribly long quarantine period, and so Rory went with his new owners as planned, a family that he was well used to, and settled with them in Rhodesia. And then after 18 months of happiness with them he fell, whilst romping beside their car in the same way he always used to greet us, and he died instantly from a broken neck. A freak accident which attached blame to no-one, but a sad end to a magnificent dog who had known three homes and owners in his short life and he had given loyalty and immense pleasure to us all. He had survived an almost fatal attack of poisoning whilst with us, a deliberate act by a gang of unscrupulous criminals who periodically fed poisoned meat to household pets hoping to immobilise them before burgling a house, and thanks to Anne's devoted nursing he managed to survive on that occasion by the canine equivalent of will-power and courage. To meet his end as the result of an accident seemed cruel fate. We may yet one day own another wolfhound, but even if we do, we will consider ourselves lucky if he is even half as splendid and lovable a pet as poor Rory, who started life in rural Norfolk and died some seven years later in Rhodesia, now Zimbabwe.

Aerial view of the Victoria Falls and the 75-year-old road and rail bridge

*Statue of Dr Livingstone
on the Zimbabwean bank
at Victoria Falls*

Stamps issued to commemorate the centenary of Dr Livingstone's death

Doughnut on a hilltop, overlooking characteristically flat Copperbelt bush country

Camp scene in typical woodland

A gaunt baobab tree beside a good tarmac road through the Zambezi valley

A J-2 helicopter on a dry dambo strewn with large and small termitaria

A Jetranger helicopter landing in a grassy clearing to collect an exploration crew

A well-established and semi-permanent bush camp at a major prospect

Bath-houses were sited to best advantage

Barry (left), Anne and Guy (right) beating their drum, 1966

The Jonas exhibit in Kitwe, April 1968

Zambian fishermen on Lake Tanganyika

Chambeshi open pit copper mine at an early stage of excavation in May 1964

Chambeshi open pit copper mine in August 1966 from the same viewpoint as the preceding photograph

My family watching an elephant at Kasaba Bay. The launch 'Sea Worker' is on the left

Kasaba Bay beach

An escorted walk for Guy and Barry at Kasaba Bay

Anne with Zara and Wattles beside a local dam at sunset

Anne with Fingal as a puppy

Anne with Rory and some of his trophies

A young lion in Kafue National Park in the early morning

An alert Korhaan in an open patch of dry grassland

Sunset over the Kafue river at Lufupa

Puku antelope in the Kafue Park

*Stamps illustrating some
Zambian fossils*

Chifubwa rock engravings, near Solwezi, in Zambia's North-Western Province

Kafue lechwe antelope on the extensive flood plains in the Lochinvar National Park

Monitor lizard at Lochinvar, well-camouflaged despite the open terrain

Guy with his hat decorated with guinea-fowl feathers

James Melek Kalukuluku   *Dickson Kamanga with Beccy*

An elephant enjoying a bath in a Luangwa Valley lagoon

Lily trotter, or Jacana, on Nile cabbage at Luamfwa

Itawa dambo, near Ndola, under gathering clouds

Kariba dam from the southern side, before the North Bank power station was constructed

Coronation Square, Kitwe, on Zambia's Independence Day; later renamed Kaunda Square

Stamps commemorating President Kaunda's Jubilee Birthday

Stamps commemorating completion of the Tanzania-Zambia railway in 1976

Blossoms of the Flame tree or Spathodea, after rain

The crane flower, or Strelitzia, one of our garden favourites

Chapter 9

KAFUE NATIONAL PARK

For our second Zambian holiday, in 1971, we had planned to visit the splendid Kafue National Park, at that time the largest full national park in Africa and still one of the largest in the world, the size of Wales or half the size of Switzerland at an impressive 8,650 square miles. Even now it is still not as internationally well-known as the slightly smaller Tsavo National Park of Kenya, or the Kruger Park of South Africa, or even the fabled Serengeti National Park of Tanzania which is only half the size of the Kafue Park. But the size of a Park is no criterion by which to judge, and Kafue had the reputation of being less spectacular and with a less concentrated and varied quota of the big game animals of Africa than many of the smaller Parks. This reputation was largely justified as there are, for example, no giraffes in the park, and one is fortunate indeed to see rhinoceros which only occur in very small numbers: in addition, the bulk of the Park consists of woodland with limited expanses of open plain or swamp so that the game which does abound is not always easy to see. But because of these drawbacks most of the game park tourists on the African circuit tended to omit Zambia from their schedules in favour of better-known reserves in South or East Africa, and even when Zambia mounted a publicity offensive to attract larger numbers of tourists, most of these visitors preferred to visit the Luangwa Valley National Park in the country's Eastern Province, admittedly one of the most outstanding game reserves of the entire continent.

And so it was that the Kafue Park was able to offer the sort of attraction that we sought, which was essentially a piece of the real Africa, unspoiled by the worst excesses of commercialisation and where we could seek out the wildlife spectacle at our own speed and in our own way. The scenes in the most popular parks of Africa, like Tsavo and Kruger, where one was more likely to see more zebra-striped minibuses than lions, or head-to-tail queues of cars crawling past a kill, were not what we were after, and the delights of the Kafue Park fulfilled amply all our expectations.

Being such a vast area we had planned to spend half of our eight day holiday in the north of the Park and half in the south. This was a logical split as there was only one camp in the Park, Ngoma, where hotel facilities were provided, and that camp was situated in the southern half: we therefore had to take with us sufficient food and supplies to last us for three or four days whilst we stayed at a non-catering camp, and we had chosen Lufupa for this more adventurous part of our holiday. We had also decided to enter the Park from the little-used and strictly non-tourist entrance at the Kabanga Post in the extreme north, which could only be reached by decidedly rough roads and tracks. Since our trip was to be right in the middle of the dry season we didn't anticipate much difficulty in reaching Lufupa by this route without a four-wheel drive vehicle, as I was quite experienced at driving in bush tracks, and felt that our Fiat 1800 saloon could negotiate all that we would encounter without too much difficulty. With a shovel in the back and some matting, with Guy, Barry and Anne to assist with any digging should we meet stretches of deep sand, we were confident that our unconventional route would be both quicker and more enjoyable than the much longer slog on better roads. In fact it turned out that our journey from Kalulushi to Lufupa, of a little over 300 miles of predominantly bad tracks and dirt roads, was substantially slower and definitely less enjoyable than we might have expected on the tedious but decidedly less hazardous alternatives of almost 500 miles and entering the Park at the normally used Chunga Post. However, it is easy to be wise after the event.

We duly set out at dawn on a Sunday morning, well provisioned, with plenty of water and a jerrycan of petrol, and wrapped in sweaters against the cold early morning air of the first day of August. The days at this time of year are truly delightful, cool to cold in the mornings and evenings but comfortably hot in the middle of the day. The skies are cloudless, though tending to be hazy with a pall of smoke from the many man-made and natural bush fires, and there is a crisp freshness of new green growth as the sap starts rising in the trees and grasses which have been burned off by the fires earlier in the dry season. Some of the bush trees and shrubs are starting to bloom, and the background brown is here and there brightened by a splash of scarlet, white or yellow, or a fuzz of pristine green buds or leaves.

We made good time on the first leg of our journey, travelling west from the Copperbelt on the well-made laterite road, after a few miles of tarmac, and were feeling calm and contented as we hummed along leaving a billow of reddish-brown dust behind us which settled only slowly in the still morning air. We crossed the little Lufwanyama River, and then the larger Lunga River, as the sleepy villages along the roadside stirred to life, chickens scurried out of the road and the African women started cooking the morning mealie porridge from their maize flour sacks. Cyclists appeared, the occasional hunter emerged onto the road from the forest, and we felt that we were seeing life of a far more attractive sort than the crowded bustle of the Copperbelt.

It was after crossing the Lunga River that our enjoyment became tempered with just a tinge of anxiety as we hit the first hilly patch of country where the relatively smooth dirt road gave way to a rocky surface of rough boulders and potholes. Our gallant Fiat crashed and plunged over the rocks as I tried to find the optimum speed at which to travel: slower, and we felt every bump and hollow; faster, and we risked the crash of exhaust on the rocks and the shock absorbers bottomed into uneven craters. This didn't last for long, but it was clearly the stretch which caused the problem which stayed with us for the rest of the trip. After twisting and turning for what seemed an endless and uncomfortable eternity, we reached Kasempa, a local district headquarters where we intended to fill up with petrol and eat our lunch. We had already travelled some 200 miles, which had taken far longer than we had allowed, and we were left with another 100 miles to go over what we knew would be worse tracks than we had used so far. The car was making all sorts of protesting clanks and rattles, and on looking carefully at the damage I realised we had all but lost our rear silencer. We also discovered that the petrol we had been assured would be available didn't exist, and a sleepy backwater of local administration, on a Sunday afternoon, was hardly the place to expect assistance even with temporary repairs and we were thankful that our spare petrol would, if the worst came to the worst, see us through to the Park where supplies could be obtained. However, we managed to run to earth a local official who was, unwillingly, persuaded to sell us five gallons of government petrol. We half expected to be told that we were not allowed to enter the Park at Kabanga without a special permit, but the official reluctantly accepted our Park reservations as being *bona fide* and allowed us to proceed.

We were by now not a little worried at the prospect of spending the night on the roadside as no private vehicles are allowed to drive in the Parks after dark and if we didn't make up some time we would not be allowed past the entry Post until the next morning. And so we pressed on, with an increasing accompaniment of protest from the rear end of the car, together with the grumbles and groans from the tired and grimy children who had so far been remarkably good. As we left Kasempa in mid-afternoon we reflected on the past state of this little town which in colonial days had shown a lot more paint and polish but now looked dirty and unkempt, with the flowering trees on its roadsides broken and torn by the local children who were no longer obliged to respect the town's appearance. The nearby Mukinge Hill mission station and hospital were still spotless and whitewashed however, and we hoped that Kasempa town would one day again look less like the broken-down shanty town that it was beginning to resemble. However, we drove on in the heat of the day and were pleased to find that the traffic-free tracks in front of us were an improvement on those behind, largely as very few vehicles came this way, and apart from several easily-negotiated sandy patches we were able to make a fairly constant speed of 40mph, our only concern being that we took the right turns at the numerous little forks in the road. We reached the Kabanga Post at about 4pm and were greatly relieved to be allowed into the Park. The Game guard on the gate was quite astonished to see any vehicle at all, let alone a white family with small children, and he waved us through after checking our reservation papers, and our holiday was started.

The first few hundred yards on the Park side of the gate, which of course was not really a gate but a long rough pole slung across the track, consisted of what at first looked like a wide, green trackless swamp. However, having advanced to the edge of this apparently impassable bog we noticed that the reeds were parted at one point and we gingerly edged our weary Fiat in that general direction, to discover a mat of various-sized logs and sticks trailing off into the middle of the obstacle and constituting a vague replica of a corduroy road. We bumped and lurched over these logs, wondering if we would ever reach the far side, but the further we went the squelchier the track became and we half expected to stick fast, embedded right in the very heart of this lush swamp. But we made it, and as we dragged up the last few damp patches I remember thinking that surely we had earned a trouble-free stay for the rest of our visit, and as we motored on with our accompanying mechanical and human complaints from car and children alike, it did indeed begin to feel worthwhile. In the dying sunlight and approaching coolness of the evening, the entire bush took on an almost luminous golden glow and shadowy antelopes leaped gracefully across the dirt track, whilst the abundant birds and insects contributed their magical noises to the scene. The last light was just fading as we reached Lufupa, and the huddle of thatched huts appeared as out of nowhere, silhouetted against a wide expanse of silvery water with the red disc of the sun slipping gracefully over the distant horizon. The camp is situated on the riverbank at the confluence of the Lufupa and Kafue Rivers, and the relief as I switched off the engine was enormous. We were all desperately tired, but none of us could imagine a more peaceful or beautiful spot in which to rest.

The non-catering camps in the Zambian game parks were staffed by Africans employed by the Tourist Board, and we were made more than welcome at Lufupa by George and Lyson. They helped us unload the car, and whilst one took away the food he would cook for our supper, the other quickly lit paraffin lamps and started a fire to heat the water for our baths. We were the only visitors at the camp for the entire three days we were there and we are all agreed that it was the most memorable stay we ever enjoyed on any of our many game park visits before or since. That first evening, as our excellently cooked food was served under the little thatched hut at the river's edge, we listened to the grunting of the hippos not far away in the gloom and the musical clanking of the blacksmith plovers which swooped down to roost nearby. Our beer was not cold, but we stacked tomorrow's supply in the clean paraffin refrigerator, together with other perishable foodstuffs that we had brought with us, butter, vegetables and meat, and reflected that a warm beer at Lufupa was worth at least ten cold beers anywhere else.

Needless to say we slept soundly that night, but were woken early, at our request, by Lyson bringing us hot water for washing, and as we quickly dressed we could smell the delicious aroma of bacon and eggs from the cookhouse. We were up and about in no time, admiring the view through the rushes across the mist-shrouded river, well bundled up against the morning chill. The pure simplicity of the camp, with not even a generator to interfere with the feeling of peace, space and solitude, reinforced our pleasure as we had half-expected to find our impressions of the night before vanished by morning. We had slept so soundly that we had not heard the lions which George assured us had been quarrelling over a nearby kill during the night, but the hippos were already grunting and blowing in the river by the time we set out in the car for our morning's game viewing drive. The best times for spotting the big game, especially, was in the early morning and late afternoon, as the heat of the day was a time of rest for most of the animals. We collected our binoculars, camera bag, water, and a supply of snacks for the boys, and after Anne had given the cook the food for our midday meal and some flour for him to bake into bread, we piled into the car. The shattering rattle on starting the engine was a total surprise, and whereas it was undoubtedly no worse than the day before, the hideous booming and clanging seemed like a scandalous intrusion into the beauty of the natural environment all around us. There was nothing we could do about it as on a quick examination I saw that the rear silencer was half off and various other oddments, of impressive original function, were dangling from the underside of the car.

Nothing daunted we set off, presuming sadly that no self-respecting wild animal would come within a couple of miles of us making such a noise, but that was fortunately not to be the case. Within a mile we came across a large pride of lions padding through the shade-speckled bush between the trees, and we noticed that several bore the blotched colouring of immature animals. They were beautiful, undoubtedly the ones heard by George during the night, and they looked extremely healthy and well fed and quite unperturbed at our dramatic approach. Thinking that they would be scared of the cacophony from our wounded Fiat, I quickly turned off the engine: but this made them appear much more wary, as though reasoning that a quiet enemy is dangerous whilst a noisy one is so stupid as to be of no threat at all. Having watched the lions until they disappeared deep into the bush, to find a suitable cool glade in which to spend the day, we drove slowly on, stopping frequently to watch the family groups of exquisite impala and the plentiful puku (both medium-sized types of antelope) and the abundance of bird life all around us. Many of the animals were new to us and I remember puzzling over our field guide in trying to identify a type of hartebeest which had a black streak down each brown flank. They were grazing on the fresh green shoots in a recently burned patch of grassland, and we eventually diagnosed that the black streaks on these animals were in fact ash, transferred to their flanks from their muzzles as they periodically rubbed away the flies between grazing on the blackened ground. It was as we were puzzling out this mystery that we became aware, or rather heard, that a large elephant had silently materialised and was watching us impressively from some 50 yards away, majestic and solitary, towering above the scrubby thorn bushes. We were late back for lunch but it was a memorable morning, and the fresh-baked bread was the highlight of our meal of which the rest was a little spoiled. That evening we had another short drive, within ten miles or so from the camp, and although we had less success than in the morning it was still delightful. The boys particularly enjoyed the comical antics of a family of warthogs, those hideous comedians of the African bush which stick their tails straight up in the air like radio aerials when on the run, and wallow ecstatically in the shallowest mud; or scuffle along on their horny densely-haired knees as they crop the short grasses or herbs, and grub out roots and tubers. As we returned noisily to the camp we saw Lyson appear from the riverside where he had caught a large and ugly catfish: he offered to cook it for us but we preferred our own less exotic fare. Our icily cold beer was deliciously refreshing that evening and set a perfect seal on our first full day at Lufupa. We watched the sun go down, listened to the hippos and the regular evening flight of the Blacksmith plovers, and wished we could stay forever.

The next day we decided to head for the far northwest of the Park, to the Busanga Plain, where we hoped to see herds of the great plains game, the buffalo, wildebeest and zebra, and with luck the rare lechwe antelope and perhaps even a cheetah or wild dog. It was a longish drive, and so we set out early, not making our accustomed stops to view the many attractive groups of impala or puku as on the day before, but pressing on at a permissible speed and ignoring the increasingly agitated roar from our shattered exhaust system. We reached the Plain in good time and spied in the distance a huge black line of slowly moving animals, and as the only way to approach nearer was by following a rough rutted road looping around the edge of the parched grassland, we bounded on over the hard packed ruts, which in the rainy season was a swampy marsh. But these deep ruts proved too much for our struggling chariot, and with a rending crash the entire rear section of the exhaust pipe and silencer collapsed and clanked to the ground. On getting out and retrieving the pieces, I noticed that one of the rear shock-absorbers had given up the ghost as well, but since there was nothing that could be done, either in the middle of the Busanga Plain or at Lufupa either, we gingerly chugged back to camp, thanking our lucky stars that we were at least still mobile. On the way back we viewed buffalo and wildebeest, zebra and impala, but we did not find lechwe, wild dog or cheetah as we had hoped. But even this disappointment was minor compared with the pleasure of just being in such lovely and remote surroundings.

It is perhaps easy to enthuse over the delights of such a trip without recalling the tribulations, as apart from the mechanical dramas of this expedition, we also had to put up with the dust and the bites of myriad insects. The tsetse flies were plentiful, and since they will follow any moving object in the hope of a feed these ravenous brutes frequently penetrated our defences: in dense shade, beloved of resting animals, the tsetse sometimes descended on us in droves, forcing us to shut the windows, and this in turn made us stiflingly hot. The only answer was to drive away, watching some of the flies follow beside the car, and then open the windows and blast with aerosol insect sprays all the tsetses which entered the vehicle. We had fortunately remembered to bring an ample supply of aerosols. It is also sometimes trying for small children during long periods between sighting the more impressive animals, and if they are hot and dusty, and bitten by tsetse and also bored, it can be hard to have to explain that they are not allowed out of the car, other than at a few authorised resting places, even if they're desperate for a pee. In looking back it is surprising that our children were as good as they were, but even so there were the inevitable frayed nerves on occasion and it was therefore not entirely with regret that we left Lufupa after three nights and headed south for the much bigger Ngoma, capital of the Kafue Park and boasting a swimming pool and bar, as well as a protected camp where the children could let off steam without any risk. We bade a fond farewell to the friendly and efficient Lyson and George, hoping one day to return to Lufupa, but sadly we never did.

We left camp after an early breakfast as usual, accompanied by the thunderous hollow roar of our shattered exhaust, and promised the boys that we would all have a refreshing swim at Ngoma camp that afternoon during the heat of the day. We only had a little over 100 miles to drive, including several planned detours on some of the circular drives, or loops as they were called in order to reach Ngoma, and since a large part of this distance was through featureless wooded stretches we were not worried about making good time that day. Our first detour was to visit the Kafwala camp, owned and maintained by the respected Wildlife Conservation Society of Zambia, of which we were members. We were quite impressed with the attractive site, on the banks of a rocky stretch of the great Kafue River, but were glad that we had chosen the less popular and more peaceful Lufupa camp in preference. Part of the loop to Kafwala was across a small plain bordering the Kafue River, an area of grassland usually flooded in the rainy season but now parched and cracked, and we noticed the small groups of waterbuck standing in the shade of the lush jungly growth and elegant palm trees alongside the river. By now we were used to the ghastly noise from our engine and I had learned to treat our suspension with considerable care, on the rutted plains roads in particular, as pot holes hit hard bounced the overworked springs up and down in an alarming way. With both rear shock absorbers gone we were utterly dependent on the leaf springs to protect the underneath of the car. But we maintained good time and as we approached the Chunga post, at the point where the main Lusaka to Mongu road bisects the Park, we reassured ourselves with the thought that we might at least be able to get our exhaust system welded at Ngoma, even if the shock absorbers were a lost cause.

We were interested to see a number of Chinese workers in their trucks in the Chunga vicinity, but noted that although they were in no way hostile they showed a sort of studied disinterest in their surroundings. Whereas Zambians in rural areas were more than likely to wave and shout a greeting, the Chinese appeared not even to notice one's presence. Their job in the area was road construction, and also the building of a major new bridge across the Kafue River on the upgraded Great West Road linking the capital city with the distant Western province. From what little we heard of the very considerable Chinese engineering endeavours in Zambia their contributions were technically quite proficient. Only the most rabid anti-Communist was able to infer any significant political indoctrination as part of the price Zambia paid for their assistance. Their policy of non-fraternisation might have seemed antisocial to the naturally friendly rural Zambians, as the Chinese kept themselves very much to themselves, but the threatened wave of yellow Socialism flooding across newly independent Africa has so far proved a figment of the imagination, and in my opinion is not a probability for the future either.

My political reflections as we passed through Chunga that day did not distract us for long from the delights of the surrounding bush, and as we boomed steadily along the hard-packed and smooth but dusty road through the woodlands of the central part of the Park, we were pleased to see a sign indicating the Mwengwa site, a clearing beside the river where we were permitted to stop and stretch our legs. There was even a tiny shack with the distinctive pattern of a bush PK so that the coy could relieve themselves in privacy without recourse to the abundant but potentially hazardous jungle along the riverbank. We stopped for half an hour or so, enjoying the opportunity to walk about, and the boys, much to Anne's dismay discovered some enticing granite boulders to climb right on the river's edge. Our picnic was uneventful however, and we resumed our journey in splendid spirits enjoying the mid-morning sunshine and with all our windows wide open and not a single tsetse in the car. We reached Ngoma in good time for lunch and were delighted with the unaccustomed space of this large hotel site, with its rows of neat and whitewashed rondavels and huge shady trees. The swimming pool was blue, clean and inviting, the bar well-stocked and our two-bedroomed hut with private bathroom and loo was airy and deliciously cool.

We soon learned that there was nothing that could be done to heal our bone-shaking and ear-deafening motor vehicle by anyone at Ngoma, and so we resigned ourselves to returning to the Copperbelt at the end of our stay in a record slow time. But in the meantime we meant to enjoy the remaining few days in the Park and we went for our usual twice-daily drives, morning and evening, and relaxed at the poolside during the heat of the day or else in our spacious chalet. I can readily remember sitting in the doorway of our hut with a pair of binoculars after lunch each day, watching the tiny but colourful red firefinches and delicate blue waxbills, as they darted about in the thorn bushes and scuffled in the dusty earth only a few yards from our chairs. It is interesting how the smaller creatures and more trivial incidents may form just as vivid memories as do the more obvious and dramatic encounters with lion or elephant, and how every day brings something different if one is observant. I think Guy and Barry almost certainly preferred Ngoma to Lufupa, and it's understandable that they were happier in the pool than sitting in a hot, noisy car waiting for some animal to appear from a likely patch of bush, and it was therefore an advantage to have the hotel facilities at hand. But whereas at Lufupa we had woken to the grunting of hippos and a total exclusion of any noises reminiscent of civilisation, at Ngoma we woke to the sound of a powerful diesel generator, the crowing of cockerels, and the chatter of hotel staff drifting to the kitchens. Anne and I preferred Lufupa and will never forget its peace, tranquillity and isolation from the humdrum modern world.

Our day of departure, which we had all been dreading, arrived all too soon, and we had the car fully loaded at the crack of dawn and were comfortably first into breakfast. We said goodbye to the pleasant staff, piled into the car with its rather dreary packed lunch provided by the Ngoma kitchen, and churned off into the pale light of early morning, startling a small but graceful herd of kudu who were crossing the sandy track just outside of camp. We had decided to make a long detour through the southern tip of the Park to Ndumdumwese Post, turn east, and head for the tar road at Kalomo. This would add a considerable distance to the journey but would also reduce significantly the amount of driving on rough dirt roads, which by August were always badly corrugated, a feature which we knew would reduce our chances of reaching the Copperbelt without shattering our springs and probably doing further extensive damage to the car. Whether or not we made the right decision we will never know, but certainly the journey proved a nightmare. We negotiated the Park roads without mishap, but no sooner had we joined the east-bound dirt road at Ndumdumwese than we realised that motoring at National Park speeds was one thing, but motoring at normal speeds to travel from A to b was quite different. Every time I tried to press on a bit we slithered and lurched on the uneven road, as the rear wheels bounced alarmingly and simultaneously lost traction, and so we made painfully slow progress. Eventually we reached the last tsetse fly barrier, the car was sprayed with insecticide from a little hand flit-gun (a hand-pumped sprayer), and a small butterfly net was probed behind the wheels and under the wheel arches in search of any crafty stowaway flies. Then we were waved on by the dozy African at the barrier. We were once more out of the big-game heart of Kafue and into the fringes of good farming country, and as we crunched and swerved on we noticed the increasingly frequent villages beside the road, a sure sign that we were approaching the main north-south road and rail arteries of Zambia.

As Kalomo appeared in the distance we all breathed a sigh of relief, though with still some 450 miles to go to reach Kalulushi I realised that all was not yet won. We spent a precious half-hour in Kalomo, stocking up with lukewarm bottles of fizzy orange at a revoltingly dirty and scruffy store, and being stared at by a vaguely hostile and insulting swarm of Zambian teenagers, totally different to the charming and courteous peoples of the interior villages and the Park's staff. We were pleased to leave Kalomo behind us. Our spirits rose as we accelerated away from the unwelcoming place, and we became almost elated when I discovered that by reaching 50mph, I could effectively reduce the head-shattering exhaust boom of the car to an almost acceptable dull roar. No sooner had I levelled out at a comfortable 50mph, however, I hit an unseen pot hole in the tar road, and with a hideous crunch and rending noise we slewed from side to side as I instantly lifted my foot off the accelerator. We slowed to a halt, and I inspected the damage, which miraculously appeared minimal. But I realised that many more pot holes hit at speed would inevitably and totally disintegrate the car, and we sadly had to face the fact that the rest of the journey, hundreds and hundreds of miles, would be accompanied by that mind-blowing exhaust boom that we had put up with for so long. The only other incident that I remember clearly from that hellish drive, apart from the entire family vowing at frequent intervals that they would never come to the bush with me again for a holiday, was when Anne suddenly burst into tears as she remembered that that day was our wedding anniversary. We reached home in one piece, apart from the bruised and battered Fiat, at two o'clock the following morning after 18 hours of almost continuous driving, and I think it must have been fully a week before our hearing was restored to what we presumed was normal.

It was over five years before we again visited the Kafue National Park, and we were sadly unable to return to Lufupa on that occasion, as the northern part of the Park is always closed to tourists during the rainy season. We had chosen to have a short holiday a week before Christmas in 1976, and although the rains had started a little late that year, many of the tracks and loops were already impassable to all but four-wheel drive vehicles, and only the main hotel camp at Ngoma was open. Many things had changed since our first trip to Kafue five years before. We had also added little Beccy to our family and so we had five of us in the car, Beccy even at just three years old already a seasoned visitor to game parks.

The most notable change to our earlier dramatic expedition was the ease and comfort of the journey to reach Ngoma. We left Kalulushi at 6.30am and were amused to be chased out of town by one of our mine policemen, in a company Land Rover, who suspected that our car was being stolen. It was at a time of frequent vehicle thefts and in the half-light of early morning, before most people were up and about, the policeman had not recognised me or the fact that it was a white man driving the car and he was covered with embarrassment on my stopping and identifying myself. Having commended him for his vigilance, and told him that he was perfectly correct to have stopped me, we proceeded on our way without mishap and drove the 450 miles to the Park entrance in eight hours, including one stop for a picnic lunch and others for equally urgent needs. Not only was the entire Lusaka to Mongu road now fully tarred, but a new tar road had been constructed to the south, linking that road with the new dam site at Itezhi-Tezhi, only 15 miles from Ngoma itself. This smooth journey was in vivid contrast to the arduous and hazardous experience of our previous visit, and despite the emptiness of this excellent road, which belies its importance, it was certainly a blessing for this remote part of the country to have such all-weather access and reliable communication with Lusaka.

The Itezhi-Tezhi dam was quite a major engineering project and one which wildlife officials and conservationists had viewed with not a few misgivings. Damning the Kafue River, at the relatively narrow Itezhi-Tezhi gorge, not only backed up a large lake in the national Park so flooding a substantial area, but by controlling the flow of this major river it was suspected that the delicate ecological balance of the floodplains downstream of the dam would be dramatically upset. This was the home, amongst many other beautiful birds and animals, of the rare and elegant Kafue lechwe, an antelope which thrives on the periodic flooding of the broad plains known as the Kafue Flats. The true effect of the new dam has still not been fully assessed, but early reports suggested that the threat to wildlife had perhaps been somewhat exaggerated.

On arriving at the dam site we became immediately aware of the sensitivity of the Zambian security officials who were constantly worried at the possibility of Rhodesian attack on any of their strategic installations. The barrier across the road was manned by Zambian police, who were deliberately slow to stroll over to our car and inspect our entry documents to the Park. Since the dam and its ancillary equipment were still under construction there was a veritable maze of tracks and dumps, sheds and quarries, covering several square miles; and since it was far from obvious which track led to the Park entrance, on the far side, the normal procedure was for vehicles heading for the Park to wait for an official escort through the sprawling dam site. But we had been warned that this could entail waiting in our car in the heat of the day for any number of hours, as the Zambian police could easily decide that they had more pressing duties than escorting tourists. And so our friends had prompted us to assure the officials at the security check that we had been through before and therefore could find our way through the site without their valuable assistance. As this meant that they could go back to sleep and not bother about finding an escort, either then or in an hour or two's time, they were usually quite happy to raise the barrier and wave one through. This tactic luckily proved effective and we drove randomly through the messy site, keeping the looming dam wall on our right, and eventually wound our way up off the valley floor into the hills on the far side of the gorge when we got our first sight of the growing lake. As we stared out over the expanse of water we realised that we had been on this spot some five years earlier, but had then had a view of the winding Kafue River stretching away into the blistering haze of a dry season landscape. Now the view was of a broad shallow lake, edged by the lush green forest of the rainy season, and nearby a new safari lodge was being constructed. It was strange to reflect that our easy journey on tar roads was progress, but that that same progress risked spoiling the Park itself by making it too accessible. More people demand more facilities, and we wondered how long it would be before Kafue would become another Kruger. Perhaps the relative inefficiency of the Zambian tourist industry would turn into a blessing in disguise in keeping the country's attractions on the simple and basic scale which make them so much more enjoyable to people like ourselves.

We arrived at Ngoma in a shower of rain, but however much we would have preferred it to have been Lufupa, it was still great to be back in Kafue, wet or dry, camp or hotel. The clouds soon cleared and the sun shone through in the late afternoon as we unloaded the car and settled into our thatched accommodation. We were out early next morning and despite the grey skies and threatening rain we headed off in the car to see what we could find. The main tracks were firm and easy going, but the loops and less frequented tracks were very variable, some boggy and impassable, whilst others could be negotiated with care. We drove through the Ngoma teak forest and saw little other than a delightful party of banded mongooses, but the birds were splendid and we spent a while in a bird hide on the Butapa loop and watched jacanas, the curious but fascinating lily-trotters which walk casually over the water-plants with their huge feet quite out of proportion to their delicate bodies. There were plentiful waterfowl on the swampy lagoons too, white-faced whistling ducks and spurwing geese, and we occasionally glimpsed the elegant head of a reedbuck as it moved cautiously through the rushes at the water's edge. Brilliantly-coloured bee-eaters were plentiful and we occasionally glimpsed a spectacular flash of the scarlet crest and wings of a loerie as it swooped through the jungly treetops of this lush and rain-soaked landscape. Early on another morning we were indeed unexpectedly lucky to come across a pride of two magnificently golden-maned lions and lionesses, resting on an anthill right beside our track. We could have passed them by had we not stopped to discuss the advisability of proceeding further, on an increasingly water-logged loop leading to the Kavuma pan, and then we saw them, barely five yards from the car. We switched off and watched them for fully half an hour, but they ignored us totally, only occasionally deigning to look towards us and yawn. There may well have been others on the far side of the ant-hill, but there was no way we could either proceed or turn the car, and so we eventually left them to themselves and reversed gingerly away until we reached ground firm enough to risk turning around.

The swimming pool again proved a great attraction during the frequent spells of hot sunshine, and the children were delighted to find that the thatched sun-shade at the poolside tables were the daytime hiding places of the many gaudy tree-frogs that were so noisy and active at night. The most common of these were spectacular, psychedelically-patterned red and white midgets of little over an inch long, with rubbery legs and suckers on their toes. They accepted being handled with some reluctance and would leap astonishing distances from a standing start, disappearing into the thatch from one's hand like a jack-in-the-box. They would land everywhere, and I remember a sticky thud as one arrived out of the blue and fixed itself unnervingly to the lens of my spectacles, much to the delight of the children: but as I was reading a book at the time this flying attack almost made me jump out of my skin. The frogs of course enjoyed the poolside nooks and crannies, as the lights at night attracted all sorts of delicious insects for their consumption, so their presence was of mutual benefit to man and frog.

One evening we joined a group of other tourists for a trip by Land Rover around the Nkale loop, a route we had found impossible by car. The Land Rover was of the large forward-control truck type, with seats on its high lorry-like body, so that we were viewing the surrounding bush from a useful vantage point. We did see one impressively horned male kudu and his herd of females, and a splendid group of sable antelope including one huge dark bull with enormous scimitar horns, but we preferred the privacy of our own car and the ability to stop, when we liked and for however long we liked, without the chatter of other tourists and the click of their camera shutters. Whilst we would be content to watch a mongoose or a ground squirrel, the average tourist is easily restless without a continual parade of elephants and buffalo. We saw plenty of the latter but only two elephants, and those in the distance, during our entire stay, but the trip was nonetheless a great success. Just a walk past the old huge sausage tree, with its enormous pendulous fruit, for an hour at the top of the observation tower on the edge of the camp, was sufficient to stimulate a feeling of great contentment as we watched the sun go down over the distant Itezhi-Tezhi hill. Our return to Kalulushi was uneventful but became tedious with all the road checks: we counted 14 stops in the 450-mile journey, some for tsetse control, others to check for poachers, but mostly routine police checks for identification, searching for weapons, or just to inspect tyres or the mechanical condition of the vehicle. We were pleased, as always, to be home, but with another haul of wonderful memories to savour over the years ahead.

Chapter 10
BRIMSTONE AND BANTU

In re-living our past memories of Zambia, it is easy for us to feel that the period of over 18 years was a long span of time; and indeed, it can be seen as a quarter of a normal human lifetime. But in terms of the history of the land it is really but a fraction of a second, and the rocks and artefacts of Zambia include a fascinating record of the past, not just of centuries, but of thousands, millions, and even billions of years. In fact the rocks of the southern half of the African continent include signs of the earliest known forms of life, and even the rocks themselves give clues to land form and climate at the time of their formation. Of course the older the rocks, then the more unlikely it becomes that any trace of life will be preserved for the modern scientist to unveil, as the physical pressures and reheating processes which periodically buckle and melt the earth's crust, equally destroy all but the most ideally-preserved fossils. Curiously enough it was not until as comparatively recently as 1964 that a young geologist at Mufulira mine, Steve Malan, first recognised what were the oldest known fossils to have been identified in Zambia. These were stromatolites, algal structures of a type very similar to those living today, and which have been recognised in rocks of immense antiquity elsewhere in the world. The exact age of these ancient rocks cannot be precisely determined, even by today's sophisticated techniques, but by a combination of methods it is possible to estimate that the stromatolites and other algal forms of the Lower Roan sequence in Zambia are perhaps in excess of 800 million years old; whilst those from even more ancient rocks in South Africa may well have lived over three billion years ago.

With one exception the fossil record in Zambia is relatively poor, and whilst evidence of other algal forms persist, from several later eras, it is largely the rocks themselves which have to tell the story on their own. We see marine environments, lakes and estuaries, sandy shore and tumbled pebbly beaches. A period of glaciation is clearly demonstrable when huge ice floes drifted south from glaciers in neighbouring Zaire, and rafted great cobbles and boulders out into the cold seas, where the ice floes melted and dropped their debris into the thick black muds below. These glacial deposits, or tillites, are widespread in the Northwestern and Copperbelt provinces of Zambia, and whilst mostly buried deep below layers of soils and later rocks, they do outcrop in a few localities where they can be examined. It is strange to walk on these dark pebbly rocks in the blistering heat of the day, and yet reflect that at the time the muds and pebbles were consolidating on the sea floor much of Central Africa was in the grip of an Ice Age, some 600 million years ago. This period of glaciation was followed by brief intervals of warmer seas, and alternating climatic changes during which a few relatively thin beds of limestone, shale and sandstone, with another minor glacial deposit, were laid down in predominantly shallow water, but these represent the end of the truly marine or geosynclinal history of Zambia. Some 100 million years later followed the last of many major distortions, and a reheating of the crustal pile of sediments and other earlier rocks like the granites which had been intruded as red-hot magmas into the buried strata. There then passed a period of little geological activity for perhaps 200 million years, and although as a geologist I find it positively indecent to dispose in so few words with such a staggering length of time, it is not until some 250 to 300 million years ago that significant accumulations of new rocks started to build again the landscape and history of today's Zambia.

This new era was heralded by a further Ice Age, represented widely throughout southern Africa by the Dwyka tillite, which sadly is not known as such in Zambia, although possibly contemporaneously fluvio-glacial deposits do exist in a few localities. But the subsequent succession of sediments, which are today known as the rocks of the Karoo era, are well-represented in the rift-like troughs forming parts of the Kafue, Luangwa and Zambezi River valleys. It is in these rocks that lie not only the economically important coal seams, but also the beautifully preserved remains of the first land animals and plants to have inhabited Zambia and of which we have any record, though clearly others must have existed in the primarily continental environment before that time.

In the Karoo period Africa was not the vast but isolated continent it is today, but was part of the colossal continental mass now termed Gondwanaland. The theory that Argentina, and the South American continent as a whole, had been torn from the western side of southern Africa; and that even Australasia in its turn had been wrenched from Antarctica, was for long discounted, but it is now virtually universally accepted amongst scientists, backed by intensive study of paleomagnetism and of related fauna and flora found fossilised in similar rocks of these present land masses. Had man lived in Karoo times it would have been possible to have walked from Quito to Calcutta, or from Durban to Darwin, without once crossing an ocean. To quote from Lord Byron: *'Tis strange – but true; for truth is always strange; stranger than fiction'.*

The creatures of the Karoo, and to a lesser extent the plants they lived amongst, have long fascinated man and include those fabulous beasts the dinosaurs, reptiles at the peak of their development. The so-called Glossopteris flora occurs over so widespread an area that it is possible to correlate rocks containing these plants from continent to continent, helping to piece together the shape of old Gondwanaland. The Karoo rocks of the Luangwa valley contain remains of these plants, as well as plentiful reptilian fossils from the age of dinosaurs. Where today modern man watches elephant and lion, once roamed Oudenodon and Rubidgea; and the recently named Zambiasaurus trod the earth. There is no doubt that the Luangwa valley of 200 million years ago was as *'red in tooth and claw'* as it is today, to quote this time from Lord Tennyson. But the dinosaurs mysteriously did not survive. Many explanations have been postulated for their abrupt extinction, but whatever the reason, we must remain satisfied with the record provided by their plentiful and worldwide fossilised remains; and with the presence of such ferocious reptiles as the crocodile, whose archetypal ancestors plundered the Luangwa swamps of their time, in a way certainly akin to their heirs' devious and sinister existence in this splendid and remote river valley.

The Karoo period in Zambia was climaxed by a flourish of volcanic activity, as it was over much of central and southern Africa. Outpourings of basaltic lava spread across the land, particularly in the southern and southwestern valleys and plains of the Zambezi and Barotse areas, damming rivers, filling depressions and streaming down hillsides, transforming yet again the face of the country. Many millions of years later, during the Cretaceous period of perhaps 100 million years ago, further deposits of sediment were laid down in the extreme southwest of Zambia. These rocks are now buried beneath the most recent sediments of the land, the sands and sandstones of the Pleistocene age known geologically as the Kalahari System, or more generally as the Kalahari Sand, which form a vast sandy blanket covering much of western Zambia and almost all of Botswana to the south, and extending into Angola and Namibia to the west and southwest respectively. It was in the early days of the Cretaceous period that the giant reptiles, the dinosaurs which had dominated the earth for so long, became extinct, most probably because of a change to a cooler climate which did not suit these cold-blooded creatures. Their dominant place was taken by the warm-blooded mammals, culminating in the evolution of man during the last five million years of the earth's history. Man's life began on the great plains of Africa a little before the start of the Kalahari period.

Thus we have seen Zambia grow from the beginnings of time, passing through periods of ice and fire, compression and rending, uplift and erosion, and smothering by wind-blown sand. Similarly the land has been populated by an astonishing variety of life, from the primordial algal ooze, to rapacious dinosaurs; and from primitive ancestral ape-men to modern man himself, this latter transition taking place in only the last few million years.

There have not been found, anywhere in Zambia, such exciting and fabled remains as those of proconsul which was found in East Africa and perhaps represents our earliest ancestors: nor have we direct evidence of such remarkable inhabitants of the continent as the Nutcracker Man of Olduvai, Southern Ape-man of South Africa, or handy Man of East Africa. But we do have every reason to believe that these links with our past must have been present, sparsely, throughout central and southern Africa prior to the Stone Age. The earliest evidence of man in Zambia was found at Kalambo Falls, on the northern border with Tanzania, where a site was excavated which contained stone and wooden tools, and evidence that fire was being used by man in the area at a time some 55,000 years ago during the Early Stone Age. Perhaps this and other riverside sites in Zambia were even occupied as long as 100,000 years ago, but it was not until 1921 that the first skeletal remains were to be found, when a skull of Stone Age man was discovered at Broken Hill, in the central part of the country. Broken Hill Man as he became known, was a cave-dweller in the Middle Stone Age, and he possessed a larger brain and was of taller stature than possessed by the Early Stone Age people. Perhaps a few thousand of these men lived and hunted in Zambia up until as recently as 10,000 years ago.

The people of the Later Stone Age still survive, precariously, in the most hostile and inhospitable parts of the African continent, as they do elsewhere in the world. The fascinating and resourceful Australian aboriginals, and certain remote tribes in southwest Asia and South America, no doubt evolved contemporaneously with the African pygmy and bushman. Most people associate the bushman in Africa with the vast and arid Kalahari Desert where these astonishing men and their families continue to survive in small numbers and against all the odds, facing incredible deprivation and using great skill in seeking and conserving the barest essentials of existence, in terrain which would destroy any other man within 48 hours.

We know that the bushmen once had much of southern Africa to themselves, long before the incursion by northern Bantu tribes, and that they enjoyed an easier life when game was abundant and ubiquitous. The bushmen were Africa's first artists and much of their art survives, decorating caves and rock shelters in Zambia as well as at such well-known sites such as the Ikanti paintings in the Drakensburg mountains of South Africa, the White Rhino site in the Matopos hills of Zimbabwe, and numerous others. I once squatted quietly in the cool shelter of the giant slab of rock which overhangs the Ikanti paintings and stared out across the rich plains far below, visualising the slow but inexorable advance of the first black peoples, and then the white, which forced the bushman from shelter to shelter, and eventually far away from their traditional and lush hunting grounds to their present final refuge in the glaring and barren sands of the Kalahari. But the bushman was far from confined to South Africa, and we have evidence of his presence in Zambia at several localities, from Mpika in the north to Solwezi in the west: his remains are essentially his art, both paintings and engravings.

Stone Age art is considered very broadly as belonging to two categories, naturalistic and schematic. Examples of the naturalistic type show clearly the forms of hunter and hunted, antelope, elephant or buffalo, and it is even frequently possible to identify precisely the species of antelope due to the accuracy and clarity of the paintings. The western escarpment of the Luangwa valley had a number of examples of such naturalistic paintings in the caves of these steep rocky hillsides. Perhaps the most curious of the schematic type are the engravings of the Chifubwa gorge near Solwezi, where the Chifubwa stream has cut through the sandy schists, and where it has been estimated that man lived more than 4,000 years ago. The engravings are curiously enigmatic, being a series of long and short vertical lines and numerous inverted U's, many of which have a central vertical line, as well as apparently random cup-like depressions. This site was first found in 1929, when it was investigated but not documented, and has been visited and excavated by professional archaeologists several times since. The rock shelter was presumably occupied for some considerable time, as the lowest engravings, some of which had a type of reddish pigment rubbed into them, were covered by several feet of alluvial sand which preserved the buried engravings in good repair, but the true purpose of the symbols remains speculative. Perhaps the significance was mystical or ritual: perhaps a form of record of hunts, or natural events; or even primitive attempts to represent man-like figures. We shall never know for certain.

The bushmen were, and remain, small in stature, and essentially followed a nomadic life-style, wandering where they wished and following the game on which they depended for their existence. Other, larger men are believed to have coexisted in Zambia, perhaps descended from Broken Hill Man, but there was no need for competition between them as food was plentiful for all and freely available until the southerly migration of the Bantu-type farming tribes of the Iron Age reached Zambia some 2,000 years ago. Farming had been in progress in the fertile valleys of the Middle East and elsewhere for thousands of years before the slow movement of these peoples reached central and southern Africa, and the initial migrations were essentially peaceful, with no cause for tribal conflict. In fact the bushmen, Africa's aptly-termed 'little people', were occasionally integrated into these new communities, and intermarriage was probably not uncommon. Some of the oral traditions of the southwestern tribes of Zambia include reference to the little people, Bakafula or Mwandibonene as they were known. Very occasionally today, a small group of bushmen may even cross the Zambezi River, from Botswana, Namibia or Angola, and briefly move into the extreme southwestern parts of Zambia in search of food.

Whereas the Tonga and Ila peoples of the southern province of today's Zambia are undoubtedly descended from the first Bantu-type peoples, and probably also mixed Bushman-Bantu descent, it was not until much later that the main territorial pressures caused real dissent and strife in the region. As the cattle farmers moved in, some carrying on to the south across the Zambezi, their iron tools and weapons were used to carve out tribal farming areas as the peoples settled and occupied large parts of the country, so forcing out the nomadic bushmen. These pressures continued over the centuries, until the incursions of Lunda and Luba peoples from the Congo, now Zaire, established the dominant Bemba, and other tribes such as the Lamba, Lima, Kaonde and many more. But it was not until the 19th century that southern Africa's greatest upheaval commenced, when Shaka of the Zulus despatched his infamous *impis* of fearless warriors, to conquer and slaughter, rape and pillage, in carving out his empire. Such was Shaka's iron rule of cruelty that some of his unsuccessful *impis* feared to return to Zululand, in what is now Natal, and they moved northwards, so reversing the earlier routes of migration which had originally brought these Bantu people south. The proud Matabele peoples of Zimbabwe are descendants of the Zulus, and were themselves raiding into southern parts of Zambia, across the Zambezi, during the last century. The Lozi peoples of the Barotse region of southern Zambia came originally from the Congo, and were in turn conquered and enslaved by the Makololo from the south, a group like the Ngoni who were fleeing north from the ravages of Shaka's *impis*. The quiet and peaceful patterns of farming and trading were upset over and over again during the last few centuries, with the inhabitants of Zambia suffering at the hands of the Bantu, Arab and European invaders alike. The tribal map of Zambia today is dominated to the north by the Bemba, and to the south by the Tonga, but the peripheral areas of the country are a hotch-potch of intermingled tribes with many different language groups and origins. 'One Zambia, One Nation' is the country's political slogan for unity, but it will be many years before this will become a reality.

The first Bantu-type farmers of the Early Iron Age, reaching Zambia some 2,000 years ago with their cattle and other domestic animals from East Africa and the Congo, gradually established themselves and planted crops, using iron tools which they made from plentiful iron ore in the area with a primitive but effective technology. Many iron smelting sites have been found, always near water, and some considerable detail of their occupants' lives and trading habits has been pieced together by archaeologists, producing a fascinating picture of the way of life of these early farmers. The principal method of farming, still used today in the rural areas, is known as *chitimene*. Trees and shrubs in an area to be planted are chopped down, at a height of two to three feet above the ground, and the branches and vegetation are then piled in heaps scattered throughout the clearing, and then burned. The salts and trace elements are thus returned to the ground in the ash from the fires and are washed into the soil by the first rains, so producing a fertile area for the crops. A clearing may be planted for two or three seasons and then abandoned, as its fertility decreases, when a new area will be slashed and burned. The stumps produce a regenerative growth of poor quality, and the abandoned clearings are easy to recognise in the bush: they are also most unpleasant to walk through, not only because of the untidy tree growth, but also because of the uneven ground resulting from the mounds on which peanuts and pumpkins were grown. We used to hate traversing these old gardens in the course of our geological and solid surveys. Shortly after Zambia's independence the government started to urge the people to 'go back to the land', to try to halt the drift of villagers towards the main population centres along the line of rail. One incentive scheme was to offer them cash awards for each acre of bush which was cleared for farming, but this scheme backfired. The method used for clearing was the familiar *chitimene* culture, rather than permanent tree felling and digging up the stumps, and so very little land was properly cleared. But additionally, it was never made clear to the villagers that the payment was intended to help them start productive farming and so what happened was a rash of slash and burn clearings which were never planted and soon returned to poor quality woodland. The villagers enjoyed being paid for this and promptly consumed the proceeds of their labours in wild beer-drinking celebrations. However, there is undoubtedly potential for major agricultural progress in the country, and a number of truly successful projects have already been tried and tested. It is vital that the full potential is realised as soon as possible, as Zambia has the soil and the land to become one of Africa's major food exporters. The Tonga peoples of 1,000 years ago, and the later Lunda and Luba tribesmen, chose their homes well indeed.

The Arab and Portuguese traders were less interested in the soils and land of Zambia than in the slaves and natural resources, ivory and copper in particular, which could be taken or traded in the heart of the dark continent. There followed the great missionary explorers of whom unquestionably the most famous, and probably the greatest, was David Livingstone, whose memory is widely respected throughout Africa and whose memorial at the place he died in 1873, Chitambo near Lake Bangweulu, is now one of Zambia's national monuments. Even today this monument is not easily accessible and few are the travellers who make the long pilgrimage to pay their respects at the spot the heart of this remarkable man was buried beneath the tree under which he died. A more imposing memorial to Dr Livingstone is his statue on the southern bank of the Zambezi River at Victoria Falls which was named after his Queen. I well remember standing beside the huge stone plinth on which the statue is erected, beside the spuming Devil's Cataract, and gazing at his towering figure as I reflected upon the arduous and dangerous journey which first brought him to this spot over 100 years previously. I noticed a silver speck high in the sky, and the streaming white contrail from a high-flying jet, the trademark of today's traveller in Africa.

There are many other fascinating national monuments in Zambia, some historical and others of scenic or political importance. These places are as diverse as the site of the Chambeshi River, in the northern province, where General von Lettow-Vorbeck surrendered the German forces of East Africa during the 1914-18 war; and the house in a Lusaka suburb from which Kenneth Kaunda led the struggle for Zambia's independence during the early 1960s. Another recent memorial has been erected to mark the site, near Ndola, where Dag Hammarskjöld, UN Secretary-General, met his death in an aircraft crash, in mysterious circumstances, whilst on a mission in 1961 to mediate in the Katangese uprising in neighbouring Zaire. A sad and tragic sequel occurred at the Hammarskjöld memorial in recent years, when a European visitor to the site was shot dead by thieves, in front of his own family, during an attempt to steal his car. A few miles from this site is another national monument, of greater age, protected by Presidential decree as recently as 1976 as a contribution to mark World Forestry Day on 21st March of that year. It is a huge brown mahogany tree, or *Mofu*, considered by the local Lamba people to be a spirit-house or *ngulu*, and therefore sacred. The tree stands between the main Kitwe to Ndola road, some 90 feet high and over 200 years old, and must have born silent witness to many of the dramas and tragedies of the surrounding forest, through the years of slavery and conquest. Many travellers must have rested in its shade, and it is to be hoped that the spirits of the traditional tribal protectors of the tree, reinforced by the President's decree, will enable it to provide shelter and inspiration for future generations. Present-day vandals periodically chop off pieces of bark and souvenirs or 'medicine' and even steal the notice board on which is written the Tree's Prayer, despite its plea:

> 'You who pass me by
> And would raise your hand against me,
> Hearken ere you harm me.
>
> I am your fire on the cold winter nights,
> The friendly shade screening you from the summer sun,
> My fruits quench your thirst on your journey.
>
> I am the beam that holds your house,
> The board of your table,
> The bed on which you lie,
> The timber that builds your boat.
>
> I am the handle of your hoe,
> The door of your house,
> The wood of your cradle,
> The shell of your coffin.
>
> You who pass by,
> Hearken to my prayer:
> Harm me not'.

This charming quotation is from *The Wayside Tree*, by an unknown poet, and was first placed on the tree by our old friend Colin Duff, in his days as Northern Rhodesia's Chief Conservator of Forests.

Since Stone Age man first travelled through central Africa, to the days of Bantu tribal warfare and subsequent colonial rule, and culminating in Zambia's independence as a black African state, there has been spasmodic progress towards a fully integrated society. This process has seen one culture absorbed into another, tribes and even races intermingling, and territorial boundaries formed and broken. It would be unrealistic to visualise the present situation as a final state, and yet it is difficult to forecast reliably the next phase of Zambia's history. With the one exception of South Africa the entire continent, for better or for worse, is now formed of independent nations in which the numerically dominant race or tribe has become the government of the land, whether by democracy, dictatorship or monarchy. But the boundaries of the vast majority of these modern states are not natural ethnic divisions, but largely remain as the imposed and physical limits dictated by past conquest of one people by another. The fear of neo-colonialism is not too far from the surface in many of these African states, and the progress of industrial and financial assistance from many nations is jealously watched by others. Past colonial masters such as the British, French, Germans and Portuguese are anxious to retain their influence, and watch carefully the machinations of Russians, Cubans, Romanians and Chinese: the latter are feared almost more than the Russians but so far have proved perhaps the most genuine in providing aid of both cash and kind without political strings attached. The Russians and their Cuban puppets are undoubtedly the most aggressive and pose the real threat to stability in the continent, with military presence already well-established in Angola and Ethiopia. With political pressures and international opinion pushing hard on South Africa, and nationalist strugglers by their numerically dominant black peoples increasing in intensity, there exists another ready source of racial tension to explode across the southern half of the continent. Tribal or racial antagonisms are never far below the surface in Africa, although, perhaps curiously, the age-old religious strife of Europe and the Mediterranean does not seem to have been adopted as readily further south, where the Muslim faith has not penetrated significantly beyond East Africa and Zaire despite the influence of early Arab traders. An obscure sect of religious deviants, known as the Lumpas, did cause some bloodshed and aggravation in Zambia is 1965, but their leader, Alice Lenshina, was swiftly jailed and her followers mostly dispersed without further trouble.

It can be stated with relative confidence that the next major upheaval in southern Africa will not be caused by religious discord; but there remains the possibility that tribal prejudices could spark off conflict. Perhaps between the Matabele and Mashona of newly-independent Zimbabwe. But the most likely of all, in my opinion, as well as that of many others, remains the dreaded racial confrontation between black and white which has been threatening South Africa and Namibia for decades and is rapidly escalating. There is time to avoid it still, but great strides will have to be made over the next few years in order to turn the tide of African nationalism and international opinion into constructive and mutual progress. It is ironic to consider that the last refuge of the Stone Age bushmen, the Kalahari Desert, is also reputed, with some authority, to be the centre of white South Africa's nuclear weapons research.

Chapter 11
LOCHINVAR

After our first trip to the vast Kafue National Park, in 1971, we had decided that not only must we continue to explore more of Zambia, but that we should do so in a similar way, by staying at non-catering camps in other wildlife refuges where we could again sense the excitement and relative isolation offered at these simple havens. The obvious choice was the teeming and exotic Luangwa valley, but this was a rather daunting prospect as by this time, August 1973, our little Beccy was just eight months old, and Luangwa was a really exhausting drive from the Copperbelt. Anne and I were well-used to long and arduous journeys with small babies, but for some reason on this occasion we felt that a shorter journey would be more propitious and so we selected the small but interesting Lochinvar estate for our visit, an area of only about 150 square miles and the most recent of Zambia's National Parks. Lochinvar had originally been a cattle ranch, situated west of Monze and south of the great Kafue River. It had been purchased by the government in 1966 with financial assistance from the World Wildlife Fund for a game management area, and then became a full National Park in 1972. The area provided a splendid habitat, in particular, for the last great herds of the unique Kafue lechwe, a species of antelope which we had sought unsuccessfully during our earlier visit to the Kafue Park. These graceful brown antelope with their elegant lyre-shaped horns thrive in the flood plains of the Kafue River, feeding close to the water and amidst the flooded grasslands, following the water's edge as it rises or sinks during the natural seasons. Their meat was also highly prized by the local people, and until quite recent times the tribes of the area organised an annual hunt, the *chila*, when hundreds of people with their dogs killed literally thousands of lechwes. Since protection of the species the lechwe have shown an encouraging increase in numbers which it is hoped will continue.

Having selected Lochinvar for our holiday we decided that we could see the best of such a small area in just three full days, allowing an additional day at each end for the journey of some 370 miles from Kalulushi and return. At that time our car was an Austin maxi, which with its five doors and roomy interior was ideal for this type of expedition. The day before our departure we spent hours packing all our requirements, which included the inevitable jerry-can of petrol, food for five days for five people, plus clothes, binoculars, my camera and its ever-increasing and bulky assortment of lenses and tripod, a toolbox, and so on. With Guy and Barry now aged 12 and ten respectively, Anne and I had almost forgotten the extraordinary plethora of gear needed for a baby's comfort and survival, but as soon as I saw the incredible mound of equipment which was apparently considered essential luggage, I almost gave up the prospect of the trip on the spot. Quite apart from the piles of disposable nappies, dozens of bottles of creams, ointments, cotton buds, special soaps and oils, waterproof sheets, row upon row of baby food jars, cans of powdered milk, feeding bottles and their assortment of cleaning and sterilising gadgets, there was a colossal plastic container of ready-boiled Kalulushi water. To the eternal credit of the Maxi, not only did this awe-inspiring pile of miscellanea fit in without my having to sacrifice any of my own gear, but there was still room to fit in Beccy's collapsible lobster-pot playpen complete with its waterproof circular foam mattress. Of course it was not just the object to fit in everything regardless, but the art was to ensure that each time an item was required during the journey it was not necessary to totally unpack the entire car.

The morning after this marathon packing session we set off on our long journey south. We were by now only too familiar with the long and dull route to Lusaka, some 220 miles away, but the roads were in relatively good shape with only a few deviations off the tarmac, over short stretches of graded earth track, to relieve the monotony. We made good time and decided to have our picnic lunch at Chilanga, just south of Lusaka, in the Munda Wanga botanical gardens and zoo, and although we didn't take the time to explore the gardens, or the snake park and animal enclosures, we did appreciate this chance to stretch our legs and sit in the shade whilst eating our lunch. Beccy had been surprisingly good so far on the journey, but it was still hard work for Anne to keep her and the boys happy in the enclosed space of the car for so long: as usual, I had decided to do all the driving as I make a rotten passenger and am less patient than Anne with fractious children. However, we soon refreshed ourselves and fitted our jigsaw of pieces back into the car and resumed the journey, confident that over half the trip was already behind us. At Monze we turned off the mostly smooth tarmac of the Great North Road, and headed westwards on a well graded and broad laterite surface, eventually turning north towards the Park and enjoying the peace and quiet of a deserted track of compacted earth that we knew only extended for a few miles before reaching the Park's entrance gate, which was itself close to the base where we were staying. The journey was one of our most uneventful in Africa and we arrived at Lochinvar Lodge feeling quite spry, and surprisingly unjaded, in time for a welcome cup of tea.

The Lodge comprises the original ranch building, with several separate bedrooms and a few communal rooms for dining, cooking and washing, and a long open verandah stretching along the entire front of the ranch. The rooms were clean, as was the linen, and other equipment, and a cook and other servants were provided. We felt it a little less idyllic than the Lufupa camp, which we had enjoyed so much in the Kafue Park, but it was certainly quite adequate and we happily unpacked the dusty Maxi and stowed away our heaps of baggage. After tea we strolled around the ranch-house and surrounding grounds, and admired the glossy starlings and bush squirrels which squabbled in the shady trees and scuffled in the dusty earth on the ground. The ranch house had been built on one of the few small hills at the southern end of the Park and enjoyed a view out over the lower ground which was a mixture of rather open woodland and scrubby grassland. A little further north of the woodland gives way to what is defined as termitaria grassland, a flat plain on which are scattered large termite mounds supporting some shrubs and trees as well as the characteristic and aptly-named candelabra cactuses. At the southern limit of the seasonal floods the termitaria die out, both the large mounds and the many small tombstone-like varieties, giving way to the flat grassy plains which are periodically inundated by the waters of the swollen Kafue River.

The water recedes during the dry season, leaving areas of desiccated mud and vistas of grassland separated by trickles of water in the centres of the streams, and it is on these plains that the herds of game are mostly seen. A few rough roads are maintained in the Park, a main north-south causeway linking a network of other tracks to points of particular interest. The north-south road leads up to the Kafue River itself, the northern boundary of the Park, but this is only passable over its entire length during the latter half of the dry season.

Since it was largely the herds of Kafue lechwe that we had come to see, it was to the north, and the grass plains, that we drove first thing in the morning after our arrival. There was a fresh breeze as we rumbled slowly on and we were surprised at the abruptness with which the termitaries disappeared at the edge of what was the southern limit of the seasonal inundation: but in August both habitats were uniformly dry and there was no apparent difference to indicate the reason for this demarcation. We soon saw our first lechwe, tiny dots on the horizon of one of Africa's marvellous, limitless landscapes, and we hoped that our track would lead us nearer to them in time, though knowing their predilection for swamp and wetland we wondered if we would indeed be lucky, as everything around us was parched and dry. But our luck held, and after several more miles of bumping and bouncing across the ruts and potholes of the track, as it stretched out across the endless plain, we reached the Nampongwe River, the only permanent watercourse in the Park. Before us, on the far bank, was a splendid herd of some 30 or 40 magnificent male lechwe, shining a handsome chestnut colour with their huge horns silhouetted against the sky. At this time of year the males form herds of their own, leaving the hornless females with the young, and all the lechwe we saw on that and subsequent days were males. We watched this herd for some half an hour until it became alarmed by some unidentified creature; the startled antelope lowered their horns back onto their shoulders, held their heads up and trotted elegantly off into the hazy distance. It was a splendid sight, and worth every inconvenience and effort in our journey. We saw many more herds of lechwe over the next few days, and neither Anne nor I grew tired of watching them, whether they were splashing through the swampy ground of a rapidly drying lagoon or grazing on the parched open plains. The lechwe is second only to the larger *sitatunga* amongst the antelopes in leading an almost aquatic existence, and will happily feed on grass and other vegetation in as much as two feet of water, standing immersed up to their white bellies.

One of the unusual aspects of Lochinvar was the absence of the larger carnivores of Africa, so that it was permissible to leave one's car and walk unaccompanied across the plains: the only animal of which one should be wary being buffalo. We soon developed a routine which proved ideal for our family group on our morning and evening expeditions. This entailed taking Beccy's playpen with us and establishing a base, near the Nampongwe riverbank, from which we could watch the prolific bird life, stalk the lechwe across the plain, or just relax with our thermos, shut our eyes and listen to the wonderful sounds all around us. The sun beat down on us every day with no thought of rain, and provided a hat was worn there was no problem from the lack of shade, as a breeze was always blowing to keep the sweating walker cool. Beccy played happily in her playpen, which was raised off the ground, and was watched in turn by whoever was on duty: the sight of a red round playpen standing on the remote plain beside our dark brown Maxi provided a strange sight. We opened all four doors of the car, as well as the large hatchback, and it looked rather like a weird and monstrous beast with wings and limbs outstretched in display. I was never able to approach nearer than about 100 yards to the lechwe herds without their noticing me and grunting and whistling to each other, but stalking was most enjoyable: I must have looked slightly threatening to them as I crept through the dry grass with my camera and tripod, with a massive 500mm telephoto lens closely resembling a bazooka. The boys and Anne enjoyed these stalks and walks too, and we even took Beccy with us on occasions, perched high in a piggy-back style with a superb view of the surrounding plains. We once all set off to investigate a speck in the distance which was the attention of a flock of white-backed vultures, to find that what we had expected to be a stroll of less than half a mile turned into a mile-long trek with Beccy getting heavier step by step, as indeed did my cumbersome camera bag. The carcase turned out to be a week or two old, with only a few dry bones and shrivelled skin with tufts of chestnut hair proclaiming the remains to be of a lechwe. There were a number of skulls and bones, and several lovely lyre-shaped horns that we came across on our walks, but although we were tempted to keep a pair of horns we were of course aware that nothing must be removed from a National park and so we resisted our acquisitive urges.

Each day we returned to the ranch for lunch, frequently late, in order to let Beccy have her full afternoon nap in the deliciously cool bedroom. At this time, Anne also enjoyed a rest from the heat, and I usually took a short trip with the boys, either by car or on foot. Our favourite spot was the well-known Gwisho Hot-Springs, a Late Stone Age site from which a number of interesting items had been excavated in the past, proving the area to have been used as a campsite almost 5,000 years ago. The early hunters at Gwisho are believed to have been very similar to the present-day Bushmen of southern Africa, and some were buried at this site at which many animal bones, stone tools and other remains were found. But Guy and Barry, though fascinated by this vision of past hunters stalking their prey amongst the plains around us, using bows and arrows and primitive stone implements, were more interested in the very real and visible phenomenon of the hot springs themselves. The water in the little pools, amongst the rocks and swampy vegetation, steamed and was too hot to touch comfortably for long. Whilst they watched one little pool a kamikaze grasshopper plunged to almost instant death in the hot water, and was helplessly boiled in a second or two, long before our startled selves could react and effect a rescue. The whole place had a rather still and eerie quality, peaceful and yet vividly menacing, as though the geological fault in the earth's surface through which these hot solutions emerged, might suddenly open wide and swallow us, Maxi and all. An old baobab tree presided over our musings and offered a suitably grotesque presence to compound the feeling of mystery: I wondered if the early hunters had also felt a magical quality at the site, which was certainly ideally suited as a base for their hunting forays over the game-rich grasslands nearby.

Another midday sortie I enjoyed with Guy and Barry was through the open woodland and bush adjacent to the ranch. We would walk a few hundred yards, find a patch of shade, and sit quietly, waiting for something to happen. It was usually the birds which would catch our attention, a hornbill cruising over the thorn bushes and preening itself in the sun, or a loerie flicking its crest and telling us to 'go away'. We would occasionally spot a group of vervet monkeys, ground squirrels or a mongoose, but never for long as these restless creatures soon passed out of sight. On trying to creep closer to a small party of vervets that day we suddenly came across a mound of beautiful guinea-fowl feathers, fresh and clean, with just a trace of the remains of the flesh and bones of the bird itself. It must have been killed earlier that day, or the night before, and we instinctively looked anxiously around, half-expecting to see a glowering leopard or civet eyeing us with displeasure: I'm sure Guy and Barry enjoyed a momentary extra dose of adrenalin as they too imagined a potential threat nearby. Forgetting our good intentions about not collecting any souvenirs from National Parks the boys quickly gathered a handful of the most elegant feathers and stuck several in the nylon leopard-skin headbands of their bush hats. For small boys they really did look the seasoned white hunters, and Anne and I realised what a splendid and adventurous life they led, compared to their friends in the Somerset preparatory school where they were boarding for most of the year.

Apart from the superb herds of lechwe, undoubtedly the most rewarding spectacle was the prolific bird-life which was to be seen wherever we went. The weavers' nests, hanging like honey-coloured balls of straw from the thorn-trees; the cheeky wattled plovers which ran alongside the tracks just in front of the car; the emerald-spotted wood-doves which exploded from the dust almost under the wheels as we threaded through the woodland. But the water-birds were even more splendid, with an endless wealth of variety, from the shimmering expanse of white pelicans dancing in the distant haze like a mirage, to the stately and magnificent crowned cranes strutting regally through the golden grass. We could watch for hours the glossy and sacred ibises, the coucals, darters, jacanas, spoonbills, spurwing and Egyptian geese, open-billed and marabou storks, grey and Goliath herons, and many, many more. We were watching just such a bewildering parade one day, from our favourite spot on the Nampongwe riverbank, when we noticed a mysterious dark blob that kept appearing then disappearing near a little rushy island a few yards from the shore. After dozens of frustratingly brief sightings, we eventually saw a slim brown shape break from the water and lope through the reeds, instantly recognisable as an otter but never clearly visible enough to be properly identified. Purely from its size, which we guessed as about four feet long overall and weighing at least 25lbs, we deduced that it must have been a clawless otter. Otters are said to be common in the waters of Zambia but that was, and remained, the only one that we ever saw.

Another fascinating and entirely unexpected sighting was made one day by Anne as we returned to the Lodge in the heat of the day. We were bumping slowly along over the cracked and rutted track just north of Chunga and close to the upper limit of the flood line, after watching a nearby herd of zebra and a few wildebeest, when Anne said that she had seen something move out on the grey wasteland. No-one else could detect anything but we were persuaded to drive over, for a better look, at a large lump of dry grey mud. As we drew nearer it took shape and became transformed into an enormous monitor lizard, incredibly well-camouflaged, in its pale grey skin mottled with pale, yellowish markings which made it blend impeccably into the arid background. It disliked our sudden appearance on its private mudflat, hissed, flicked its thick grey tongue in investigation of the intruders, and lashed its huge tail in disgust at the sight of my instantly-produced camera. The monster was even larger than the beast I had unfairly and ignominiously strapped to my Land Rover bonnet in my early years in Zambia, and was the first monitor lizard that the rest of my family had ever seen: we measured it, visually, as best we could, and reckoned it to be very little short of seven feet long from the end of its snout to the tip of its tail. It's curious that this unexpected encounter with an ostensibly unattractive creature should have been so memorable, but we were all thoroughly excited by our unlikely meeting in such a blatantly open environment. We felt sure it would have given a good account of itself if attacked by one of its few natural enemies, but it certainly had no place to hide, and relied entirely upon its remarkable ability to merge into the inhospitable background.

Back at the ranch house in the evenings there was usually a division of labour in assisting Anne to get Beccy bathed, fed and put to sleep, by which time the boys were also normally quite ready for bed. Dusk was always one of our favourite times in Africa, not just for the alcoholic sundowner which we could happily go without, but for the sheer tranquillity which descended over the bush and permeated the scene. The sun's final few minutes above the horizon were always glorious, as the yellow orb settled lower, became orange and eventually a fiery red as it slipped down through the smoky haze and sunk behind the horizon. Frequently, as we sat watching this never-failing light-show from the comfort of the ranch's verandah, we would see shadowy shapes slide silently through the grasslands below us, as eland or bushbuck surreptitiously moved from one clump of thorn bush to another, seeking a place of safety for the night. The owls and nightjars would drift effortlessly past, ignoring the flightpaths of purposefully flitting bats which swooped and swerved with unerring accuracy round the trees and buildings, scything through the air, which was scented with a mixture of woodsmoke and plant fragrance. As the last light finally faded and complete darkness descended we would regretfully move inside, away from the insects, and settle to the evening chores such as they were. By nightfall the bath-boy had always got a blazing fire going to heat the tank of water outside the ranch, and while Anne ran Beccy's bath, Guy and Barry often escaped from view and rushed outside to chat and play with the pleasant and ancient Zambian who tended the fire and who was always kind to the children. Drawing a bath was always a little hazardous and usually entailed a variety of ancillary tasks: such as sweeping away the blizzard of flying bats which appeared as if by magic as the first light was switched on; and skimming the miscellaneous assortment of grubs, ants and flakes of rust off the surface of the water as these objects spewed forth from the antique taps. It was always doubtful whether one emerged cleaner after a bath but the hot water certainly had a soporific effect on Beccy and she slept well at Lochinvar. After Beccy, the boys were forcibly immersed in a refreshed tubful of hot water, ants and rust, and then began the ritual of tucking them into bed and tying down the mosquito nets all around them. These nets hung from hooks in the rafters, via a system of bent wire coat hangers, and it was quite an art to arrange the support such that an adequate amount of net could be tucked in all around the bed, avoiding the numerous large holes which previous occupants had no doubt caused by their similar endeavours. Of course, having got Barry suitably ensconced he would remember that he needed to go to the loo; then Guy, tied down for the night, had forgotten to put his torch under his pillow; then drinks were required; and so it went on, seemingly for hours, as we tied and untied the nets repeatedly until our own turn for bed arrived and we tumbled in exhausted, just tucking in any available fold of net as best we could. It doesn't take long to realise that you have trapped one or two mosquitoes inside the net with you. The high-pitched whine increases in pitch as one hones in on its target, and then there is an ominous silence as it prepares for the stab into some juicy patch of flesh: this sequence always reminded me of the doodlebugs which I had seen and heard over London as a very small boy, first the ominous drone as the bomb approached, then the even more terrifying silence as the engine cut and it glided to earth, and finally the shattering crunch of the impact and explosion. Fortunately one could despatch mosquitos, unlike doodlebugs, with insect sprays, and there was always fierce competition to capture a can of aerosol to put under one's pillow: but, by one of Murphy's laws, those with aerosols never tucked up mosquitos inside their nets, and those with mosquitos never had the aerosols.

On our final morning at Lochinvar we again drove northwards to Chunga, and the Nampongwe River and continued as far as the banks of the Kafue River itself. We passed a herd of 120 eland browsing on the crest of a low ridge, stopped to view a small family group of zebra, and tried stalking a dainty pair of oribi (small, slender antelope) that slipped in and out of the tall grass and which proved far too shy and elusive to allow me to approach close enough for a photograph. We also watched a magnificent marsh harrier quartering the ground with supreme skill and precision, and stopped to inspect a few weavers' nests, but having reached the Kafue we pitched our odd little encampment, lobster-pot and all, and settled down to let the scene produce what it could. We were puzzled for a while by some large animals which we spotted in the distance, and which were mingling with a herd of lechwe, until we realised that they were cattle, owned by the Tonga people who had a few huts of reeds and thatch on the raised north bank of the Kafue some quarter of a mile away. We were also viewed ourselves by villagers in canoes as they lazily paddled past on their way to go fishing in the lagoons and ponds nearby, and I speculated on the probability that their ancestors had been rearing cattle and fishing in this very area for perhaps the last 1,000 years or more. It was interesting to see how naturally they fitted in to this environment and how they blended with the scenery so that they appeared to be an entirely natural part of it. To them, although Europeans were no novelty in the National Park, nor of course in the Southern Province or elsewhere in Zambia, we must appear thoroughly alien with our noisy cars and extravagant culture, with vacuum flasks, and ice, binoculars and cameras, disposable nappies and canned beer. Whilst we feel lost without a daily news broadcast telling us what is happening in London or New York, Tokyo or Moscow, the local villagers are not interested in any real way in what happens in Lusaka, or even Monze, as very little affects their own way of life which depends completely on such natural events as the seasons and the dramas of their own families and tribal groups. As we watched the grey loeries in the tree tops outside the ranch that evening, we reluctantly realised that the next morning we had to do as they counselled us and 'go away' from Lochinvar, to return to the self-imposed discipline and rules of the so-called civilised world on the Copperbelt. But we were grateful that we had enjoyed so much these few days of tranquillity in this lovely spot.

The following morning we completed the rituals of packing for the long journey ahead, and this was an easier task than previously since we had by now eaten virtually all the supplies. With everything on board we said our farewells to the cheerful staff and thankfully slipped away just as two carloads of new arrivals noisily debauched at the entrance to the Lodge. Quite clearly there were now too many tourists for the limited accommodation, even allowing for our vacated beds, and we just heard the first few voices raised in argument at the carelessness of the Tourist Board official in Lusaka who had obviously made a double-booking, as we drove off. This disharmonious theme was aggravated by our reception at the gate through which we had to check out on leaving the Park. Just occasionally we had come across junior government officials who relished being discourteous and awkward, and as we waited overly long at the barrier, we sensed that one of those occasions was at hand. Sure enough, a surly Park official eventually strolled over from his little hut, and we saw his eyes light up as he glanced around the inside of the car: he had spotted the guinea-fowl feathers in the boys' hat bands and he proceeded to lay down the law about trophies and National Parks. He had certainly understood the letter of the law but we felt he should also have been told about the spirit of the law as quite obviously the impact of removing a handful of feathers was scarcely earth-shattering. However, the law is the law and since technically he was correct we had to agree to his confiscating the offending feathers and the boys were near to tears as they removed them to the gloating Zambian. Despite the fact that, as soon as we had been allowed to proceed, I assured the boys that we still had a handful of only slightly less elegant feathers in one of our cases in the boot of the car, the incident cast a gloom on the journey.

We stopped for a proper visit to the Munda Wanga Gardens in Chilanga on our way home, and our bad start was compounded when we saw how neglected these once lovely ornamental gardens had become. It was not difficult to imagine the glorious picture they had once presented, and we're told that they have again been revived to a reasonable standard, but the untrimmed lawns and scruffy paths, unclipped hedges and general air of neglect was depressing. Even a peacock, though elegant in itself, chose to preen and parade itself against a background of rusty and unpainted galvanised iron as though to exaggerate the degree of deterioration that we saw all around us. I have wondered subsequently whether we viewed Munda Wanga with an unfairly jaundiced eye that day, because of our contretemps over the guinea-fowl feathers, but I suspect that was not the case. There were many other examples of past care and attention being allowed to decay due to disinterest, lack of finance, or inability of the Zambians to preserve certain worthwhile achievements of the colonial days, though of course others had been well-cared for and respected.

On returning to Kalulushi, we all considered that Beccy had been an exemplary baby during our five day trip, and whilst we had all taken turns to keep her quiet and out of mischief, she deserved a small reward for her contribution to our enjoyment. At that time there was an embarrassing shortage of toys in the shops, in fact an irritating shortage of everything, and so we racked our brains to think of something suitable. Not being near Christmas there was not even an anticipated arrival of any orders to the big stores, and we almost resigned ourselves to finding some second-hand item advertised in the paper, or on the Mine Club notice board, when we heard that some Chinese goods had arrived in Kitwe. The traditional sources of toys, from England and the rest of Europe as well as from America and South Africa, had long since dried up either due to problems of foreign exchange or political realignment. We had nothing against Chinese goods so we dashed off to Kitwe, with our fingers crossed, and were delighted to find some new toys in the one surviving toy shop. Amongst the collection of tin and wooden bits and pieces, which were admittedly colourful though of dubious durability, we found some cuddly toys, including a splendid and enormous panda which we knew at once was exactly right. We bought the panda for about eight pounds, which we considered a bargain, and Beccy absolutely loved it from the word go, even though it was about twice her size. It was christened Lochinvar in memory of our trip, and it today has pride of place in Beccy's collection of dolls and teddies on the top bunk of her bedroom in our Cornish cottage. A Chinese panda, bought in Zambia, called Lochinvar, and still in splendid shape, is destined to become a family heirloom and we hope one day to see Beccy's children taking good care of it.

Chapter 12
SERVANTS AND SKELEMS

As a topic of conversation amongst expatriates in Zambia, servants took the place of the proverbial weather in England. There was always some new horror or indiscretion, skill or revelation, which could be discussed involving either one's own or someone else's servants; and there was always a ready stream of applicants for any sort of household vacancy. One expatriate woman, who advertised in the local paper for a paraffin refrigerator, had a reply from some hopeful, who stated, 'I wish to apply for the vacancy of a paraffin refrigeratory, I do not have any experience as a refrigeratory, since I have not worked as a refrigerator before. But I have worked with paraffin.' Some other optimist answered a different advertisement, this time for a 'talking African grey parrot', stating he would like the job even though he was rather a dark grey.

When we arrived in Zambia, during the last decade of the colonial era, there were three distinct categories of domestic servant, cook-boy, house-boy and garden-boy; and depending on one's own social standing in the expatriate community one employed one or more of these servants. The newly-arrived white man and his family would be expected to engage at least a garden-boy, in order to keep the outside of the premises neat and tidy, and his wife was quickly urged to add a house-boy to the establishment. The latter would be expected to do all the domestic work starting by bringing in an early morning cup of tea and carrying on all day, with a couple of short breaks, until he had finished washing up the pile of dishes after the evening meal. His duties would include all sweeping and cleaning, kitchen chores, washing and ironing all the household linen and personal laundry, and numerous other tasks. The hours were long, the work hard and on a seven-day basis, and the rewards extremely small. But the widespread unemployment problem meant that there was never a shortage of applicants for jobs as domestic servants, and those who secured these posts were considered the lucky ones. Favoured house-boys were also provided with overalls, either khaki or white, but because of the high turnover of servants it was quite often many months, or even years, before uniforms were bought, in case they could not be retrieved in the event that the man was fired. The senior establishments were easily identified by the number of servants and their dress, if by no other means, and the top management normally boasted at least one gardener, sometimes two, clad in overalls; one or more house-boys in white uniform; and also a cook-boy. Uniforms were sometimes embellished by the addition of white gloves and a red fez with a black tassel, and the normally bare feet might perhaps be clad in white gym shoes as a final elegance. Some of the older and well-established servants were delightful characters and assumed the air of favoured retainers, becoming almost a part of the family, but in our experience this was very much the exception rather than the rule, and generally speaking Zambians were not good servants in the sense understood of, say, those of the colonial period in Asia or even elsewhere in Africa. Acquiring a good servant was often a case of trial and error, and we found that whereas one servant might suit a particular employer he would be hopelessly unable to cope with another. A large part of this problem most definitely stemmed from a natural incompatibility of temperaments, between the essentially easy-going Zambians and a certain type of European who was not only unused to having a servant, but was also not prepared to make the effort to understand that a successful employer-to-servant relationship requires mutual respect. We noticed some households where the servant was considered a necessary nuisance, and it was astonishing how much abuse some were prepared to tolerate in order to hang on to their livelihood, however meagre. But it would be wrong to create the impression that servants were either favoured retainers, or abused serfs, as the majority of expatriate households employed one or more who enjoyed a perfectly pleasant and satisfactory working relationship.

As the social revolution of independence approached, and then passed, it was clear that some Zambian servants became disillusioned, as they had expected, if not a reversal of roles, at least some significant reallocation of property. Some, in common with many other Zambians, had presumed that the servants would overnight become masters, and that the white man would leave their goods and belongings and depart the country, so that a great share-out of houses, furniture and cars would take place. One noticeable trend was the rapid rise to eminence of black politicians and businessmen, as well as the increased opportunities throughout the industrial scene, so that Zambians acquired posts of social status which required the addition of servants to their households. It then became apparent that these servants showed a marked lack of enthusiasm for working for fellow Zambians, who proved less charitable as employers than did the expatriates. Perhaps this trend will in time be overcome, but it was certainly at least in part due to the relative role of the wife in Zambian traditional life, which made it unpalatable for a Zambian servant to accept instructions from a woman, however important her husband's role in society. Many senior Zambians had wives who had always played a thoroughly subordinate role, and who might well have never had the benefit of education outside their tribal systems. They additionally often had no experience of how to keep house and entertain, in the western sense that they were expected to adopt, and so servants of such unfortunate women could find themselves in a position from which they had to instruct, rather than be instructed, whilst retaining a menial role which was utterly confusing and unacceptable to them.

Following independence, a new trend developed, in that a different type of expatriate became more and more prevalent. Europeans joined the vast mining companies and other industries on a shorter term basis, no longer coming to make a career and establish a future for themselves in the country, but in order to gain experience to further careers elsewhere, and also to earn and save as much money as possible in the shortest possible time. Three-year contracts were introduced, or in some cases even shorter periods of commitment, and servants were then often dispensed with as an avoidable luxury. Others combined servants' roles, so that more and more expatriates sought a general factotum who would sweep the yard and cut the grass, as well as do the laundry and washing-up, and even manage some of the cooking. In order to save money, wages tended to be kept artificially low and did not keep up with increased salary levels of expatriates and the parallel increases in the cost of living. It was not until nine years after independence, in 1973, that the government introduced a mandatory provident fund for domestic servants to which employers were required to contribute a monthly sum, to which was added a further small contribution which could be deducted from the servant's wage. Many expatriates were happy to make this provision for their servants' old age, and readily paid both contributions, but others dismissed their servants or even refused to register them with the National Provident Fund. Yet others avoided the need to pay contributions by hiring and firing in quick succession, or by paying under-age or piece-work employees on a day-to-day basis.

Another noticeable change over the years was in the accommodation provided for servants. As I have already described, in an earlier chapter, the big towns and rural administration centres of the country had all been designed on the basis of separated zones for blacks and whites, with the big well-spaced houses for the latter in one area, and the cramped compounds of small huts in another. But this proved inconvenient where the servants had to travel long distances to and from work, and so small huts were built for the servants at the end of the whites' gardens; incidentally, making it easy to increase their working hours by having their servants constantly nearby. It was also beneficial to the servants as housing was always hard to find, and although small, these servants' quarters were at least dry, usually brick-built, and had the relative luxury of running water on tap, as well as a lavatory. But over the years it became more of a nuisance than it was worth to have servants living so close to their employers' houses, as the extended family principle of the Africans ensured that for every servant there resulted in not only a wife and children, often numerous, but also various brothers and sisters, uncles and aunts, who all piled into what was frequently a one-roomed hut. Gradually the servants were moved out of these *kaiyas*. Sometimes a compassionate employer would build a small house elsewhere, if ground was available; others would rent accommodation in the compounds; others again would make an additional payment of a housing allowance, and let the servant find his own dwelling; whilst yet others would make no provision whatsoever, and callously adopted the attitude that it wasn't their problem, and that if their servant didn't want the job then there were plenty of others who did. The traditional servants' kaiyas at the bottom of the gardens rapidly became tool sheds and repositories for old rubbish. In the mining towns the companies recognised the problems and allocated a limited number of mine houses, in the compounds, to domestic servants of its officials, and although there was always a waiting list we were fortunate in being able to obtain quarters fairly rapidly for our own servants. Some of our less fortunate colleagues, in desperation, reverted to using their kaiyas for their servants' accommodation, but this became frowned upon eventually due to the increased security risks in the late 60s and 70s.

Like most other expatriates, our experience with our own servants were extremely mixed, and we went through periods of rapid disenchantment alternating with happy spells when we enjoyed the loyal attentions of some delightful characters. Our first employee was a disaster by the name of Ignatius, and within just one month with us we lost virtually all our hand-embroidered linen which we had received as wedding presents. We eventually caught him red-handed, but rather than turning him over to the pretty ruthless colonial police we merely dismissed him without a reference, hoping that he would thereby learn his lesson and mend his ways. He was only a young lad, rather churlish and unable to speak much English, and we never saw him again: the temptations must have been extreme and we undoubtedly were too soft on him by the standards of the day, as our leniency was quite probably seen as a sign of weakness.

We then went through a succession of mediocre garden-boys and house-boys, with some bright spots and other less amusing incidents. I remember some of them better than others of course, from the ultra-respectful Pelekamoyo, ancient and unctuous, who always bowed and saluted us; to the enormous and overpowering Yebeta, a colossal Lozi tribesman from Barotse, who approached with extreme stealth, without meaning any offence, and then spoke with a voice like a bellows which made us jump out of our skins. Yebeta was an ex-police constable, and he must have looked most impressive in full charge, but we found him to have a delightful childlike mentality quite out of keeping with his bulk and looks. Anne's mother paid us a visit for a few months when Guy was born, and I'm sure she never quite got used to Yebeta, stripped to the waist as he worked in the garden, looking as though he had just stepped down from striking J Arthur Rank's gong. He had a disarming grin, an extraordinary capacity for hard work, and an insatiable appetite: he also smoked heavily, and for every cigarette he smoked he appeared to use an entire box of matches. In fact his constant silent approaches, culminating in a grin and a booming request for another box of matches, eventually proved rather irritating, and although he was a thoroughly nice man we were not altogether sorry to see him go when he decided to re-join the police. We wished him well and soon missed this cheerful hulk, as we found it hard to replace him at first.

Simon Wellington followed Pelekamoyo as our house-boy, and at first we found him relatively adept and quick to learn, but whereas Pelican, as we called his predecessor, had once been a waiter and knew some of the rudiments of setting a table, and other household chores, Simon had to be shown almost everything and had come to us without a reference. We realised that this was a little unusual, as not only was he not a young man anymore but he also had what appeared to be a well-used khaki uniform. However, knowing the way in which clothes were bought and sold in the various compounds and local markets, we felt that perhaps he had bought the uniform to impress us, and anyway we gave him the benefit of the doubt. We took several months to see through the guile, when it slowly dawned on us that not only were the groceries not going as far as they used to, but that it appeared extremely likely that dear Simon was so attentive when Anne demonstrated some new house-keeping skill because, the more Anne demonstrated, the less work Simon actually had to do himself. He became more and more open with his craftiness, and the groceries thinned so rapidly that we eventually gave him a week's notice. This was another mistake which we didn't make again, as at the end of the week we lost another haul of groceries and a few handfuls of the week's washing into the bargain. Far better, as we discovered, to give instant dismissal with an extra week's wages, than risk a help-yourself act at the end of a period of notice.

It was not until 1963 that we acquired our most faithful and likeable servant, Dickson Kamanga, who started work as a gardener in October of that year. Dicky, as he rapidly became known, served us faithfully and well for almost 15 years and we always enjoyed having this cheerful and willing worker around. He not only became part of the family but also a companion for the children: he always greeted the boys with warmth and friendship when they arrived back in Zambia for their school holidays after a term away in England. Dicky, like many of the most faithful servants that we got to know in Zambia, was actually a Malawian, his home being at Nkhata Bay on the spectacular western shores of Lake Nyasaland, now of course Lake Malawi. We believe his father to be a local chief, and certainly Dicky had all the natural courtesy and politeness one would expect from such heritage, as well as a dignified bearing. He was not a large man, wiry and of small to average build, and he normally had a strangely serious and dead-pan expression which belied a very ready sense of humour. He did not speak very good English but enough for us to communicate, and it was a great pleasure to share a joke at the end of long and complicated instructions when he would suddenly realise what we were talking about; his face would be instantly transformed into a broad grin, accompanied by a slightly embarrassed and strangely girlish giggle, when we would all go into fits of laughter. During Dicky's many years with us he did the hard work in constructing, or reconstructing four of the five gardens that we made in Kalulushi, digging hundreds of yards of trenches for hedges, countless holes for shrubs and fruit trees, and doing all the heavy work of digging and clipping, chopping and carrying, laying paving slabs and mixing concrete. His small frame was as strong as a horse and he really did achieve a prodigious amount of manual work, although never mastering the finer points of planting seedlings or cuttings. Many were the times when he inadvertently weeded out Anne's carefully planted flowers, or cut down a young shrub, but we were usually at fault ourselves for not having adequately explained the task required.

During our long leave away from Zambia we were happy to leave Dicky in charge of our gardens, to weed them in the rainy season, and water them in the dry months, and on those occasions our friends would take over the payroll and visit our garden weekly to see that all was well. Dicky was always faithful on these occasions and worked happily without supervision, apparently not content to leave all to a last-minute blitz a few weeks before our return, a habit well-known amongst other gardeners. We could also happily leave our cats in his care, and he would feed them daily for us, from a supply of tins which we left with him for the purpose, thus avoiding the need to kennel them for long periods: cats hate confinement and this alternative was always a great relief to us as Dicky was so reliable. Of course no-one is perfect, but we first really appreciated what a splendid servant Dicky was during a period of almost a year when he left us to return to Malawi: he was uncertain whether he would wish to return to us or might decide to remain in his lakeside village and so we paid him off, and never expected to see him again. We very rapidly missed his steady reliability and became thoroughly disenchanted with the idle, and often deceitful succession of replacements, of whom there were six in as many months, from the plausible Banda, to the idle Bwalya; the idiot Boniface, to the ungrateful Albert; and the incredible oaf Button to the slick but slothful Vincent. All these people were forever asking for advances of pay or loans, 'balance' as it was known; none were in any way co-operative or energetic after the familiar first few days' enthusiasm, which was intended to impress and lull us into a sense of security; and most of them we fired in desperation. Some disappeared after obtaining 'balance', and others just moved off on payday without telling us that they would not be back, but we were so pleased to see them all go. We then thought that we would at least be charitable, and pay someone whom we knew would not be able to work hard, rather than expect a fair day's work from an able-bodied gardener, and so we employed the one-armed Sixpence. He was an elderly man, courteous and pleasant enough, but quite obviously limited in usefulness in what was essentially a labourer's job. We got on well enough, Sixpence doing what he could, and we were thankful not to have the annoying need to be forever checking his work because, quite simply, he couldn't really do very much. Perhaps our charity was good for our souls, but it certainly wasn't good for our garden which slowly but surely deteriorated without Dicky's care. Anne and I both found that we would be working like mad, after Sixpence left us each afternoon, in order to tidy up after him and so as not to offend the poor man who probably thought he was doing well, since we seldom had the heart to reprimand him.

Whilst Dicky was away we occasionally had well-written letters from him, polite and charming in his use of expression. His first letter, after reaching Malawi, told us that 'It was a very nice journey through the way, and it took me one and half weeks to arrive home'. We knew that he always laughed when we asked about his passport, since he never obtained one. He experienced no difficulty in crossing the border, at various points between Zambia and Malawi, leaving the bus either at Chipata in the south or Nakonde in the north, and filtering through by small footpaths and tracks, before once again boarding a bus on the Malawi side. It was therefore scarcely surprising that his journey had taken some ten days, but we were delighted to read that he intended to return to us in a few months' time. He ended his letter with the courteous instruction to me to 'Pass hot greetings to the family. I beg to drop the pen down. Goodbye. Your servant Kamanga.' A later letter told us that he was now arranging his journey and ended with yet more hot greetings. Dicky's letters had one notable difference from the letters we received from other servants, or employees, in that he never asked for money. This latter tendency was always irritating. We had one letter from a lad named Christopher, who had proved a most unreliable and idle employee and had been fired for these characteristics, after working for us for only 16 days. Some two years later we had a cheerful letter from him asking for a Christmas present: 'Now I beg you to post me Christmas about £2.10s0d,' and passing 'greetings on your wife, wishing her a very happy life. With many wishes, Christopher.' In due course Dicky arrived back in Kalulushi and we were relieved to be able to explain to Sixpence that we would have to end his employment: we gave him a bonus and a good reference for his honesty and he was quite happy to leave. Dicky soon slotted back into his hard-working but comfortable routine, and our family and household started to tick over once again in its familiar way. The only other time we were without Dicky during our remaining 11 years in Zambia was always puzzling. Our house-servant, James Melek, arrived as usual one morning and told us that Dicky had been arrested for shop-lifting at a store in Kalulushi. This was so out of character for Dicky, who had never stolen from us and yet had had ample opportunities, that I rushed to the police station on the assumption that it was a mistake. But I was assured that Dicky had been caught red-handed taking a petticoat from the store without paying for it, and he was duly tried in the local court and sentenced to a few months in jail. I appeared briefly in court on his behalf, to give him a good character reference, but he was duly taken off to Kamfinsa prison, near Kitwe, and later to Solwezi where he was made to work on a farm. I never convinced myself that he genuinely intended to steal the petticoat, and to this day I still feel that it was either a put-up job by the Zambian police, who did occasionally harass the local Malawians, or else that Dicky had a mental lapse. In all his 15 years' service with us, Dicky had proved totally loyal: in fact he had frequently brought us items which we had lost in the garden and he subsequently found, and we had of course on plenty of occasions entrusted our property as well as pets to him, during often long absences. I still trust Dicky implicitly, and we had absolutely no misgivings about re-employing him after his release. He joked about his days in prison and told us that he had not minded it, earning about one penny a day whilst working on the land at Solwezi. He had missed being able to buy his beloved cigarettes, but otherwise was none the worse for this unfortunate experience, and re-joined us as if nothing had happened. He clearly had not picked up any bad habits from his criminal fellow-prisoners.

James Melek Kalukuluku joined us as our house servant in 1966 and stayed with us until the year before we left Zambia. James was a Zambian, of the Kaonde tribe, who are generally regarded to be one of the more industrious of the indigenous peoples. His home town was in Mumbwa, a rural town and administrative centre about 100 miles northwest of Lusaka, the country's capital city. Like Dicky, James proved a reliable and pleasant member of our household, and although perhaps a little more moody than Dicky, he nevertheless served us faithfully and well for a full 11 years; together they formed a happy and memorable team. James was a small man, but well able to give a verbally good account of himself, and we were often amused at the way he bossed Dicky around, since a house-servant is a senior social post to the gardener and he was always anxious to maintain the distinction. His spoken English was also better than Dicky's, and so he was an invaluable interpreter to use on occasions. There were many notable occasions when James Melek amused us immensely, sometimes intentionally, but more often purely by accident: perhaps the funniest of all was one of the latter. On one of our trips on leave to England Anne and I had taken Guy and Barry to Hamley's the world-famous toy shop in London, and amongst the items bought with their pocket money was a joke tin labelled as peanuts: on opening the lid, out leapt a coiled spring, covered in cloth to resemble a snake, accompanied by a piercing shriek. This tin had long been abandoned by the boys and turned up years later amongst the toys that Beccy acquired from her big brothers and was one day left lying around in the dining room looking for all the world like an innocent tin of salted peanuts. We were all sitting in the drawing room nearby one day when we heard the familiar high-pitched squeak, but followed instantaneously by a blood-curdling yell of terror. We rushed in to find James looking ashen and faint, and also covered in confusion: he attempted to explain that he had opened the tin to dust inside, but I think even he found his explanation unconvincing as we tried to keep straight faces and nodded reassuringly to cover his embarrassment. We had long known of James' weakness for the odd spoon of sugar, or handful of nuts or other oddments, but had accepted these items as part of the perks of the job and never found him guilty of taking anything that could really be considered stealing. Like Dicky, James had many temptations and opportunities to steal from us, and we had found him totally trustworthy, but we were all enormously amused at the sight of the shaken James eyeing the sneaky cloth snake as he slowly regained his natural aplomb.

Both Dicky and James were loyal in protecting our property, and they frequently assisted us in repelling the occasional invasion by hordes of picannins who periodically climbed our garden fences to steal mangoes or guavas from our fruit trees. Adults were also not slow to avail themselves of fruit, or other desirable items left lying around in gardens on occasions, not to mention the incursions by professional thieves and burglars who posed a more serious problem. We were suddenly alerted one day by a terrific hullabaloo from the far end of the garden as our Rory, joined by two particularly vicious-looking Dobermans owned by our neighbours, gave vent to their impressive voices. James, who was preparing vegetables in the kitchen at the time, muttered 'skelems', and dashed off into the garden still carrying a large solid wood chopping board. Anne and I were both slow to follow for some reason, but we arrived in time to see, and hear, little James looking wrathful in his white uniform, landing a colossal blow on the head of a much bigger man who was desperately scrambling over our six-foot-high wire fence, scattering mangoes in every direction. The sound of the chopping board crashing onto the woolly skull of the intruder would surely have been heard for miles, accompanied by the screams of abuse from James and the crescendo of canine noises from the three enormous dogs. If the thief managed to retain a single mango it was undoubtedly hard-earned, and we almost felt sorry for him as he loped off into the bush, nursing what was undoubtedly going to be a monumental headache. We congratulated James on his creditably swift and courageous action, and he visibly swelled with pride, adding some scathing remark about garden-boys to Dickson who had also by then arrived from the opposite end of the garden.

Poor James was not a particularly strong person and he had several medical problems whilst he was with us. The mine hospital treated domestic servants of employers, as well as the employees themselves, and so we were lucky to have ready medical attention for his troubles. He was not a shirker of work but sometimes found it genuinely hard going and we were obliged at times to give him extensive time off duty. We found that most Africans are extremely stoical about pain and so it was sometimes difficult to know whether a complaint was related to a serious ailment or not. Anne remembers only too well an occasion on our early days in Zambia when a servant said he had a tummy-ache: Anne told him to take the day off, but as she watched him walk slowly down our driveway on his way home she felt rather uneasy about the way he was clutching his side, and so she got the car out and took him at once to the hospital. Fortunate indeed that she did, as he was admitted for an emergency operation with acute appendicitis, and she was told that the appendix would certainly have burst within an hour or two. From that day on we were always most cautious about dismissing complaints as minor and James had to spend several months in hospital over the years. His pains seemed also to upset him, understandably, and on his off-days he would be most unlike his usually cheerful self and would sulk unnecessarily if Anne reminded him of a task undone or skimped. These periods became more frequent over the years and we eventually decided that we should pension James off and let him return to his village near Mumbwa where he could lead a less tiring life. The house which we rented for James in the township was some couple of miles from ours, and since he came to work in the morning, left after lunch, and returned again at tea-time as a rule, he was travelling quite a distance each day; and although we had bought him a bicycle some years before, as a present for looking after our property during one of our long leaves, it still meant a strenuous bicycle ride of some ten miles each day for him. He left us some nine months before our departure, and we were delighted to see him again when he visited us shortly before we finally left the country. He had established himself near Mumbwa, where he had built a house some years previously, and had cleared a few acres of land on which he was growing maize and tobacco with some success: he looked extremely well and prosperous and we were glad he had taken our advice and accepted his early retirement, since the change was obviously suiting him.

When James left us we already knew that we would ourselves be leaving within a year, and we could not bring ourselves to train a brand new house-servant to our ways. James and Dicky had become such an established team that we felt it better to ask Dicky to become the house-servant and for him to find a suitable and temporary assistant to look after the garden. Thus it was that we employed Sam Kondowe, a young man who came from the same part of Malawi as Dicky did himself. Sam was fit and strong, pleasant and polite, and we found him ideally suited to our household. Dicky rapidly became a fine house-servant, amusing us with his expression, like 'the kettle, she is cooked!' and his courtesy became even more noticeable. He would always approach us from a lower level if he wished to address us, gently bending at the knees if we were standing, or kneeling if we were seated, holding the palms of his hands together, courtesies we found charming in an old-fashioned way and not at all obsequious. We barely had time to get to know young Sam, but from what we saw of him we felt that in time he too would have made an excellent and trustworthy servant.

When we left Zambia Dicky and Sam both returned to Malawi. Dicky told us, flatteringly, that he would not like to work for anyone else and we assured him, much to his delight, that if we ever found ourselves in Malawi in the future that we would be sure to visit him in his village at Usisya near Nkhata Bay. We had visited Lake Malawi for a holiday one year and had found it an idyllic setting, with good soil and plenty of fish in the freshwater lake, making subsistence by farming and fishing an attractive life. On several occasions since, we have let our thoughts slide back to that holiday and we can easily picture, and even envy, Dicky's simple existence on the edge of the lake. We have written to him, and he to us, and we would all of us be delighted to renew our friendship one day. Our last photograph of Dicky, in front of our large house in Kalulushi in the garden he worked so hard on, shows him resplendent in a Cheviot tweed suit which I gave him, with white shirt and smart tie, looking like the aristocrat which we felt he really was, despite his menial though happy role in our lives. All the children were devoted to Dicky and remember him with the same fondness as do Anne and I.

One characteristic common to all our servants, and to a large extent to African people as a whole, was their delight in bright clothes and what we might consider as outlandish garments. The more garish the better seemed to be the rule, and the fact that there was no truly national costume meant that imagination was the only limiting factor. After independence there was a rash of the most bizarre outfits, made, patriotically, in the national colours of Zambia, themselves an essentially anaesthetic juxtaposition of black, red, orange and green, the saving grace being a fish eagle emblem. The colours were intended to symbolise the country's background: black for the people; red for the blood shed during the struggle for independence; orange for the copper, mainstay of the nation's economy; and green for the fertility of the land. This dazzling array of stripes and blotches were combined in fantastic array in items from shirts to umbrellas, and overshadowed the other exotic but colourful clothes at every political rally or function. But away from the nationalistically aware centres of population, it was mainly the women who wore the most colour, in bewilderingly intense shades and patterns. Amongst the domestic servants it was as much the incongruous cast-off clothing of their employers as the sheer colourfulness of their attire which caught our attention. One might see an otherwise insignificant soul wearing a tattered shirt and a large black homburg; or a cricket blazer in some famous colours, worn with khaki shorts, a furled black umbrella, and a bright red mining helmet. James was particularly fond of a weird vinyl hat that would have looked fine on a Chicago gangster. Dicky's tastes were a little more circumspect, but possibly because he owned a large quantity of my abandoned or presented clothes and my own tastes are fairly conventional; he certainly was happy to acquire as large a wardrobe as possible, and both his wife and James' also owned a lot of Anne's clothes over the years.

Just before we left Zambia we had a final share-out between Dicky and Sam, strictly according to service and status of course, and we gave them a great deal of odds and ends; kitchen items and crockery, blankets and tools, clothes and other oddments. On the evening of this share-out they both left our house laden with their spoils, only to arrive back in the custody of mine police, with huge grins on their faces. They had been arrested on suspicion of being burglars, and after their initial fright had managed to persuade the police to come to our house to verify their stories. We quickly satisfied police enquiries and we all enjoyed a good laugh, commending the police on their action and assuring them that Dicky and Sam were indeed our employees and had been given the items they carried. All's well that ends well, and our servants had certainly earned their trophies.

Chapter 13

LUANGWA VALLEY

Our final holiday within Zambia was a week's visit, in August 1975, to the South Luangwa National Park, certainly the most spectacular game park in the country and in my opinion amongst the very best in the whole of Africa for the sheer abundance of the wildlife. The valley of the mighty Luangwa sweeps down to the southwest from its headwaters, near the Malawian and Tanzanian borders, widening out into broad plains through which the river meanders and frequently shifts its course, before cutting through gorges and finally debouching into the massive Zambezi River at Feira, on the border with Mozambique, some 350 miles from its source. There are actually three National Parks within the valley itself, the South being by far the largest: the others are Luambe, a small Park of predominantly woodland, situated on the east of the river; and the somewhat larger but more remote North Park. The northern part of the South Park is the centre for the wilderness trail safaris promoted and run by the redoubtable Norman Carr, who has done so much both to conserve and publicise the fabled wildlife of his beloved valley. Guy and Barry were later to experience the unique quality of one of Norman Carr's safari camps, and more of that later, but Anne and I never managed a second visit to Luangwa, much to our regret. Perhaps some day we'll be lucky enough to return.

My first sight of the Luangwa valley, in 1969, was several years before our family visit, and from the unusual vantage point of a small Bell G-2 helicopter. We had established an exploration base at Mpika, high on the plateau to the west of the valley, and the reconnaissance team was assigned the task of searching and sampling the area of the western escarpment and the valley itself. Much of the terrain prospected was extremely remote and the work was somewhat hazardous, the only efficient and cost-effective access being by helicopter, since tracks were virtually non-existent. When I visited the geologist in charge of the programme, I accompanied him for a first-hand look at the river-ground which he was working. The pilot flew the two of us from the Mpika airfield, which we had reached by our fixed-wing aircraft earlier that morning, and whilst the little chopper lifted off and cloppered its way eastwards towards the escarpment, we looked down on the rough and virtually uninhabited ground beneath us as we slowly approached what looked like the edge of the world. The view as we crested the final ridge of the scarp was stupendous. Spread out below us, at the foot of the near-vertical wall of the Muchinga escarpment, was a flat plain stretching to apparent infinity where it disappeared in the haze. We flew first along the side of the scarp, which was streaked here and there, by the white slashes of waterfalls where small streams tumbled frenziedly over the jumbled rocks in their haste to reach the valley below. We then flew low above the valley floor, startling antelope from the shade of shrubs and patches of woodland, disturbing occasionally some larger animals, and finally reaching the lazy Luangwa River itself, the only water for many miles in the centre of the valley during the dry season. At the point where we crossed the river for the first time the murky water was occupied by a group of some 30 hippos, partly submerged and with just their backs, snouts and eyes exposed, as they dozed idly through the heat of late morning. We hovered, momentarily above them, but they instantly churned the water in alarm as their peaceful reverie was shattered by the whirling clatter of the chopper: some opened their gaping jaws displaying massive, razor-sharp incisors in a gesture of threat and anger at our intrusion; others splashed and slithered into the deeper water, and sank out of sight. Further down the river, other family groups reacted in a similar way, and we mused on the incredible ease with which one could study the distribution and population of the hippo by using a helicopter-borne survey, not to mention the countless other uses of this versatile aircraft. In fact one benefactor of Zambia and its wildlife, the internationally-renowned artist David Shepherd, had donated a magnificent Bell Jet Ranger helicopter to the country's Game Department using the proceeds of an auction of his pictures, and this machine was used particularly effectively in the war against poachers in the country's National Parks. We followed the river for a few miles, seeking a landmark to identify our position accurately on the aerial photograph we were using as a map and on rounding one major curve of the river, which pinpointed our position precisely, we were delighted to see a small herd of elephants surprised in mid-stream as they crossed from one bank to another. Like the hippos, the elephants were startled at our noisy arrival and trumpeted in rage, striding out through the water and causing giant bow-waves to surge towards the shore. On reaching the broad sweep of sand, which stretched for 100 yards from the water's edge to the steep banks, they trundled hurriedly on, throwing their trunks from side to side. As they crushed their way up and over the high bank and into the shady refuge of the sparse woodland, the sheer power of their impressive bulk and overwhelming strength remained indelibly imprinted on my memory. However, immensely pleasurable though game-viewing was, our task was a geological one and we reluctantly set a course for home, taking us over a couple of features which were of interest to us. We were also well aware, as was of course the pilot, that our little G-2 had a rather limited range, added to which was the need for this airborne food-mixer to claw itself up into the sky in order to clear the top of the escarpment which was looming far above in the distance. As the pilot skilfully hauled us higher and higher, and finally levelled off above the rim of the valley, I glanced reluctantly back and determined that one day I would return to this enchanting and awesome valley, which was truly a naturalist's Shangri-La. Even though we had seen relatively little wildlife from our brief aerial sortie, we knew that this valley, once the haunt of dinosaurs, was now the domain of perhaps the largest population of elephants in the whole of Africa, probably numbering in excess of 100,000 of these spectacular monsters.

When I did eventually set foot in the Luangwa valley, in 1975, it was with my entire family, including little Beccy who was by now becoming a seasoned traveller and National Park connoisseur. After her inauguration at Lochinvar, which had proved so successful, Anne and I had taken her on a brief visit to the splendid Amboseli National Park in Tanzania when she was still only one and a half years old. Now, at the ripe old age of two and a half, we felt that she could stand the rigours of a more taxing trip and so we planned our expedition to Luangwa with some confidence, at least as far as Beccy was concerned. Any long journey in Zambia had become slightly hazardous, for a variety of reasons, as the escalating terrorism in neighbouring Rhodesia had caused the Zambian authorities to become very jumpy and suspicious, and both the military and police in the country were somewhat arbitrary and unpredictable in their actions. All the major strategic installations were under guard by armed soldiers or police, and we had good reason to expect a certain harassment at the bridge over the Luangwa River on the Great East Road, as this was the only permanent road link between the Eastern Province, in which the park lies, and the rest of Zambia. This major bridge had been completely re-built some years earlier after the original bridge had been sabotaged by Rhodesian agents, and not only were the approaches now heavily guarded but we were advised that it was necessary to show passports before being allowed to cross between these two parts of Zambia, regardless of one's origin or destination.

We did, in fact, already know first-hand how particular one had to be, from an experience on one of our earlier expeditions, when we had visited the wonderful montane grasslands of the Nyika National Park in Malawi and had returned via the Great East Road, in 1970. On that occasion the Great East Road was not completely tarred, and the route on the east of the Luangwa valley was particularly rough and treacherous such that we were pretty tired by the time we arrived, gratefully, at the smooth tar on the bridge itself. In fact we were so delighted to have reached the bridge successfully, without knocking a hole in the car's sump, that we patiently tolerated the rude flurry of officialdom. There were also several notice boards declaring the area to be one in which photography was strictly prohibited, but as we were waved on after our car had been carelessly searched, I foolishly decided to take a photograph of the impressive bridge from a point some few hundred yards up the road. I stopped the car and took one snapshot through the window. Just as I let in the clutch to move off the peace was shattered by an ear-splitting yell, whistles blowing, and the crash of undergrowth as an armed policeman came hurtling down the hillside straight towards us. Instantly regretting my photographic folly I stopped the car and waited for the verbal onslaught, and worse, which I felt sure was imminent. The hot and panting Zambian crunched to a halt by the driver's door and thrust his head almost down my throat: 'couldn't I read?'; 'why had I stopped?'; 'where was I going?' A stream of questions, some quite irrelevant and all in broken English, continued to pour over us until he ran out of both breath and ideas almost simultaneously. Just as I was about to attempt some sort of reply, he suddenly spotted my gleaming camera with its telephoto zoom lens sitting innocently in my lap, and I then realised that I had not been stopped for photographing the bridge, which had apparently escaped notice, but for stopping the car in a no-stopping zone. 'What is that?' With no hint of sarcasm, I replied that it was a camera. 'Did you take a photo?' No, I lied, never expecting for a moment that I would be believed. 'Drive on'. None of us dared breathe as I drove slowly on, marvelling at the naivety of this security official, and also at our luck: whilst far from proud of lying, I couldn't help feeling that the means justified the end, as the prospect of being detained with my entire family at this hot and inhospitable place was most daunting. Rounding the first bend, as we gathered speed for the next long and tedious leg of the journey, we were all horrified to see two more armed policemen waving us down. With a sense of impending doom I stopped once again, and both men thrust their heads through the open windows, eyeing the piles of luggage and my sweating family in what I felt looked a thoroughly evil and predatory way. Breaking into a delicious smile the larger of the two men asked for a lift! We were all so surprised and relieved that we almost laughed, and despite our obviously bulging car I instantly agreed to give them both a lift to the next small town. As we pushed and squeezed and redistributed our pile of chattels I couldn't help feeling that this charitable act in some way atoned for my lie to the puffing and gullible constable who had so generously overlooked my previous unlawful halt. The next 50-odd miles, before our two passengers alighted, were certainly penance for my foolishness: they were both hot and sweating, and undoubtedly unwashed, and the resultant aroma as we sped on through the heat of the day was quite overwhelming. On bidding them farewell I felt thoroughly purged.

That experience of five years earlier was still at the back of my mind as we set off, at three o'clock in the morning, for our Luangwa holiday. But we made good progress on a fair and empty road, reaching the outskirts of Lusaka just as dawn was breaking. Beccy had slept soundly for three and a half hours, and the boys, and even Anne, had managed to sleep for part of the way: so with some 220 miles behind us, it left the rest of the day to complete the remaining 400 miles. The African dawn, like dusk, is a magical time in the bush, and as the sun slowly lifted above the hazy horizon we looked forward with great anticipation to the next daybreak which we would witness from the haven of our rondavel in the south of the Luangwa valley itself. As we drove into Lusaka there was an increasing bustle of activity while a swelling stream of people emerged from dusty tracks and footpaths on to the main road; walkers, cyclists, and some old vans and lorries bringing the workers into the city from their poor houses in the squatter townships and compounds which spread out for miles beyond the modern buildings of the capital. Grossly overloaded lorries, with perhaps 50 people clinging on to the back, clanked and groaned their way past the walkers and cyclists, and the familiar U.B.Z. buses crawled crabwise into the rush-hour build-up as we slipped gratefully out of Lusaka and all its urban dreariness. We stopped only long enough to fill up with petrol and sped gratefully out along the Great East Road, admiring the sentinel-like Borassus palms scattered across the surrounding farmland, until we found a suitable place to halt for our breakfast picnic. It was still cool, and we settled ourselves in a comfortingly warm patch of sunlight to drink our hot tea and prepare for the long trek ahead. We soon warmed up and stripped off our sweaters, re-stowed the car and moved off in good spirits on the excellent tarmac surface, humming happily along and eating up the miles. We reached and passed the infamous Luangwa bridge and were delighted to find that the road now continued as modern full-width tar, unlike our previous journey when long stretches were still rocky and treacherous. The worst problem on the road was now the occasional herd of goats which seemed to enjoy crossing on corners, so that one came across them unexpectedly, but we successfully negotiated these bleating hazards and arrived at Nyimba for our final intake of petrol before leaving the main road.

We had booked our holiday at a hotel lodge, Luamfwa, in the extreme south of the Park, partly because it was in this area that we would be most likely to see the rare Thornicroft's giraffe, and partly because it was well away from the main package-tour frequented lodges. This meant that we could knock a considerable mileage off our journey by cutting up to the Park on dirt roads from the south, rather than using the more conventional but longer route through Chipata and approaching from the east. So it was that we turned off the tar beyond Petauke and travelled the remaining 90 miles on little-used tracks through sparsely-populated hilly woodland country. This last leg of the journey was both pleasant and uneventful, apart from a few momentary alarms when we trusted to luck and judgement at un-signposted intersections, and we arrived tired but relaxed at the Luamfwa Lodge just 14 hours after leaving home in Kalulushi. It was a journey of exactly 1,000 kilometres, or about 620 miles, and with no major dramas apart from a few fractious squabbles amongst the children we felt this was a most auspicious start to our holiday.

Luamfwa is pleasantly situated on the edge of a swampy lagoon which is dressed in the luscious-looking bright green water lettuce, or Nile Cabbage, so typical of these oxbow lakes. Our accommodation was in a thatched building, with twin-bedded rooms and its own bathroom and lavatory, similar to several other units which housed the visitors. The main building comprised a large lounge, dining room and verandah, joined by a paved terrace to a kidney-shaped swimming pool. The whole area was perched on the bank of the lagoon, shaded by mature trees and providing a view of the broad and peaceful haunt of elephant, hippo, crocodile and lesser creatures. Of course the hotel was less popular than the somewhat grander and longer-established Mfuwe Lodge, further north, but the facilities were perfectly adequate and we were more than prepared for the few shortcomings. I recall the running hot and cold water in our bathroom which was so thick and red that it looked like tomato soup concentrate; and the entirely opaque water in the swimming pool which closely resembled pale green milk. But in the heat of the day, once one had explored the underwater morphology of the pool bottom, it was perfectly safe to dive in and be both refreshed and chlorinated at the same time. There are very few places where you can wallow in a swimming pool and watch elephant and hippo browsing in a lagoon only 50 yards away from your iced beer. The manager of the hotel, a Mr Katate, was a pleasant and helpful man and did his best to overcome the many logistical problems during our stay, none of which caused more than an occasional minor inconvenience.

On the first morning after our arrival we drove off to explore the Park, nearby the Lodge, and were delighted at the large number of elephants we saw, a dramatic difference to our experience in the Kafue Park where we had seen so few. There were jumbos everywhere and we soon appreciated the problems which they were reputed to create. They thrive within the relative safety of the Park, but their numbers swell at the expense of the mopane woodland, and also the thorn trees, on which they feed. We saw several areas of ravaged forest and began to understand why some scientists considered an annual cull of this vast elephant population was necessary. The subject was, and remains, somewhat controversial, but there can be no doubt that these animals are in places producing a detrimental change in their environment. They have also become rather crafty, leaving the confines of the Park at night, raiding the mature gardens and crops east of the river during the darkness, and then returning to the protection of the Park in the morning. In fact the morning parade of herds of elephant crossing the Luangwa River, at first light, has become one of the tourist sights, so these pillaging giants play the rules of survival very much to their favour and lay on an undoubtedly beautiful spectacle as they head for safety: rather as human criminals once sought the sanctuary of the church in an earlier age. Perhaps, as some conservationists believe, the imbalance of the elephant population in Luangwa will correct itself, but meanwhile their superb concentration can still be seen and provides a thrilling memory for all lucky enough to visit this marvellous Park.

Elephants are everywhere in Luangwa but we were also able to see many other species of wild animals and birds. The graceful Thornicroft's giraffe we found quite plentiful in the Luamfwa region, and there were also large herds of buffalo, plentiful hippo and crocodile, many water-buck, zebra, impala, puku, bushbuck and others. The bird life too is outstanding, particularly in and near the lagoons, and by the mighty Luangwa River itself: we saw many colourful bee-eaters, including the white-fronted, but sadly we did not find the fabulous carmine bee-eater which nests in huge colonies in the sandy riverbanks in the northern part of the Park. The brilliant flashes of glittering crimson, as these elegant birds twist and turn over the water, is justly considered amongst the finest sights for the bird watcher. But we enjoyed the ubiquitous pied kingfishers, and also the solitary giant kingfisher which regularly visited the trees beside the Luamfwa Lodge, as well as the many geese and other water-birds, spoonbills, saddle-billed and yellow-billed storks, and the stately herons. One of our favourites, perhaps because there was always one or two to be seen from our strategic viewpoint, as we relaxed after lunch beside the pool, were the curiously refined jacanas or lily-trotters which tip-toed fastidiously amongst the water lettuce for all the world like prancing ballet dancers. Sometimes, as we watched, there would be a sudden eruption from the water beneath the carpet of lettuce and the jacanas would scuttle away, or fly off, as the bulk of a hippo surfaced through the floating vegetation and waddled over to a sandbank, there to slowly collapse in its rolls of flesh like a tethered pinkish-brown dirigible. In the background, on the dry flats above the water-level of the lagoon, it was possible to watch the occasional animals break through the edge of the woodland and trek across the open ground before disappearing once more into the shade of the trees. Elephants of course were frequent visitors and would sometimes progress slowly through the reeds and water plants, crossing the entire lagoon, often up to their tusks in the cooling water and revelling in the refreshing mud. On the far side of the lagoon, were several clumps of the rather straggly Hyphaene palm trees, less impressive than the Borassus palms we had seen near Lusaka, but nonetheless attractive with their top knots of fan-like leaves and rather tropical-looking, especially in silhouette against the sky at dusk. The fruit are the size of tennis balls and have a tough fibrous shell protecting a hard white kernel known as vegetable ivory: this can indeed be carved into useful and decorative items rather like ivory itself. Elephants enjoy the fibrous coating of these palm nuts and we frequently saw elephant dung containing the indigestible kernels, especially along the river terraces where the palms grew, but also in other areas many miles from the habitat of these trees. In this way the seeds of many trees and shrubs are distributed, so the elephant plays an important part in spreading and propagating plants as well as in destroying them. The fortunate nuts of the Hyphaene palm, after the coarse husk had been digested by elephants, are thus strewn around the valley within cannonball-sized dung heaps like instant growbags.

Another impressive tree of the valley is the sausage tree, which is common throughout large parts of Zambia. I remember one huge tree in particular. As we stopped briefly beneath its shade, to admire the less usually noticed but large and beautifully coloured purplish blooms, Anne suddenly spotted a slight movement in the long yellow grass some 50 yards away. We drove very slowly on and were just in time to see a splendid leopard melt away into the background; but although we searched the surrounding area scrupulously, with our binoculars, we could not find where the beast had gone to ground and that tantalising brief glimpse was all we managed to get. Shortly afterwards we had our first encounter, also, with a spotted hyena. Normally one associates the hyena with the scavengers, hanging around other animals' kills and competing with the vultures for the scraps. But our first meeting was extremely dramatic and unexpected. We were driving slowly along, in a wooded area, when a couple of large warthogs crashed through the bushes at the other side of the road, swerved madly to avoid actually hitting the car, and then thundered on along the dusty track accompanied by a frenzied and panic-stricken squealing: in hot pursuit was a hyena, momentarily delayed as it saw our car and lost sight of the warthogs, and then it too hurtled off down the road. Within a few hundred yards the quarry and their persecutor left the track, but we heard no obvious culmination to the chase. We were able to persuade ourselves that these weird comedians of the African bush had escaped their equally unattractive and unwelcome escort. Despite their undoubted ugliness we had always had rather a soft spot for the plentiful warthogs, and would have been saddened had this pair failed to escape, but during all our many visits to game parks in Africa we never witnessed a kill, for which we were quite thankful.

We subsequently saw other hyenas, one insolently stretched across the road at dusk one day and apparently determined to entirely ignore us: as it was late and we had to reach the Lodge before darkness we were not particularly amused, but as we approached nearer and nearer it eventually stretched, yawned and strolled casually off into the long grass, stopping only to turn and offer us a lingering sneer of disdain. The massively powerful jaws and hunched shoulders made it look particularly menacing and evil, and we were quite pleased to see it go, even though we were of course quite safe in the car. We were also occasionally halted by elephants, either crossing the roads or just browsing the trees alongside, and on one occasion we were clearly being warned by a large female elephant that she had taken possession of that particular piece of road and was not prepared to share it. As we inched nearer to her she would bellow her disapproval, wave her trunk menacingly and trample the ground in rage, so that I felt obliged to reverse rapidly away: we repeated this manoeuvre several times until we all got rather impatient, and as she had wandered some yards from the road I decided to call her bluff and accelerated rapidly past her. At a safe distance we slowed down and looked back, to see the elephant cow ripping up great chunks of vegetation and flailing about in a thoroughly bad-tempered way. Elephants, like humans, are reputed to have off-days, and we felt sure that this display was because that particular day was such a day for that aggressive cow. Normally we displayed every courtesy and caution when approaching any animals, but seldom had we felt so deliberately provoked.

On most days we travelled about 75 miles on the tracks and roads around the southern end of the Park and so we soon ran low on petrol. Luamfwa was advertised as having petrol supplies, but we were somewhat dismayed to find that we were only allowed four gallons, since their stocks were virtually finished. We had sufficient with us to get us back to the nearest garage on the Great East Road at the end of our stay, but if we saved that then we would be unable to leave the Lodge during the rest of our visit and we still had several areas that we wanted to see. The Lodge manager was polite and sympathetic but appeared to be entirely in the hands of some nameless official in Lusaka who was responsible for ensuring a regular supply of fuel and provisions. Radio contact with the main Lodge at Mfuwe solicited the information that they had plenty of petrol but that anyone who wanted any would have to go and get it: since we didn't fancy a round trip of some 100 miles, on tracks of dubious negotiability and mostly outside the Park, we said so in no uncertain terms to the wretched Mr Katete and told him to sort it out or else we would expect free accommodation in his Lodge until petrol arrived to enable us to leave. This dire threat seemed sufficient, as the following evening the only official vehicle at the Lodge, a battered Land Rover driven by Mr Katete himself, limped into camp, having made the journey on our behalf and returned with two 44-gallon drums of petrol as well as some most welcome fresh vegetables. We learned from Mr Katete that his journey had been unusually arduous as several stretches of road were passable only to four-wheel drive vehicles, and so we were most thankful that we had not been tempted to make the trip ourselves. He also told us that not only did his ancient Land Rover have no spare wheel, but that his colleagues at Mfuwe had also refused to lend him one: with his heavy load he was indeed fortunate not to have had a puncture. That night we were all roused by truly horrific and hideous screams, and we wondered if Mr Katete was perhaps engaged in some ritual witchcraft aimed at his inefficient and unhelpful bosses and colleagues. However, the waiters assured us next morning that the rumpus had merely been the shrieks of a baboon which had been caught by a leopard: we saw no signs of a struggle, even though the screams had appeared to have come from right beneath our bedroom windows, but we accepted the explanations as being perhaps the more likely that our own imagined version. We enjoyed both the vegetables and the feeling of security at once again having a full tank of petrol.

A number of distinguished visitors have been in the Luangwa valley from time to time, perhaps the most well-known being Dr Kenneth Kaunda, Zambia's President. In fact the President's Lodge in Luangwa is a sort of Camp David to 'KK' who visits the Park at least once every year and who clearly thoroughly enjoys the magnificent sense of remoteness he can achieve there, even when surrounded by his aides and friends and security officials. Another famous visitor was Jacques Cousteau, the celebrated naturalist and marine scientist, who brought his team both to Luangwa Valley and Kasaba Bay during the making of his remarkable film *The Hippo*. The dangers of filming these huge beasts are considerable and some of the underwater photography in this film is truly remarkable: we saw the film, in Zambia, the year before our visit to Luangwa, and we were all most impressed with both the skill and persistence shown by Cousteau and his team. Other visitors to Luangwa have of course been numerous, including both Sir Peter Scott and David Shepherd amongst artist naturalists, as well as many visiting heads of state and politicians all of whom could hardly have failed to have been impressed by this wildlife showplace. Various prestige projects have been completed in recent years, including a major new airport to serve the package-tour tourists who fly from Lusaka for short visits, and a large new hotel lodge to cater for the increased numbers of visitors which are anticipated. It is to be hoped that these facilities will be well-used, but one cannot help being a little cynical about the general inefficiency which tends to pervade the Zambian tourist industry. Despite improved facilities it remains the attitudes of the staff which determine whether or not such enterprises are successful, and in general we found that a spirit of apathy was quite widespread, providing a poor comparison with similar attractions in the more popular game parks of East Africa, as well as South Africa. Time of course will tell, but the international traveller who expects, and pays for, the best in service as well as facilities, has so far been disappointed in these aspects of the country, whilst remaining unfailingly enthusiastic about the splendour and abundance of the animals of the valley.

Our time in Luangwa ran out all too quickly and we determined to make the most of our last day at Luangwa. We were up early for a drive before breakfast and were lucky enough to get a brief glimpse of a black rhino as it trotted along the earth track in front of the car, only to swerve off as it sensed our approach, when it was instantly lost to sight in a dense tangle of buffalo thorn, leaving only the noise of its bulldozing passage through the thicket as proof of what we'd seen. The buffalo thorn is a particularly unpleasant type of bush, or small tree, as its thorns point out in opposite directions, so earning its other name of 'wait a bit thorn' because of the difficulty of untangling oneself once snagged on the sharp spikes. Remarkably enough, elephants are quite partial to browsing on the buffalo thorn, as indeed on many of the other thorn trees, and its hard to understand how they can do so with such obvious impunity. After losing sight of the rhino, the only one we saw in the valley, we found little else other than a small but graceful herd of kudu and returned for a hurried breakfast before setting out again for a longer excursion. We had decided to head for the river, at a point where it was sluggishly meandering through a wide expanse of sand flats which we had noticed were usually occupied by crocodiles and hippos basking in the hot sun of mid-morning. The riverbanks, some ten to 20 feet above the largely dry river bed, were well shaded by mature trees and we could park the car, switch off the engine, and quietly watch comings and goings of the valley's inhabitants ourselves whilst remaining quite inconspicuous. Behind us was a dry gully, opening out into a flat plain or dambo, over which grazed groups of impalas, puku and water-buck: families of baboons played along the edge of the dambo, and colourful birds were everywhere. Elephant would move gently and silently through the trees, pausing occasionally to tear off leaves and branches as they browsed, sometimes leaning their great bulk against a convenient tree for a good scratch. We could have watched the peaceful and primitive scene for ever, but there was always the urge to see what was around the next corner and so we eventually moved off, clumsily and noisily compared to the ease and grace of the elephants which we had been watching. The track followed the riverbank quite closely and we stopped frequently, scouring the patches of shade ahead with our binoculars, searching the likely spots for new interest; the wild date palms with the dense jungle of fronds and branches of dangling orange fruit, and the dry dongas in particular (narrow steep-sided ravines formed by water erosion, usually dry, except in the rainy season). Always nearby were the elephants, and in the background the beautiful and haunting cries of the fish eagles.

Tired at the end of the day, hot and aching from hours sitting in the car, caked with dust and with sand on everything, we slowly drove back along the same riverside drive and were rewarded with an unforgettable sight. The sun was sinking rapidly and the whole sky, orange and gold, was reflected from the broad and smooth expanse of the lazy Luangwa River stretched between the broad sweeps of yellow-tinged sand bars: silhouetted against the dull red orb of the sun were a pair of fruiting Hyphaene palms. We drank in the scene, like rich wine, but as we absorbed the sheer beauty and wildness of this tranquil vision the peace was shattered by the rumbling clank of a Land Rover, as it rushed past us in a cloud of dust. It was the only other vehicle we had seen all day and it ruthlessly brought us down to earth. By the time the dust had settled the best of the sunset was gone, and although I managed to photograph what was left, the magic had slipped away.

Back at the Lodge we packed the car ready for an early start next morning and were all agreed that it had been a splendid holiday. We slept most soundly that night, and despite the prospect of the long and tedious journey which lay ahead, there was no doubt in our minds that this was one of the wildest and most interesting places which we had ever visited. The next day dawned and we sadly bade farewell to Luamfwa, slowly driving the few miles out of the park, passing as we did so a family of giraffes and other early risers before reaching the barrier and leaving the valley behind us. Our journey was mostly uneventful until we had crossed the Luangwa bridge, which we achieved without incident, but it was ironic that after successfully negotiating the rough and rocky tracks through the valley foothills, I drove round a bend at fair speed on the wide tar surface of the Great East Road and ran straight into a rock fall, badly dislocating a track rod and crunching the exhaust pipe and front silencer. We limped the rest of the way home and gratefully fell into bed in Kalulushi, some time in the middle of the night, physically exhausted but mentally refreshed.

For Anne and I that was the last we were to see of Luangwa, but we were able to give Guy and Barry the chance, precisely two years later, to spend a week at Norman Carr's Chibembe camp in that great valley. Our boys were by then 16 and 14 years old, well able to cope for themselves, and since we were able to send them with a party from the Kitwe Camera Club, including our very good friends John and Lesley Wheeler and their own though younger children, as well as several other friends, Anne and I had no qualms about their wellbeing. It proved a fabulous trip for them, not only for the chance to experience the thrill of a walking safari but also for the privilege of meeting and getting to know Norman Carr himself. They were given a twin-bedded hut, near the edge of the camp, and spent a full week in the Park during which they spent several days on walking excursions and others being driven on game-viewing trips in Land Rovers. One of their day's walking provided them with what will no doubt remain one of the highlights of their lives.

On that particular day, Guy and Barry chose to accompany Norman Carr on a long hike through the bush and were joined by just two other visitors, a middle-aged Scots woman and a young man, neither of whom they had previously met. Norman Carr, who was always unarmed but took with him an armed and experienced African guard, was a fund of knowledge and good-naturedly chastised the boys for their inability to identify very many of the bird calls which were all around them. They walked through open bush and woodland, crossed dry dongas and small watercourses still holding small pools, always led by the guard who was closely followed by Carr himself and the group of walkers behind. Stops were frequent to allow time for the animals to be identified and photographed and the boys revelled in the thrill of being on foot in this marvellous wilderness. On reaching a large dry gully the party disturbed a very young elephant, which on being startled, struggled up the far bank and disappeared into the green undergrowth beyond: the party also crossed the gully, and on reaching the opposite side began walking along the edge in the direction taken by the young elephant. Suddenly there was a blood-curdling scream of rage, accompanied by a thunderous crashing in the dense bush, and an enraged cow elephant burst into view not ten yards from the group, thrashing its trunk from side to side, flapping its ears like berserk windmills and stabbing the air with its tusks. The visitors' legs turned to jelly, but Norman Carr quietly pushed them behind him and urged them to rapidly retreat across the gully and up the other side, whilst the armed guard instantly brought his rifle to the ready and held his ground. As the group half fell and half scrambled down the bank, across the donga and up the other side, the young man courageously helping the Scots woman ahead of him, Guy and Barry heard a deafening roar as the guard fired his rifle. On reaching what was hoped would be safety, the quivering group was joined by Norman Carr who had brought up the rear, armed as always with nothing but his walking stick; but whilst they could see and hear only too plainly the furious trumpeting matriarch on the far bank, there was no sign of the guard. Seconds later, however, when all sorts of dramatic thoughts had flashed through the boys' minds, up bobbed the grinning black face of the tiny and courageous African, one tooth shining splendidly in his ancient gums, to re-join them. It all happened so quickly that the only thought in the tourists' heads was escape, and none of them needless to say had time to even think about taking a photograph. Nervous laughter followed Norman Carr's assurance that the still furious cow would not follow them over the donga, since the banks were steep and would involve the elephant in an uncomfortable and undignified scramble, but it was some time before the adrenaline stopped gushing through everyone's veins and their limbs started to resume their normal abilities. The party were obliged to return to the donga, as they had to cross it to reach the camp, and this time they descended almost on to the back of a dozing hippo, which fortunately took off in the opposite direction after a noisy and threating display of ire. By the time the group reached camp their nerves were shattered, and Guy and Barry told us how they had nearly jumped out of their skin when a small flock of doves had unexpectedly clattered into the air beside them, a full hour after the encounter with the elephant.

Another, less exotic but amusing incident, occurred in camp: in fact, inside the boys' thatched hut at night. They became accustomed to being awakened by the rumbling and gurgling guts of elephants which favoured a nearby tree for feeding during the darkness. On one evening they were actually prevented from getting any supper, as an impressive grey hulk browsed casually between their hut and the main building of the camp, flapping its ears impertinently each time Guy and Barry, becoming increasingly hungry and correspondingly bold, attempted to sidle stealthily past. But one particular night, after the camp staff and visitors had all turned in and the electricity generator had been switched off, the boys were woken as usual by the musical burping and belching of a browsing elephant: once awake however, Guy noticed another sound, a sort of rustling, chewing noise right beside his ear. With visions of scorpions and baboon spiders, and even more alarming unknowns, he courageously groped for a box of matches and struck a light, but there was nothing to be seen except a somewhat ravaged-looking tube of barley sugars on the bedside table. Barry was by now awake, and with the light of a candle to guide them, he assisted Guy in constructing a cunningly-contrived trap to capture the intruding sweet-toothed thief. The design featured the lid of a travelling chess-set, weighted by a glass ashtray propped up by a matchstick, to which was attached a long thread. Guy held the end of the thread, then blew out the candle, and waited. Lying awake and listening to the ruminating jumbos, the boys speculated on both the ingenious design of the trap and on what they would find if it proved successful. Sure enough, within ten minutes or so, they heard the resumption of the attack on the barley sugars. With a smooth jerk Guy sprang the trap and the box-lid descended, with a thud, over the packet of sweets and its assailant. The candle was lit and Guy and Barry watched the box, scampering about as if by magic. With due care the trap was inverted, and there, cowering in a corner and shivering with fright, was a minute and wide-eyed mouse, with guilt all over its tiny face. Not having the heart to despatch such an insignificant and terrified creature, the boys cautiously opened the hut door and released the thief into the night: they returned to bed and slept soundly for the rest of the night. Next morning, they were amazed and dismayed to find not a sign of their barley sugars, but only a trail of chewed wrappers leading to the door and on into the bush beyond. The intrepid and persistent mouse had had the last laugh after all.

At the end of their weeks' safari Guy and Barry returned to the Copperbelt. At the impressive new Luangwa airport they were amused to notice that the smart new control tower and terminal buildings were still locked and empty, and their chartered HS748 aircraft was one of two being loaded by a melee of disorganised Zambia Airways ground staff who were attempting to resolve discrepancies, between seats available and the considerably larger number of passengers with valid tickets. The centre of operations was a small corrugated iron shack in the shade of one of the elegant new buildings. Eventually the problems were resolved, presumably not satisfactorily for everyone, and Guy and Barry returned to the familiar scene at Southdowns airport, near Kitwe, where we met them. They could hardly wait to tell us of their adventures, which were far more memorable than any of us could have anticipated, and we have no doubt that their stories will even improve with age in the way of the fisherman's tale. Whether they do or not, the boys certainly had the holiday of a lifetime and they will always remember Luangwa valley, and their Norman Carr safari, as the zenith of their childhood in Zambia.

Chapter 14
ODDS AND ENDS

It is strange the way in which fairly minor incidents sometimes lodge in the dark recesses of one's mind, later to spring out, quite arbitrarily and unexpectedly. But it is in this way that my attempts to illustrate my family's many years in Kalulushi have been influenced by a kaleidoscopic jumble of largely unrelated experiences, rather than by a steady, chronological analysis of our existence. Of course it is frequently the unusual, the amusing, or the dramatic events, rather than the mundane, that tumble out like this, and so perhaps there is after all some method in the madness of the mind, if it provides an excuse to omit the dull routine.

Natural phenomena have always been particularly interesting to me and the weather and climate of Zambia provided, as in many other lands, a frequent topic of conversation. One of our earlier memories of the spectacular extremes of Kalulushi's weather, was of a shattering storm, in April 1961. We were quite used to Africa's violent ways by then, and took the many electrical storms and torrential downpours in our stride, but at that time Anne's mother was with us, on her first visit overseas, both for a holiday and to see her first grandson, Guy. On the particular night of this storm Anne and I had gone to the cinema in Kitwe, leaving in broad daylight in late afternoon, with Anne's mother staying in Kalulushi to baby-sit for us. When we left the cinema it was dark and raining lightly as we drove back home quite unprepared for what was awaiting us. In these few short hours, Kalulushi had been hit by a manic storm and the whole town had been reduced to chaos: our first intimation of something amiss was when we were stopped, on the outskirts, by a policeman who warned us that a number of roads were blocked by fallen trees and several diversions were in force. We threaded our way home as best we could, by a roundabout route, incredulous at the size of some of the felled trees which had been blown about like matchsticks. Several houses had had miraculous escapes, others had been partly crushed, and a number of cars were pinned to their driveways by colossal canopies of leaves and branches. On reaching our home we were greatly relieved to find that we had been lucky, only one small flamboyant tree having been blown over, but Anne's mother had been terrified by the sheer frightening force of the storm, which was utterly unexpected and unlike anything else she had ever witnessed. It was one of the worst storms the Copperbelt had ever experienced, localised though it was in Kalulushi, but more than 400 trees, some over 100 feet high, had been either ripped out by the roots or snapped in half. Rain had been driven almost horizontally by the force of the wind, and two young African children had been killed, one by a lightning strike and the other after touching live electric cables brought down by the gales. This furious storm was the culmination of the highest annual rainfall that Kalulushi, or the Copperbelt, ever experienced: a total of over 79 inches against an average of around 51 inches. Every year there are reports of several deaths by lightning strikes and the violent electrical storms of the Copperbelt which has a reputation as one of the world's worst areas for such occurrences. The charismatic darkening of the skies, to a deep velvety indigo, frequently whilst sunlight still illuminates the vivid colours of the flowering trees in the foreground, provides an unforgettable though certainly menacing spectacle, whether it be in the towns or out on the open tree-dotted plains. Then come the first few drops of rain, warm and heavy, and absorbed thirstily by the baked ground, followed by a steady downpour, the intermittent flashes of lightning, and the deafening crash of thunder. As the eye of the storm moves nearer, and the flashes and crashes become almost simultaneous, it is perhaps easy to see why primitive man both feared and worshipped the elements over which we still have virtually no control.

When the Ngoni people arrived in Zambia, crossing the Zambezi River from the south, another natural phenomenon occurred which dates this occasion precisely. We were lucky enough to witness, from our garden in Kalulushi, a perfect annular eclipse of the sun on April 18th 1977. This rare incident was extraordinarily eerie, even though the press and other media had thoroughly informed the entire population as to exactly what to expect and when it would occur. The prediction of the event was almost as mystical to the majority of the indigenous people as was the event itself, and it was fascinating to speculate as to the effect such a weird event must have had on a superstitious tribal culture over 140 years previously. Even our relatively westernised and educated servants, James and Dicky, were quite unable to comprehend our explanation of the phenomenon, particularly when we embellished our description with the information that the black central mass, the moon, had been visited by space-suited American astronauts some years earlier. We naturally were viewing the sight through protective film, but a number of cases of eye damage were reported, after the event, from both black and white people. But what we found so impressive was not the eclipse itself, nor the accompanying semi-darkness in the middle of the day, but the reaction all around us in the garden and surrounding bush. Not a bird called, nor a single insect hummed or buzzed, and the absolute silence was quite overpowering. It was rather like the oppressive quietness of the country after a long stay in an industrial city, so that the absence of sound became temporarily more noticeable than the sounds that were missing.

Unlike our great friends John and Lesley Wheeler, Beccy's godparents who had both been born and bred in the southern hemisphere, I never became competent at star-spotting in Zambia. John would patiently point out this and that constellation and relationship in the heavens, but my purely northern hemisphere upbringing seemed to provide a natural barrier to such stellar education. In fact early on in our time in Zambia I had foolishly got lost by taking natural bearings from the sun, quite forgetting that I was now in the south, not north of the equator. But one particular event had got me fascinated once again in the sky and that was the prediction that a spectacular comet, Kohoutek, was likely to be visible from the Copperbelt on a certain day. I was determined to photograph this rare event and planned a trip to the nearest point to home from which we could get an unobstructed view of the appropriate horizon. The best viewpoint appeared to be from the edge of a local lake, known as the *Seventeen Mile Dambo*, not because it was 17 miles long, or even around, but for the rather unimaginative reason that it was situated 17 miles away from Kitwe. It was a lovely spot, once a private game area, but now a national bird sanctuary administered largely by the

Copperbelt branch of the Wildlife Conservation Society of Zambia. Thus we planned a pleasant afternoon's bird-watching followed by a comet-spotting session. Unfortunately enough, just as we were about to set off, we received a visit from some Kitwe friends who were accompanied by a young American student, whose reason for being there I forget: but I do recall very clearly that I was hard put to it to explain afterwards to the children, who were fascinated by the young American's appearance, that some people these days just liked to wear both a beard and a plaited pigtail! The pigtail was really the only exceptional thing about the otherwise perfectly normal and very pleasant young man, but I couldn't help thinking that his hairstyle looked rather like a comet's tail, and I was champing all the time at the delay in our leaving for the dambo. Eventually, niceties satisfied, we excused our lack of hospitality and our visitors left, closely followed by ourselves. We never saw Kohoutek, despite very lively imaginations from all members of the family, and apart from almost getting the car stuck in the mud, as it was well into the rainy season, and to be precise, December 30th 1973, we had to be content with a poor view of a woolly-headed stork peacefully fishing in the reeds. We learned later that Kohoutek's comet was in fact something of an astronomical washout, and that far from being easily visible to the naked eye, it was so remote as to be decidedly a non-event. But at least honour was satisfied and we had tried to find the elusive object: we would have been most disappointed if it had lived up to expectations and we had then missed it, delayed by an American pigtail.

One of the most curious mysteries that I recall from Kalulushi concerned the arrival, overnight, of a single baby elephant only a few months old, which was found wandering on our private bush airfield next to our geochemical laboratory. Soon after arriving at my office that morning I received what I thought must be a hoax 'phone call, stating that a baby elephant was totally disrupting work at the laboratory: I arrived to find a swarm of Africans struggling to restrain a terrified young animal, barely three feet high, which they were attempting to tether to a large flamboyant tree. The babel of laughing and shouting, as everyone present gave instructions at once, was clearly distressing the elephant, and I quickly sent for one of our most experienced wildlife enthusiasts to put in charge of the operation to calm and capture it. This he did, with much difficulty, and it was only by threatening to take action against the laboratory workers for being absent from their places of work, that we were able to restore some sort of semblance of order. We managed to manoeuvre the young jumbo into a shed, where he was hosed down and allowed to move freely without interference; meanwhile, we had telephoned for a ranger, from the Zambian Game department, to decide what was to be done. I had also fetched Anne, who was always very knowledgeable about young animals and who immediately established a rapport with this immensely strong and bristly creature which behaved like a grey leather tank, knocking people over left, right and centre. It appeared to welcome Anne, nuzzling against her and probing with its rubbery little trunk. By the time the ranger arrived the elephant was more calm, but there was no sign of the herd or the mother from which it must have been separated. There was a well-known herd which roamed between Chingola and Kalulushi, never coming nearer than several miles away from the towns and seldom seen, but no-one knew of the herd's present whereabouts. And it was highly suspicious that the baby should be on its own, since the protective instincts of elephants are well known, and never will they abandon their young from choice. The most likely explanation of the baby's presence was that the mother had been shot and the baby had either been left to wander or else put on a poacher's truck from which it had later fallen. I never discovered the true explanation of our unusual visitor, and am sad to say that the story had an unhappy ending, as the little jumbo died at the Game Department's headquarters in Chilanga where it had been taken. A post-mortem showed that it had died from pneumonia, and also had a broken rib, but it had struggled for life for some time before succumbing to its ailments.

The young man who had helped disentangle the baby elephant from the Kalulushi laboratory workers almost lost his own life at the tusks of a mature elephant some years later. Gys, a Dutchman who had been brought up in Kenya, was a natural bushboy, both hunter and wildlife enthusiast, and his knowledge and love of the bush made his choice of work as a prospector an easy one. After marrying Sheila, a charming and attractive young Irish nurse, he continued to enjoy working in the bush and his wife frequently accompanied him. One day in June, 1975, Gys and Sheila, with two young English geologists, left their camp on the Musondweji River and drove east past the grim ironstone hulk of Kevamba Hill in search of an elephant herd, from which one of the local chiefs had asked Gys to shoot the one tusker for which he had a licence. They found the herd, in the tsetse-infested country some miles from Kevamba, and they watched the animals push through the tall elephant grass of a dambo before following at what they thought was a safe distance. One of the beasts must either have waited deliberately in ambush or else just dropped behind the others. There was a mighty trumpeting and screaming, and as the party of four scattered from the path of the charging elephant, Sheila was knocked to the ground and gored: one of the tusks went through her groin and she was dreadfully injured, but for some reason the elephant left her without trampling her body or tossing it as is often the habit of these beasts when enraged. The journey back to the camp was a nightmare, and the incredibly courageous girl's senses stayed with her long enough to instruct the men on how to stop the massive bleeding, using all her nursing skill and willpower. Back at camp, radio contact was established and the company's chief medical officer was flown out at once to attempt to save Sheila's life. Back in hospital, with both medical skill and her own sheer determination, she made a slow recovery and was later able to lead a normal life. How Gys' natural flair and experience let him lead his party into this terrible accident he could never explain, but many a natural hunter has lost his life, as a result either a momentary lapse or else a totally unpredictable encounter. On that occasion, luck was against them in allowing the accident to happen; but for them, mercifully, in providing the happy ending.

Undoubtedly one of the memories of Zambia which will live with us the longest, certainly for Anne in particular, were the vicissitudes and excitement of shopping. Not for exotic gifts or clothes, but for the essentials of day-to-day living, and for feeding a growing family. In our early days the shops were full, the choice was tremendous, and prices were quite reasonable. But in the 70s the situation got progressively worse, until shopping became not only most unpleasant, but a distinct worry for the expatriate housewife. Of course, the problems were undoubtedly worse for the wretched Zambians, who had to fight and struggle, queue and bribe, in order to obtain their bare necessities of mealie meal, sugar, salt, cooking oil and other basic items; but whilst we were sorry about their plight we were more concerned with our own. Perhaps the problems appeared worse than they really were, as on reflection I cannot recall that we were in any way deprived, and indeed we actually managed to sustain a pretty agreeable standard of living, but effort was involved, and the subterfuge required, were considerable. There were times, and months on end were not unusual, when it was quite impossible to buy flour, sugar, oil or butter; and to get meat and milk was definitely tiresome to say the least. Many contacts were established with local farmers, and housewives would club together to make periodic visits to these farms and buy in milk. I well remember working away late one evening with Anne, hacking up lumps of fat and meat which had been brought as half a cow and roughly butchered, in order to pack it into manageable joints for the freezer: I certainly wouldn't recommend this as a very rewarding evening's entertainment, and I was sick of the sight of meat for a day or two afterwards. But there was a comfortably satisfied feeling as the piles slowly reached the lid of the freezer. We did the same with pork on occasions, and Anne used to buy chickens by the dozen when other meats became quite unobtainable. All sorts of liaisons were established amongst the expatriate housewives, and teams of cars would stream out of town, to different destinations, at the first report of the appearance of some rare commodity at one or other of the Copperbelt towns. At various times we acquired such unlikely packages as crates of toilet paper, sacks of flour and sugar, or huge cartons of butter. These would be assiduously divided or bartered amongst our friends, and although there were those who hoarded huge stocks of items for their own use, this was really the exception rather than the rule. Near to Christmas one year an unexpected luxury arrived in the form of Chinese chocolate. Now although we missed not being able to buy chocolate when it was available we hardly ever bought any. But when Anne fortuitously happened to be in the one shop which suddenly trundled out these exotica she compulsively, and instinctively, bought two whole crates, some 300 bars of chocolate as far as I recall. This trophy was triumphantly driven home to Kalulushi, where the telephoning and bargaining began; and whilst some ladies jumped into their cars and raced to Kitwe in an effort to emulate Anne's coup, others settled down to the serious business of bartering. What was the exchange rate for Chinese chocolates versus loo paper? Would Anne be interested in swapping a few bars for some tinned cheese, or perhaps an illicit South African apple or two? That was an exciting week.

Most of the mundane fare, that we normally take for granted, became unavailable over the years, particularly such items as tea and coffee. Many were the packets of Earl Grey or Nescafé, which were innocently imported with the luggage of expatriate schoolboys returning to Zambia for their holidays. Guy and Barry used to bring a regular supply of such light and small items, usually accompanied by a batch of magazines hastily grabbed at Heathrow, and occasionally spiced with a pound or two of mousetrap cheese. In return we would send monster avocado pears, weighing up to a pound or more and which grew in our garden on four enormous trees thoughtfully planted by our predecessors. These avocadoes really were huge and utterly delicious, and the crop was frequently so prolific that some fruit were left lying on the ground for the dogs to enjoy; and Rory simply adored them. Fortunately, the Zambians did not acquire a taste for this epicurean fruit and concentrated on stealing mangoes, and so at least we had a welcome commodity with which to return our overseas suppliers' kindness. On one return trip Guy had his hand luggage stuffed with some half dozen of these colossal avocadoes and was taken aback when the airport search at Lusaka revealed the horde. The customs official menacingly demanded to know what Guy was doing with the fruit, a curiously unimaginative question, but when Guy said that he was going to eat them on the journey this appeared to satisfy the man and he was allowed to keep them, much to his relief. Other children suffered less successful encounters with the mercurial and inconsistent Zambian customs officers, many having tearful scenes, or worse, when items had been confiscated.

One particular expatriate suburb in Kitwe, known as Parklands, had its own small shopping centre consisting largely of Asian and Greek supermarkets and delicatessens. The owners of these continued, for a number of years, to manage to import items unobtainable elsewhere, and Parklands became our favourite shopping haunt for a while. This was so until late in our stay in Zambia, but was spoiled by the revelation of a friend that the shops were the homes of a large and thriving community of rats. Although we had never been very happy about the obviously haphazard approach to hygiene in these shops, particularly those which had been taken over by Zambian proprietors but also those still in Greek or Asian hands, we were not prepared for the discovery of the rats. As it happened, the premises used for the meetings of the Kitwe Photographic Society, to which I belonged, were located above one of the shops in the Parklands arcade, and as these meetings were held in the evenings we found ourselves walking past the shop windows sometimes quite late at night. It was then easy to see the sleek, furry scavengers preening themselves in full view, scrambling about amongst the groceries in the windows and on the shelves, thoroughly enjoying the many freely available left-overs from the day's trading. We never bought anything at Parklands again that wasn't either in a bottle or tin, and then only if there was a desperate need and we couldn't obtain the item elsewhere. The last item we purchased at Parklands is recorded in my diary, a one-pound jar of Robertson's Golden Shred, for which we paid the equivalent of just over one pound sterling in 1977: I'm sure we would have paid even more, if necessary, as such items were rare indeed and jealously conserved.

Just after the inauguration of the Tazara railway, in 1974, there was a predictable increase in both the variety and quantity of Chinese items in the shops. These ranged from the now familiar toys, such as Beccy's panda Lochinvar, to other more general goods such as clothes and domestic articles, pots and pans and some quite good quality and very inexpensive crockery. I still have an astonishingly cheap cashmere cardigan, made in China and bought in Zambia, and although our other Chinese clothes have since passed on, these all proved to be surprisingly good value and wore well. Our surprise at associating good value and quality with Chinese goods was curious, as we had never before had any experience of the East or its products, and I presume it must have arisen from an instinctive western prejudice. We have since learned to respect the achievements of the Chinese and are less suspicious of their intentions in Africa. The ancient Chinese cultures have always commanded widespread respect and admiration, but since the Revolution one tends to think of these cultivated people as solely a political and philosophical adversary. I would love to know what their impressions are of the Zambian people, and what are their true aspirations on the international scene.

One of the most worrisome aspects of the perpetual shortages was the difficulty of feeding small babies and getting the numerous accessories which a baby's welfare appears to demand. Things like feeding bottles, nappies and plastic pants, baby foods in jars and tins, pots and tubes of creams for all sorts of lavish and no doubt essential ministrations, all these were at one time or another either unobtainable or in critically short supply. The modern white baby is an astonishingly pampered creature. Whereas the Zambian mother in her bush village might perhaps interrupt her daily routine marginally, both to produce and care for her infant, the European mother expects a great deal more. One of the chores of the expatriates' house-servants was the easing of the burden that the newly-arrived baby thrust on to the household, and we wondered what was the effect, on the servant's own families, of seeing the complex panoply of a white baby's nursery. Of course many of the European mothers enjoyed the chores of motherhood, as did Anne, but there was certainly a great advantage in having a servant who was not only a laundryman but also a washer-upper and cleaner of all messes, as well as someone to push the pram to quiet the yelling brat at times of stress. Our James Kalukuluku was good at all these chores and was, I'm sure, also quite genuinely fond of our children: though it was only Beccy who he knew as a real baby. The nickname for such all-purpose servants-cum-baby-minders was 'muntumatic', a slightly unkind concoction based on the word *muntu* meaning simply a person. When we first arrived in Zambia the blacks were referred to as 'munts', a word which lends itself to being spoken with a derogatory tone, but it soon lost favour, for good reasons. The better-known South African equivalent, kaffir, lost its use even earlier for the same reason, although it is still used despisingly in South Africa very widely today. However, whilst 'munt' is a nasty word, by inference, 'muntamatic' seems to be rather a nice word which was generally used in a flattering rather than offensive way, in discussing the many attributes of one's servants.

In the absence of either James or a member of the family to quieten Beccy during her seemingly frequent bouts of squawling for attention, we often resorted to the use of a dummy, another item of the baby's kit which was periodically impossible to buy. We must have got through dozens of these curious gob-stoppers during Beccy's babyhood and she became most attached to particular models. However, they were easily lost, at least temporarily, and we tried to maintain a stock for emergencies. At one period of hardship, I remember scouring the Copperbelt's chemists and Asian stores in an attempt to replace these dummies, and I eventually tracked down two: one all-rubber luxury contraption with a flat rim, the size of a coffee saucer, which half concealed Beccy's face when in use; and a nasty cheap plastic one in a sickly pink colour which was so tiny I was afraid she might simply inhale it, ring and all. However, these two dummies became firm favourites and were known lovingly, as 'Wubber Dummy' and 'Pink Dummy'. Much to our shame, Beccy retained these until she was three, despite numerous attempts by us to accidentally lose them, but since she had avoided what we considered to be worse and less attractive habits like sucking thumbs or rags, we bore with it until her third birthday. We had earlier persuaded little Beccy, with difficulty, that big girls of three couldn't possibly have dummies and so she had agreed to discard them both on that day. When her third birthday arrived, true to her word, though with obvious sadness, Beccy ceremoniously consigned her beloved Wubber Dummy and Pink Dummy to the dustbin and there was never a mention of them again. But considering the immense trouble to which I had gone to find and buy these hideous appendages I was quite sad myself to see them go, though delighted at the prospect of not seeing them sticking out of Beccy's mouth any more. Such were the triumphs and trials of shopping in Zambia that these ridiculous and trivial moments leave their mark.

Some of the colonial terminology lived on, at least unofficially, leaving a legacy of the earlier days of segregation and racial privilege. Thus it is that the shopping areas of African townships, built originally to supply the black inhabitants of the compounds, are still referred to as the Second Class Trading Areas. Many of these stores were owned by the Asian traders, and plenty still are despite the repercussions, throughout Africa, of the cruel policies of Idi Amin in Uganda; but the Zambians, like many Africans, have long resented and hated the exploitative role of the less moral of these well-established Asian families. From time-to-time difficulties have arisen, in political terms, for many Asians and these traders now have virtually all been obliged to seek Zambian citizenship, as indeed have a fair number of white farmers and businessmen. The small businesses, mostly centred in the so-called second-class trading areas, are now a real ethnic hotchpotch, with a curious mixture of Zambians, alien Africans, Asians, Greeks, Italians, and other Europeans. Now that the Zambia-Zimbabwean border is once again wide open, perhaps these emporia and stores will revive and thrive as they did in the fifties and sixties. It was in stores such as these that we sometimes managed to find the scarce commodities that made shopping in the seventies so exasperating and yet so exciting. With persistence and the right contacts even these shabby and run-down stores sometimes provided a real prize, like an antique tin of bully beef, or even a revered Wubber Dummy.

Perhaps the search for food was one of the major objectives of the expatriate housewives, but there was no question that this was almost a total preoccupation for many of the poorer Zambian families, who would eat what to us appeared the strangest things. I remember checking a friend's house and garden in his absence and being puzzled by a muffled squeaking noise as I accompanied the gardener around the plot inspecting what little he had accomplished during his employer's absence. Eventually I realised that the noise was coming from one of the pockets in the gardener's overalls and so I asked what he was carrying. This he reluctantly showed me, pulling from his pocket a plastic bag, into which was stuffed an exquisite and protesting Paradise Flycatcher. These are tiny birds, exotically coloured, with a vivid blue ring around the eye, silvery grey and rufous plumage, and a long and elegant tail like a chestnut-coloured streamer. The gardener assured me that this dejected bird was a potential mouthful and would be cooked as a relish to accompany his mealie meal. I bought the bird for about ten pence and later released it, unharmed though offended, in our own garden: to our extreme delight, within ten minutes of releasing this beautiful creature, it's calls were answered by a similar bird with which it eventually flew off into the bush.

Birds and small rodents were of course plentiful and often eaten by the Africans, but certain tribes enjoyed regular seasonal treats. I have a note in my diary recording an item on the television service, TVZ, during an evening's broadcast in November 1975, in which the newsreader urged that 'those in the Serenje district who are away catching caterpillars should return to cast their votes in the local government elections'. How these itinerant gourmets were supposed to take heed of a television broadcast remains unclear, especially as Serenje itself was a distinctly fringe area for TV reception. On the Copperbelt, few of the caterpillars were considered a delicacy and we often regretted that the so-called army worms, which were actually the caterpillar of the Noctuid moth, were not consumed. These black and yellow striped caterpillars often swarmed in large numbers and would devastate lawns and vegetation in astoundingly little time if allowed to proceed unmolested. Apparently more palatable were the locusts, or green grasshoppers which sometimes appeared in large numbers, although never in plague proportions so far south. I think it was the long-horned grasshoppers which were mostly favoured. It was a common sight at night to see the swarms of insects flying around the fluorescent streetlamps, whilst almost equally numerous swarms of picannins, below, grabbed the dazed creatures on the ground and stuffed them into a truly nauseating writhing mass down the necks of empty Coca-Cola bottles. It was certainly not a sight for the squeamish, let alone a food source for which any expatriate was competing, even during the direst shortage of more conventional nourishment.

Another aggravating shortage was a recurring one which persisted throughout our long stay in Kalulushi, namely an inadequate water supply. During the latter part of the dry season there would be the inevitable irritation of water rationing, when pipes periodically ran dry and gardens could not be kept fertile. These were really minor problems for the expatriates compared to the desperate situation in the African compounds where supplies were even more limited: we seldom had more than a few hours without water, and could provide for such easily anticipated shortages, but the densely-populated townships suffered far more and for far longer. We complained at having to tell our servant to fetch a bucket of water from the swimming pool with which to flush the loo, and grumbled as our lush green lawns turned a little brown, but it was easy to allow such things to assume gigantic proportions during times of general difficulty. It was a little chastening to experience both a water shortage and a sugar shortage in England, on one of our long leaves, and to realise that such problems were not unique to the third world. A sad state of affairs nonetheless, but particularly in respect of England where there is little excuse, rather than of Zambia which still faces enormous problems of development and finance.

Whilst we were in Zambia we got used to the many inadequacies and inefficiencies of the civil service and public sector of that country and any delay, deficiency, or general malaise, was accepted philosophically as being yet another manifestation of the ubiquitous 'Z-Factor'. But after two years back in England we are astonished to realise that the Z-Factor appears to be almost as prevalent in this country, although Anne and I were not aware of it 20 years ago. Perhaps we were just too young to have noticed, but there does seem to have been a marked deterioration in the concept of providing a service, and in some respects the Zambian situation is even preferable as the difficulties to be overcome are greater. In 18 years we only lost one letter to our knowledge; and whilst we mocked the system when a mailbag full of letters, luckily none of ours, was discovered abandoned by a postal worker in the bush behind Kalulushi, it never occurred to us that this could happen anywhere but in Zambia. But an attic-full of undelivered letters was found in a postman's house in England just the other day. Similarly, our drama over attempting to obtain a duplicated driving licence for Anne in Zambia is little worse that our experience in trying to renew our expired British licence through the ill-fated Swansea computer on our return. One aspect of living overseas, is the mistaken concept, as memories fade and blur, that the grass elsewhere is always greener than in one's own backyard. There must always be compromise as nowhere is perfect.

There were a number of personal or family watersheds during our years in Zambia, and many would be familiar to other expatriates, both there and elsewhere in the world. After our first few years in the country, during which we became certain that we enjoyed living there, we determined we would make it our home as long as it met certain requirements. The first of these was that my job should remain both satisfying and rewarding, and this it did, until the financial and technical constraints of the last two or three years of our stay with which I don't propose to bore the reader. The second condition was that our lifestyle should not be constrained by either legal or political considerations, and that the safety of ourselves and our children should not be prejudiced in any foreseeable way. Despite a number of alarms and excursions this condition was met throughout our lives in Kalulushi. A third criterion was that the mining companies' hospitals and medical services should continue to provide the excellent personnel and facilities for which they had already earned a high reputation by the time of our arrival. Whilst we became more than a little critical of the expertise available on one or two occasions, and particularly when Guy developed a mysterious and recurring high fever and other symptoms, we were generally quite satisfied. On the first occasion when Guy was being treated for his alarming fever, he became covered from head to toe with a horrifying rash of giant red blotches and angry weals, eventually traced to an allergy to penicillin, an allergy shared by Anne and Beccy. However, by and large, we lived a pretty healthy existence and did not feel unduly concerned by any risks of a medical nature.

The fourth and final criterion was that the children's education should not suffer, and it was in 1970 that this aspect gave us very serious cause for concern, when the boys were respectively nine and a half and seven and a half years old. The primary schools had been racially integrated by that time and the teaching staff, although all expatriate still at the previously all-white schools, were experiencing a high turnover; and the influx of black children, many of whom understandably had communication problems, was tending to slow down the classes' progress. We decided that boarding school was the answer, but although we had booked places for Guy and Barry at Springvale School, near Marandellas in Southern Rhodesia, the travel problems between Zambia and that country had become increasingly severe and fraught with all sorts of awful complications. We therefore changed plans and decided on an English preparatory school, with the attendant advantages of relatives at hand in case of problems, and the fact that we would one day return ourselves. The school was a success and the boys enjoyed the advantages of a good education on the one hand, and exciting holidays in Africa three times a year on the other, but the complications of their travel became intense. On arrival in England we ensured that the boys were met by a Universal Aunt, a splendid organisation which we continued to use, mainly for our own peace of mind, until well after Guy and Barry were able to fend for themselves. The Aunts took all problems in their stride, taking the boys home for the night when required, meeting them off flights at absurd times of the night, filling in time with visits to the Tower of London or Madame Tussaud's and buying cricket or ping-pong bats at Lillywhites. Nothing was too much trouble, and nothing ever went wrong once the boys were in England, during the days of the Aunts. On one occasion their tickets were not reconfirmed by the school and a belligerent, umbrella-waving Aunt so dominated the airways' officials that not only did she get them a seat after all, but they came first class. By contrast, several years later when we belatedly allowed Guy and Barry to travel alone, much to their relief, in the same situation they missed their flight and had to spend two nights in London waiting for another. Their expenses were paid by the airline and the boys rather enjoyed it, but communications being what they were we were distraught on discovering in Zambia that they had mysteriously vanished. There is nothing so exasperating as watching streams of children disembarking at the end of a 5,000-mile journey and joyfully reuniting with their parents, whilst you wait with your heart in your mouth as the last passenger alights and the aircrew disperse. The air service from London to Lusaka was usually well-organised and predictable, but the shuttle service feeding the Copperbelt from Lusaka was a disgrace. Not only was it often impossible to be sure whether flights would arrive at Kitwe Southdowns aerodrome or at Ndola, 50 miles away, but once having opted for one or the other it was normally a wait-and-see situation even for the Zambia Airways ground-staff. When Guy and Barry failed to appear off the aircraft we discovered that there was no passenger list to check whether they had arrived at Lusaka. By driving between Kitwe and Ndola we eventually, after several hours of much agitation, established that the boys had not embarked in London and we did eventually get a telegram from their grandfather explaining the delay. In fact my mother had valiantly tried to phone from Kent, but although she thought at one time that she was talking to our servant Dicky in Kalulushi, she was quite unable to get her message understood and was repeatedly asked by some mysterious Zambian exchange telephonist, 'Why you want speak Kalulushi?' That was perhaps the most confusing journey, but there were many others involving waiting at Kitwe when they arrived at Ndola; some vice versa; and once when they arrived at Ndola while we were at Kitwe, we drove over to collect them, only to pass them going in the opposite direction on the road in a Zambia Airways bus.

But undoubtedly the most alarming occasion was when the boys were still quite young. Having waved a tearful goodbye at Ndola we returned home to reflect on how unsatisfactory these partings were, and whether we shouldn't quit Zambia and establish a more normal existence elsewhere. Six times a year we had the hassle of these flights, and three times a year we parted with the boys. The following morning, in the comparatively quiet and empty house, we were still in a morose and dejected mood when the phone rang. Anne answered it and nearly fainted as the voice on the line announced that he was the airline manager and that he had some bad news for us! Before Anne could think of anything to say the manager added that the aircraft carrying Guy and Barry had been grounded at Entebbe airport in Uganda with engine trouble. The boys stayed at a luxury hotel with a swimming pool, and ample charming air hostesses to look after them, and had the time of their lives at British Caledonian's expense for a full 36 hours. Meanwhile, telexes flew about and all the anxious parents chewed their nails in Zambia, as this was one of the so-called 'lollipop specials' which carried dozens of returning school children. Having ourselves travelled on such a flight we always felt that the air hostesses deserved danger money to compensate them for the pranks of the unaccompanied minors: little monsters who are all tears and short grey flannels as they kiss their parents' goodbye, and then undergo a metamorphosis as soon as they are on the plane, stuffing barley sugars and ringing bells for the hostesses, asking for gin and tonic as they hurl their teddy bears about. The first-timers initially sit and try bravely to stifle sniffs and mop up the welling tears, but after a few journeys even the most timid come out of their sad little shells and sneak off to the loo for a quick illicit smoke, coming out reeking of airways' aftershave. The girls tend to be less offensive or adventurous, but many a transformation occurs nonetheless from the pigtail and school blazer, to the instant teenage poppet doused liberally with perfume, outlined in lipstick and eye pencil.

Our own travel experiences were scarcely more satisfactory than the boys' school flights and we dreaded the first and last leg of every journey, from the Copperbelt to Lusaka and vice versa on the return. Our worst homecoming was in October one year, when Beccy was still tiny, when we arrived at Lusaka on time in the early morning. Unfortunately, it was only a few days before the tenth anniversary of Zambia's independence and chaos everywhere was supreme. The flights within Zambia were in hopeless disarray as various top government officials commandeered aircraft, as they rushed around the country, and there quite simply was no aircraft available to fly passengers to the Copperbelt. After hours of scuffling around the almost deserted, though impressive, Lusaka International Airport, attempting to find someone to whom to complain, we eventually established contact with some senior official. The restaurant was shut, the phones were all out of order, and there was no chance of getting any accommodation in Lusaka as every last bed was packed with party officials and visiting dignitaries who had come for the independence celebrations. Our only hope was clearly to nag the junior official into providing a bus to take all 25 passengers on to the Copperbelt. Some time after midday we finally succeeded in commandeering a run-down coach which we felt had a 50/50 chance of lasting the 200 miles to Ndola. The journey was long, slow and ghastly, October seeming even hotter than ever before, and we arrived home that night completely exhausted. Anne had inadvisably taken her shoes off, to ease her throbbing feet, but since they had swollen up to the size of over-filled hot water bottles there was no way in which she could get back into her shoes until next morning when the swelling had receded. It was at times like this that we practically quit, exasperated beyond measure at the frustration of travelling, but it was only usually a week or two before the mood wore off and we relaxed again into the comfortable and pleasant life of near-normality that we had come to enjoy so much.

Chapter 15
TRIUMPHS AND TURMOILS

When I arrived in Northern Rhodesia, in October 1959, one of the greatest engineering feats in the whole of central Africa was virtually complete. Kariba Dam, built to provide electricity for the power-hungry Copperbelt, and also of course for Southern Rhodesia, was steadily backing up what was to become the largest man-made lake in the world. This vast area of inundation extends for some 180 miles along the Zambezi valley, and fully 56,000 of the local Tonga villagers had had to be resettled since the works had started, in 1955. But challenging and difficult though this operation had been, since the peoples of the valley quite naturally resented having to leave their traditional lands, the phase of the project which most caught my imagination was neither the immensity of the engineering achievements, nor the human problems, but the astonishing bid to save the wildlife. This latter exercise, known as Operation Noah, was organised jointly by the Game Departments of Northern and Southern Rhodesia, assisted by a number of dedicated volunteers, many of whom came from the Copperbelt. As the level of the lake rose, as in fact it continued to do until 1961, so numbers of animals became trapped on islands which gradually but relentlessly shrank in size. Most of the largest animals, elephants, buffalo and others, seemed able to cope with the situation and either waded or swam ashore of their own volition before the distances became too great. But literally thousands of other creatures, from the huge kudu antelopes to the smallest rodents, became marooned and increasingly distraught as their island land masses dwindled in size, and many must have drowned before rescue could be affected. The work of both European and African helpers, however, was tremendously successful, and although both hazardous and arduous, they worked unselfishly and methodically to capture the often-frantic animals and liberate them on the mainland; even venomous snakes and viciously fighting monkeys and such, being patiently and carefully rescued. The volunteers had to provide their own supplies and stores, and worked desperately hard, in appallingly unpleasant conditions, in order to complete what was certainly a triumph of conservation.

The Kariba hydro-electric scheme was itself a tremendous boost to the Copperbelt mining industry which was being faced with increasing problems in meeting the power requirements of the expanding mines. Electricity from the Congo provided part of this need, whilst other sources of energy included coal from Wankie in Southern Rhodesia, imported oil, and local produced cordwood: in fact some quarter of a million acres of forest had been used to fill the mines' needs, for both fuel and timber. And so it was with relief and celebration that the switching of power from Kariba, to join the Congo grid, was achieved late in 1959, the huge steel pylons standing proud along the wide swathe cut for 275 miles through the bush between the dam and the Copperbelt. Almost 1,000 pylons, placed on average a little over a quarter of a mile apart, carried power to the central switching station at Kitwe, to which electricity also came from the Congo's Le Marinel project on the Lualaba River a further 320 miles to the north. Since that day in 1959, when the power came from massive turbines sunk in the south side of the Kariba gorge, a new project had been completed to build another colossal generating plant at Kariba, this time on the Zambian side of the gorge. I visited the project in May 1976, and was most impressed by both the sheer scale of this huge task and by the engineering complexity. The Kariba North Bank project was then well advanced and one of the four huge turbines was already in operation: the power was generated by the fall of water over a vertical distance of 92 metres, whilst travelling from inlet to outfall a distance of 250 meters. The generating hall, deep in the hillside, was 130 metres long, 25 metres wide and a spectacular 45 metres high: we walked in the vast concrete-lined spirals through which the water would hurl itself onto the turbine blades, and strolled through the gently inclined tunnel to the outfall, where a Zambian was casually fishing. The might of the Zambezi has now been tamed at the small power station at Victoria Falls; at both north and south banks of Kariba; and at the enormous Cahora Bassa site in northern Mozambique; thus providing electricity for Zambia, Zimbabwe and Mozambique as well as surplus for export to Zaire, Malawi and South Africa. From its modest beginnings as a trickle, at its source in the extreme north-western corner of Zambia, the Zambezi has certainly played a major role in the history and economy of much of central and southern Africa.

It was in February 1960, only three months after our arrival in Africa, that Harold MacMillan made a speech in Cape Town including the now much-quoted phrase that 'the wind of change is blowing through the continent'. These winds reached gale force in the Belgian Congo only five months later, when Katanga erupted in such a tragic way lending force to MacMillan's statement. Our reaction on the Copperbelt was perhaps a little complacent, as we felt that the British colonial ways were far less likely to permit a similar uprising, and after all, we were still at that time part of the Federation as well as a full British colony. But the next two years, until collapse of the Federation in 1962, did provide a few uneasy times as the rising tide of African nationalism gathered strength and produced the occasional incident which revealed how close we were to flashpoint. I have mentioned my enrolment as a Special Constable in 1961, when a nervous expatriate and colonial population prepared for any eventuality, but the end of the unhappy federation between Northern and Southern Rhodesia and Nyasaland was then in sight, and a Congo situation never seemed probable.

At the elections in 1962, when the various nationalist parties were seeking seats in the new Northern Rhodesian Legislative Council, I was one of a number of mining company employees who were inspanned to assist with the simple mechanics of the electoral process when the Africans first exercised their right to vote. My task, for which I attended a two and a half hour briefing and for which I was paid 25 shillings, was as a Thumb Marker. I had one African assistant whose plausible title, of which he was inordinately proud, was Assistant Thumb Marker. My instructions were not elaborate and so when the allotted time for the general election arrived, at 6.15am on 20th October 1962, I duly reported to the Polling Station in my official capacity as Thumb Marker for the Copperbelt West Electoral Area and signed a declaration of secrecy. The instructions for thumb markers, under Section 74 (1) (c) of the Electoral Schedule, 1962, consisted of the following sequence:

Check both thumbs are unmarked

Dip left thumb into bottle of ink to depth of nail

Issue a tissue

If a person is left-handed, he may dip his right thumb: if no thumbs, one finger.

I actually dipped 172 thumbs in the first hour of polling, and issued a similar number of tissues, but I have no records beyond the first hour by which time the novelty had decidedly worn off: we stayed at our posts until 8pm, when thankfully we were dismissed. We all later received notes of appreciation from both the local District Commissioner and His Excellency the Governor of Northern Rhodesia, together with a cheque for three guineas. It was all so wonderfully British and courteous, and yet rather sad as we realised that it was the end of an era. Only two years earlier, one of the last English DC's at Kalulushi, one Mickey Chittenden, whom I never had the pleasure of meeting, had responded to a typically officious government circular on effective ways of prolonging the life of rubber stamps. He had requested 'six toothbrushes, old, for the cleaning of rubber stamps'. He duly received what he had indented for, in a velvet-lined box, together with instructions to use the toothbrushes with 'a caressing, though reverent, motion'. It would be nice to think that some humour remains in government circles in Zambia, but I have a feeling that what exists is, unfortunately largely unintentional.

And so it was that the various candidates were elected and the Legislative Council was formed, with members either Reserved National, Higher Franchise or Lower Franchise, depending upon the complexities of the agreed formula. The ensuing two years passed rapidly, with much rivalry between the main parties, the United National Independence Party and the African national Congress, with the United Federal Party and the Liberal Party, on the side-lines. Incidents amongst the African supporters were numerous, but occasionally tragedy also struck the expatriate community, such as when a murderous mob attacked an innocent white housewife, incinerating her in her own car by pouring petrol over her and lighting a human pyre. The bereaved husband courageously appealed to the white population to forgive, if not forget, and was supported by most right-minded people, but this was a sign to all that the situation could get out of control during the highly charged months leading up to independence. Some frightened whites left, but most stayed on, confident that the country still had a future to offer.

On October 24th, 1964, Zambia achieved independence, following in the tradition of those British colonies in Africa which had already reached this status, such as Nigeria, Ghana, Kenya and several others of lesser international importance. The white community played a very low-key role in the proceedings, as was indeed both fitting and prudent, but the scenes of jubilation and excitement amongst the Africans was intensely emotional; it was immediately apparent how deeply significant they felt the occasion to be, and how profoundly different life would be in the future in all sorts of major and minor ways. The majority black rule of the past two years had provided a useful psychological buffer to pave the way for the new government, and many whites had appreciated during this period that in Kenneth Kaunda the country had both a fair and capable leader, with a commendable standard of moral integrity and consistency. The fact that Dr Kaunda remains (at the time of writing) Zambia's President to this day, despite many political, diplomatic and economic setbacks, is a tremendous tribute to his personal qualities of leadership, attributes which the whites were quick to realise. Many friends of ours shared our view that as long as KK was in the chair then there would be justice and equality for all in the years to come, and although we often wished that the President had more men of his own honesty and consistency to assist him, we held, and still hold, great respect for the way in which he has earned his undoubted reputation as one of the true statesmen of black Africa.

Undoubtedly the most serious and persistent of Zambia's numerous problems since achieving independence was the proclamation of UDI by Ian Smith, in Rhodesia, one short year after KK took office as President and continuing from November 1965 until April 1980 when Zimbabwe was born. Shortly before UDI my family and I were returning to Zambia from a European holiday and we had chosen to return by sea, through the Suez Canal and down the Red Sea and east coast of Africa, to Beira in Mozambique. Each day we avidly read the ship's bulletins as the prospect of UDI loomed ever more imminent, hoping that the situation wouldn't be precipitated at all, but specifically that it wouldn't prevent our driving through Mozambique and Southern Rhodesia as we had planned. As it turned out we got back a few days before UDI but in the week before that fateful decree the country was alive with gossip and speculation. Many of the whites in Zambia applauded Smith's decision, some privately and others, tactlessly and rashly, in public. Despite the obvious bad feeling that this caused, some foolhardy expatriates in subsequent years held parties on the anniversary of UDI and drank the health of Smith and his cronies, wishing him success in his venture. These taunting gestures understandably infuriated KK and his countrymen, who wished to see majority rule established in Rhodesia, and throughout Africa, and a number of white parties were broken up by police and celebrators thrown into prison with pretty rough justice. Other expatriates, who inadvertently chose a UDI anniversary for their private parties sometimes found their houses raided as well, and a great deal of animosity was generated between the races each year on and around this date in November. But by and large, support for Smith amongst Zambia's whites was expressed in terms of irritation and frustration at the trade and other restrictions which followed UDI. However, necessity is the mother of invention, and it was not only the problems which the illegal regime to our south generated for Zambia. An oil pipeline was built from the Tanzanian port of Dar Es Salaam to Ndola on the Copperbelt; the long dreamed-of rail link between Zambia and Dar Es Salaam was completed, using Chinese aid and skills; alternative power sources were constructed; and many communication systems were improved in our land-locked country. There were those, both black and white, who resented KK's refusal to deal with Rhodesia, and the eventual closure of the border brought undoubted hardship to all Zambians as well as to the large expatriate community, who were then denied many of the commodities which had previously been imported from and through Rhodesia. Dr Kaunda faced several crises, both internal and external, resulting from the reinforcement of his principles, and there were those that predicted his overthrow as his policies brought extreme economic hardship to his country. There were political threats from the African National Congress veteran Harry Nkumbula and from KK's lifelong friend and colleague Simon Kapwepwe, as well as other internal challenges to his leadership, but Kaunda's answer was to declare a one-party democratic state. This contradictory philosophy was imposed on Zambia with surprising ease, and at the time of writing, only the United National Independence Party exists in the political sphere. But despite aspects of the President's leadership which were anathema to the whites, such as his refusal to import badly-needed industrial and agricultural items through Rhodesia, as well as his occasional unstatesmanlike outbursts at political rallies or on emotional state occasions, the majority of expatriates admired his courage and consistency, and he is revered by most of his countrymen despite recurring undercurrents of discontent and a few educated cells of opposition.

One of KK's apparent failings was in backing the wrong horse elsewhere in the continent. He supported the Biafran revolutionary, Colonel Ojukwu, during the Ibo uprising in Nigeria: I also backed Biafra, not for political reasons as I only had a shallow knowledge of the issues involved, but because I had been at school with Ojukwu and knew him well and liked him. Although Colonel Ojukwu had served in Zaire, with a Nigerian contingent of the United Nations peace-keeping force there, in the early sixties, I had not seen him since a meeting at Oxford in 1954 where he was studying at Lincoln College, but I felt it would be nice to count a President amongst one's ex-schoolfriends. On that occasion both KK and I backed the loser, but whereas my commitment was purely a mental and personal one, Kaunda had to unravel and heal the diplomatic sores left by his support for a defeated regime. In Angola, too, Kaunda backed the bearded Dr Jonas Savimbi of UNITA, who was to lose the contest for leadership after independence of that country. Again, most recently in Zimbabwe, Kaunda was strongly in favour of Joshua Nkomo rather than Robert Mugabe, and whilst supporting their perilous alliance as the Patriotic Front it was Nkomo who was favoured for eventual leadership. All these diplomatic trials have posed problems for this Zambian leader, but in each case he has had the courage of his convictions, publicly stated his allegiance, and has skilfully and honestly accepted the inevitable, once events have moved in the opposite direction to those he would have preferred. It is refreshing and unusual, to see a politician make a decision rather than shilly-shally and sit on the fence, however much one may disagree with the decision: a wrong decision is eminently preferable to no decision at all.

The end of the sixties saw the continued rise of nationalism in Zambia and a flourish of acquisition of assets owned by external organisations including the multi-nationals. In due course, in 1969, the country's dominant industry, the copper mines, were nationalised, the vast mining companies being 'invited' to sell a 51% interest in the producing mines to the government. Despite much concern by the many thousands of essential expatriate skilled workers, the transition to state control was commendably smooth and trouble-free, and the management contracts which were negotiated ensured that the day-to-day running of the mines was barely affected. For some years both of the colossal mining companies, the Anglo-American Corporation and Rhodesian Selection Trust Ltd, had pursued enlightened policies of Zambianisation and training, and industrial relations have remained essentially sweet throughout all the most difficult times of the past 20 years. Integration has progressed at all levels and the tendency to window-dress the companies' management accounts had been kept to a minimum. The only racial tension which reached the stage of union negotiation in my own department was in the seventies, and concerned an unfortunately-named clerk called Rosemary whose personal hygiene belied her name. An accountant told her so in a regrettably tactless, and one might almost say colonial, style. Since the alleged remark was twisted to imply a racial insult the machinations of official unionism were brought to bear, and although the rash expatriate was truthful, if tactless, it was difficult to pacify the black union members for some time. But such trivial incidents are the staff of life to unions, especially where there are racial implications, and the waste of time for all concerned was enormous.

The '70s dawned with a spate of robberies, a feature to which Copperbelt expatriates became increasingly accustomed over the ensuing years. As the guerrilla war in Rhodesia escalated, and the number of guerrillas in Zambian bases increased, so the availability of firearms became greater, and the robberies and burglaries became more frequent and accompanied by armed thuggery and murder. Expatriates of course, being mainly skilled or professional people and therefore comparatively wealthy, were the prime target, though plenty of Zambian businessmen were also robbed. Living in a mining community and town we were fortunate in having the additional protection of the well-disciplined mine police force, and so whilst robberies were certainly commonplace in Kalulushi and everyone took sensible precautions, we were not constantly worrying about either our safety or the security of our belongings. The Zambian state police force, however were often found to be both lacking in diligence and resources. There are many stories to be told of distraught householders arriving home at night to find their houses had been robbed, but on phoning the police for assistance, being told that if they wished to report the details they would have to drive to the police station to do so as the police had no vehicle at their disposal.

One very pronounced aggravation to the general malaise of robberies was the ease with which criminals could slip across the border into Zaire with their ill-gotten gains. There are numerous small tracks and paths through the bush and I have several times wandered across the border between Zambia and Zaire whilst working on a survey in the Copperbelt. Plenty of these paths are wide enough to allow a car or van to thread between the trees, particularly in the dry season, and this did often happen. The shortage of essential commodities in Zaire, coupled with the rife corruption in that state, meant that Copperbelt loot made excellent profits for Zairean criminals. Not that all robberies were master-minded from Zaire by any means, but a fair number undoubtedly were. Perhaps the prime targets for thieves were cars, and there was a steady stream of private and company-owned vehicles that disappeared overnight, even when protected by the most elaborate and bizarre security systems. I well remember returning from leave once and taking delivery of a new company car, one of the Fiats which were assembled under licence in Livingstone and which were becoming more ubiquitous than the previously favoured Peugeots which have proved so reliable in central Africa. After a tedious journey driving Guy and Barry to Ndola airport, for their long journey back to school in England, Anne and Beccy were with me in the new Fiat as we returned wearily home, Beccy for some reason having opted to travel on the floor at Anne's feet in the front. As I drove home, and just as it became dark, the car's engine suddenly cut out. After an amateurish attempt to check all the various electrical components I gave up diagnosing the fault and we were luckily able to hitch a ride with a passing motorist. I returned, after seeing Anne and Beccy home, with our good friend John Wheeler who is a handyman par excellence, to attempt to restart the erring Fiat, failing which we would tow it back to Kalulushi mine garage for repair. It should be said that to leave an unattended vehicle on a Copperbelt road at night was to court certain disaster, as by morning every movable piece would have vanished, or walked off into the bush as we would say, and a wheel-less, engine-less, window-less hulk would be all that remained. However, with John's knowledgeable help we checked all the obvious and less obvious potential faults to no avail. John asked if the car had one of the mine's newest anti-theft devices, and ignition cut-out, of which I was not aware. On assuring him that the mine had delivered the car to me with no comment about such a device, we checked anyway, and there it was. A cunningly concealed switch hidden under the dashboard on the front passenger's side. Beccy had clearly amused herself on the floor by investigating under the dashboard and switching off the ignition as I drove along. With the switch returned to normal I finished the journey, but took a long time to live down the cause of the breakdown. As an afterthought I checked with other mine officials who drove similar company cars and found several who were unaware of the secret cut-outs: these devices became known, and possibly still are, as Beccy switches.

Another exasperating safety device, in addition to the locking steering column, Beccy Switch and 'Krooklok', was a gadget that could set off the car's hooter if the car was moved or rocked without first switching off the alarm. The sensitivity of these devices was adjustable, but a fine tuning was required to establish just the right degree of response to various pressures. It was also easy to forget that the system was in operation and to return to your car, open the door, and find everyone rushing at you as the hooter went off alerting everyone within earshot. Even more maddening was to be awoken in the middle of the night as the hooter alarm blared into the neighbourhood, to dash out grabbing a stick on the way, only to find our large blonde cat sitting on the car's bonnet and cleaning its whiskers or dismembering a mouse. Bonny, the cat in question, was enormous, and if the alarm was set to be insensitive to one of his leaps then it could also be driven or pushed away: we were once woken three times in one night by Bonny, and thereafter never used the hooter alarm again, relying on a combination of the Beccy Switch, steering lock and 'Krooklok'. Our car was never stolen.

Zambia had its high points in the '70s, as well as the uncertainties which were responsible for a very high turnover of skilled expatriate workers and a similarly difficult job in recruiting replacements. Isolated incidents reported in English newspapers were frequently exaggerated, or written up in an alarmist way, whilst the country's achievements were largely overlooked. Perhaps the most significant of these achievements in the '70s was the completion of the Tazara, the Tanzania Zambia Railway, or Uhuru railway as it became known in Tanzania. The first freight train from the post of Dar Es Salaam reached Nakonde on the Zambian border on the 7th of April, 1974, and from then on it has become a major lifeline for both Zambia's exports and imports which had traditionally been hitherto routed through either the Rhodesian railways to the south, or the Benguela railway, through Zaire and Angola to Lobito Bay in the west, depending upon political and logistical problems. It was not until October the next year that passengers were carried by Tazara, the first departure being on Anne's birthday. We never managed to make the train journey, from Kapiri Mposhi in Zambia to Dar Es Salaam, but friends who have done so consider it a very worthwhile experience. The opening fares for this 1,200-mile journey, which took 48 hours, were as little as £4.25 for a third-class ticket to a modest £18.20 for first class passengers: even in 1975 that represented tremendous value for money and made East Africa accessible for the first time not just to the relatively wealthy expatriates and tourists, but to many Tanzanians who worked on the Copperbelt's mines.

Sadly, some six months before Tazara's passenger service was inaugurated, one of the most unpleasant government purges of alien Africans on the

Copperbelt took place. Reasons for the purge were complex, but included a genuine desire to rid the country, at a time of high unemployment of aliens who had no work permits or legitimate reasons for being in Zambia. The crime wave was attributed, rightly or wrongly, to these unemployed aliens, and for various diplomatic and political reasons the Zaireans and Tanzanians were hardest hit, being rounded up and then given from one to two weeks to leave the country. The Malawians, a larger number of whom lived and worked on the Copperbelt, were given from two to three weeks to leave, but I suspect that many managed to avoid the police and the decree and simply melted away, to return some few months later when the alarm was over.

Regrettably, the last few years of our stay in Zambia were not celebrated for any great or far-seeing accomplishments by the government; partly because the world-wide depression hit that country like any other, particularly as it depends so heavily on copper for its wealth and foreign exchange. At times of depression, copper is in considerable over-supply and prices plummet. Combined with the poor availability of the basic needs of the country, and the inability to buy and pay for badly needed replacements, the general air of malaise made the second half of the seventies a time of hardship in Zambia, and a period which compared poorly with the previous one and a half decades for all their dramas. Crime increased and armed thuggery became hard to contain. We sincerely hope that the '80s, which dawned with the end of Britain's colonial history in Africa and the independence of Zimbabwe, will see a resurgence of prosperity and a resumption of real development in Zambia.

Chapter 16

EXIT AND FAREWELL

To spend over 18 years of one's life in a single place it is necessary to be either, without choice, or happy. My family and I were indeed happy in Kalulushi, and at the time of our departure I had spent close to half of my life, and all of my married life, in that small Copperbelt town. But all good things are supposed to come to an end and we all of us experienced mixed feelings when our time to leave finally arrived. Our many years of happiness had been sprinkled with times of worry and frustration, and the proportion of these had increased over the last few years to such an extent that it seemed that to leave when we did would ensure, on balance, that our memories would remain on the credit side. During this time we had passed many milestones, at any of which we might have decided to leave Africa and our expatriate existence, but the attractions of our Kalulushi cornucopia had always outweighed the disadvantages. When the decision to leave was finally made for us, by the closure of my entire department due to the disastrous and desperate economic situation of the copper mining industry, and its consequent inability to maintain an effective exploration effort, we felt that perhaps this unceremonial exit from our luxurious rut was proof that it was time to move on. Back in England we would at least be on hand during the final years of our sons' education, as they reached maturity and made their own way in the world, and we had often regretted being so far away from our families. So it was with very mixed emotions that we faced the task of winding up our affairs in Zambia and put in hand the awe-inspiring transactions which the government requires of those emigrating the country. We never really considered ourselves as immigrants in the first place, rather as long-term visitors, but officially we became emigrants and had no option but to embark upon all the formalities with which this status required us to comply. On first learning of all the intricacies of the emigration procedure our immediate tendency was to stay in Zambia. It was clearly much easier to get in than it was to get out, and it was quite clear why so many expatriates had found it so tempting to renew their contracts, rather than face the blizzard of forms and negotiations which departure demanded.

After assembling a monumental plethora of there were various government and other officials to be seen, from customs officers to bank managers, company accountants to auctioneers, doctors to travel agents, and others. Slowly our documentation progressed and we began to cross off items on the huge checklist that we had compiled. Some thoughtful company official had provided a diagrammatic summary which showed not only the components of the departure process, but also the sequence to follow, rather like a lunatic snakes and ladders. If you got your assets valued and listed, for Bank of Zambia exchange clearance, you went back to square one if the value of your car was not officially certified beforehand, and so on. But apart from the sheer complexity and tedious form-filling, and the toing and froing which this necessitated, Anne and I were agreed that the most distasteful part of our departure was the disposal of items which we couldn't, or didn't want to, take with us.

Various friends had tried all the alternatives and none were pleasant, or simple, though perhaps the easiest of all was to have an in-house auction and get rid of everything at once, resigning oneself to paying a whacking fee to the auctioneer. We tended to prefer selling our bits and pieces privately and so advertised, by word of mouth and on various notice boards: some goods were unobtainable locally and both expatriates and Zambians were always keen to pick up sought-after second-hand items at house sales. First pick went to one's close friends, then the servants, next other friends and acquaintances, and finally to all-comers. We hated the whole process, particularly when Zambians would haggle: this was less irritating when they were clearly poor and in need of the goods for personal use, but there were also the professional vultures who would buy from European house-sales at knock-down prices and then make a huge profit on resale in the compounds. We were lucky in having a large outbuilding in which to lock up our sale items and we opened shop every afternoon during the week for some two months before we left. Everything was there from tables to pictures to books and records, kitchen utensils and toys, garden tools and hosepipes. Most of it went relatively smoothly, but in the end we were left with a motley collection which we sold as a job lot to a Kitwe auctioneer: we had decided that we should have done that in the first place.

The problem of shipping goods to Europe from Zambia was complicated by the virtual impossibility of exporting by road or rail to southern or eastern Africa, for onward transit by sea, with any likelihood of goods arriving at all; and let alone intact. We were therefore virtually limited to air freight, a costly business for the ton or more of items we wished to send home. A large proportion of this amount, by weight, were books, with the rest comprising clothes, linen, some crockery and pictures, and all our small ornaments and other items of sentimental value, as well as my not inconsiderable collection of rocks and minerals.

We had arranged to have these goods professionally packed, and the great day eventually dawned when the freight agents were due to descend on us and pack up. The time they were due arrived, then passed, and there was no sign of them. After waiting a couple of hours we tried telephoning to find out the cause of the delay, hoping against hope that they had not forgotten to assign us a lorry and a team of packers. This seemed unlikely though as I had personally checked their schedule two days earlier as a natural protection. We phoned and phoned for almost another hour before abandoning the telephone in disgust: it was one of the frequent off-days for the telephone service and it was impossible to contact the Kitwe freight agents, so I was obliged to drive the ten miles to their office. The explanation for the delay was that the lorry which they had consigned to us had broken down, on another job, and was still several hundred miles away in another Province. I was assured that a different lorry and its team would be sent later that day, a promise I had no choice but to accept with a good grace, though strongly doubting the likelihood of this actually happening. However, just before dusk a vast pantechnicon arrived with a team of burly Zambian packers and a myriad of empty tea chests. By the end of two hours hard work they had packed no less than 16 tea chests and five other large crates, and despite our worried checking all appeared to have been expertly accomplished. Sure enough, just over a month later the entire consignment was delivered to our cottage door in Cornwall, even the carpets having been individually crated and shrouded in polythene sheeting prior to despatch from Kitwe. This achievement fully restored our faith in the shippers, especially when we found almost no damage to our goods. It was ironic that the delivery in Cornwall was made by a single driver, with no mate or assistant, and since some of the crates were far too heavy or awkward to be handled by the two of us, let alone by the driver on his own, I had to send them away to be returned the following day with a couple of extra helpers and a small trolley. Contrary to our recollections, standards of service in England have proved little if at all more prompt or efficient that the service we had scathingly grown used to in Zambia. Although there are, happily, some exceptions to this generalisation, the Z-Factor seems to have followed us.

We are frequently asked what it is that we miss most now that we have left Zambia, and this is a surprisingly difficult question to answer. There are some obvious aspects, such as the superb climate, and the ready availability of servants, but these are not the Pandora's box that might be expected. The climate is magnificent, and we do miss the sunshine, but perhaps the most delightful aspect of the Zambian weather is its predictability, rather than the actual temperatures or number of hours of blue skies. One can plan holidays with complete confidence, eat one's meals in the garden, arrange children's parties or picnics, and know that for virtually six months of the year there is no risk of rain affecting such activities. To plan a picnic in England is to court disaster, and if my family is in any way typical, the preparations can be quite traumatic as the car becomes increasingly loaded with an endless variety of items designed to meet every eventuality. A huge groundsheet to ensure no one catches a chill sitting on wet grass; umbrellas in case there is no handy shelter from the inevitable rainstorm; an incredible heap of anoraks and wellington boots; a change of clothes for Beccy, who inevitably falls or runs into a river on these occasions; at least one towel to dry ourselves after getting soaked; a rug in case it turns chilly; a thermos of hot coffee to warm us if it rains, and a giant plastic cauldron of orange squash in case we get hot; and so on. Our picnic expeditions in England require, or so Anne insists, preparations more fitting to a trans- Arctic assault. Whilst in Zambia we just dumped our hats and a cooler of water in the car and we were off. And whilst perhaps we were nostalgic for the primroses and bluebell woods of the valley near our Cornish home when in Zambia, I now feel a yearning for the vivid splashes of scarlet Combretum and the wild gladioli, orchids and red-hot pokers of the bush which we have left behind. The smell of honeysuckle in the English hedgerows is no more delicious than the scents of many African blossoms, and there is nothing to compare with the smell of charcoal burning, once common in England but now only associated, in our minds, with the woodlands of Zambia.

Our own garden in Kalulushi provided us with a host of delightful sights and scents which we now miss, from the huge white blossoms of the Queen of the Night, an exotic import from Central America which thrived in the Copperbelt climate and opened its bloom whilst you watched at sundown, only to die by morning; to the familiar hibiscus and bougainvillea which provided such brilliant splashes of colour. One particular shrub we remember especially well was a night-flowering cestrum, which produced prolific sprays of greenish-white flowers from which an overpowering scent filled the night air, attracting squadrons of hawk moths to hover and sip from its nectar. In one of our gardens we planted this shrub at the side of our back verandah, but after one flowering season we had to move it to the far end of the garden, as the intoxicating scent was so overpowering that we couldn't escape from it even inside the house with the windows shut.

The children climbed avocado trees instead of conker trees, and collected huge tropical moths and butterflies instead of red admirals and meadow browns. Guy constructed a ramshackle butterfly trap which he loaded with bananas laced with rum or sometimes with Rory's droppings, or even both, and then hauled this evil-smelling offering into the top-most branches of a huge mahogany tree which grew beside our swimming pool. As he lazed in the pool, floating on an inflatable bed, he would gaze up at his nauseous contraption and the swarms of depraved swallowtails which were attracted to it, periodically disturbing himself long enough to lower the trap to the ground and remove the latest butterfly prize and release the drunken remainder. Little wonder that his butterfly collecting ceased on returning to England, where considerably greater effort is required to catch considerably less exotic creatures.

Apart from the climate, its warmth and predictability, Anne and I do miss the servants which made life so much more pleasant. But those who have not lived in countries where domestic servants are readily available do not seem to appreciate the implications and responsibilities which are inherent in employing a servant. A frequent impression is that African or other foreign servants in the lands of our lost empire are virtually slaves, who do all the white man's chores at a wage bordering on the bread-line or even below it. But this is far from the truth, and whilst certain of the new breed of British expatriate are undoubtedly unfit to employ servants, the large majority realise their responsibilities as employers and treat their servants with both respect and warmth. The economics of supply and demand control servants wages, and the generally low amounts paid are often offset by provision of such perks as food and housing, and many employers also take an interest in the welfare of their servants' entire families. The servant-employer relationship should be a happy one, and ours certainly was: we felt our servants to be happy to work for us and we certainly always considered that we had a responsibility towards them and frequently assisted in any problem which they experienced, whether it be in illness or merely aiding them in the form of loans or providing security, filling in forms, or in fact in any area where an employer would normally help an employee. But in essence we enjoyed their loyalty and having them around, as an extension of the family. Guy and Barry will always remember the warm greetings they received from James and Dicky on arrival home for their school holidays at the end of each term, and the formal and sad handshakes on their departure. The boys had a special relationship with Dicky who was always ready to abandon his weeding or grass-cutting in order to play football, or teach them some basic Nyanja words. There was a mutual respect between us all which made for a happy household, of which James and Dicky were an essential part, and we shall always remember them with affection.

Apart from the sunshine and servants syndrome, undoubtedly our happiest memories of Zambia relate to the magnificent spectacles of wildlife with which that country is so richly endowed, and thanks to our large collection of colour slides we can recapture these sights and relive our experience at will. A sunset over the broad sweep of the Luangwa valley, or a picture of a young lion padding through the dry sun-dappled bush beside a dirt track in the Kafue bush, stir memories of sight and sound with great facility so that all the associated happenings parade through our minds as though it was yesterday. We have many mementoes other than these pictures too, and they all generate special memories, whether they be the thumb-piano

I acquired by barter in a remote village, the impressive wooden bust of an African bought from a Zairean curio seller in a Kitwe market, or the lump of vegetable ivory from a Hyphaene palm nut. Guy has his butterflies, Barry his little hide-covered drum and copper mementoes, Beccy her wooden animals, Anne her lace and bead work; and I have my rocks, minerals and gemstones. Our house is full of bits of Africana, and it is fascinating to stop sometimes, examine one of these items, and allow oneself to be mentally transported to the place of origin thousands of miles away where we spent so much of our lives.

It is scarcely surprising that it is the happy memories, and the best aspects of Zambia, which most readily spring to mind, whilst the dark days and tragedies stay buried. But during the occasional fit of nostalgia we do permit ourselves of course to remember that all was not sweetness and light throughout our stay. We recall the uncertainties and worries of the Congo uprising; the heartaches and frustrations of parting with the children at the end of short school holidays; the increasingly aggravating shortages of essential commodities; and the occasional anti-white demonstrations and sullen hostility which contributed to the general feeling that we were no longer welcome, however badly our skills might be needed. Whilst the Zambians individually could be charming and gracious, there was something vaguely sinister in the rapid change of character as soon as a crowd gathered, as though they felt a collective need to dominate the race which had once dominated them.

Perhaps we had become over-sensitive, but we no longer felt the natural rapport in the towns which undoubtedly still prevails in the rural areas. The process of gaining political maturity appears to have degraded the traditional values and courtesies of the Zambians, such that they have little with which to replace the rapidly eroding tribal loyalties. The one-party participatory democracy of Zambia is a strangely anomalous political answer to the conglomerate of Bantu peoples who are its citizens, and whilst President Kaunda has set a moral and strong leadership precedent, which is admired and envied by much of Africa, it is difficult to predict an undisturbed future for the country. No doubt the independence of Zimbabwe, which almost completes the circle of African-ruled states around Zambia's borders, will contribute to a brief euphoria as import and export problems are eased. But much of Zambia's economic depression, so easily blamed on the past 15 years on the 'Rhodesian problem', may be seen to be less than previously supposed a direct result of the political repercussions of UDI. It has become too easy to blame administrative shortcomings and ineptitude upon the mysterious implications of the closed Zambian-Rhodesian border, and now that this no longer presents an excuse it is quite possible that other, internal, scapegoats will be needed, to account for gross inefficiencies. In the short term it is probable that confusion and rival antagonisms will prevail in Zambia, adversely affecting the quality of life enjoyed by the expatriates and indigenous inhabitant alike, whereas the long-term future of this rich and underpopulated country, with its wealth of natural resources, must be secure.

In making our personal farewell to Zambia, we certainly wish all her peoples a happy and prosperous future, and will always be grateful for the many wonderful experiences which we shared and enjoyed whilst guests in that exciting country.